WOMEN'S WORK

In Memory of Sarah Hannah
(June 1, 1966 – May 23, 2007)
"You Furze, Me Gorse"

WOMEN'S WORK

MODERN WOMEN POETS
WRITING IN ENGLISH

Edited by Eva Salzman & Amy Wack

seren

Seren is the book imprint of
Poetry Wales Press Ltd.
57 Nolton Street, Bridgend, Wales, CF31 3AE
01656 663018
www.seren-books.com

The right of the poets to be identified as
the authors of their work has been asserted in accordance
with the Copyright, Designs and Patents Act, 1988.

The poems © individual poets (see Credits)
Introductions © respectively, Eva Salzman and Amy Wack, 2008

ISBN 978-1-85411-430-3 cased
ISBN 978-1-85411-431-0 paperback

A CIP record for this title is available from the British Library.

The publisher acknowledges the financial assistance of the Welsh Books Council.

Cover Art: 'Falling Jug' by Shani Rhys James, courtesy of Martin Tinney Gallery.

Printed in Bembo by Bell & Bain, Glasgow

Contents

Eva Salzman: Introduction

I

This anthology presents a panoramic selection of leading English-speaking modern poets, with an emphasis on bridging the US, UK and Ireland divides. You'll find here a dazzling plurality of idiom, style and subject, well-established poets appearing with lesser known and newer voices deserving of a wider audience: the latest contemporary writers set in context against their heritage, to represent the full sweep of the modern period.

Given the space – and a more perfect world – these poets should appear alongside their male counterparts. That book is also overdue. Given the space...well, usually there is not the space. All things being equal (which, mostly, things are not) editors largely agree that more men than women deserve more pages in mainstream anthologies purporting to reflect the canon; the 'indispensable' list is still comprised predominantly of 'men poets'. (Stephen Pain recommends the universal adoption of this phrase: " 'man poet' Ted Hughes, poet Sylvia Plath[1], 'man poet' Dylan Thomas, etc." Imagine the *Times Literary Supplement* review of the 'man-poet' Seamus Heaney! The long-awaited publication of *Men Poets of the Twentieth Century*!)

How to address a problem not seen as such? In the UK, any glaring gender imbalance is typically explained away as a 'coincidence' here, an 'accident' there. In that case, one should send for the doctors. If the selection criteria are in fact gender-blind, based on quality alone, this implied opinion of women's writing is an offence demanding a response.

Many women poets disagree with the separatist ideology to which anthologies like this are assumed to subscribe. Some distance themselves from what Germaine Greer calls "the spirit that produced anthologies such as Diane Scott's *Bread and Roses* and Louise Bernikow's *The World Split Open*..." and "the reinvention of poetry as a propaganda tool of the women's movement [that] must have galled independent women poets who had been toiling away for most of a lifetime, only to see their small market overwhelmed by a froth of publishing on the part of literature co-operatives and writers' workshops."[2] Irritatingly, anthologies sometimes do perpetuate the very stereotypes about women's subjects we aim to disarm in this volume.[3] An anthology compiled to prove a point would be top-heavy with its own agenda. Nevertheless, my own internal, and heated, debate on this subject – and some poets' ambivalent feelings about women's anthologies – impelled me to address not only what is a routine gender bias, but also our problematical relationship with efforts to redress it. Hence, this polemic before the poetic. Hence the launching of this spectacular wealth of talent with a modulated celebratory note. Aren't women's anthologies self-defeating – 'own-goals', as they say? Doesn't positive discrimination undermine a work's legitimacy? True or not, the merest hint that the critical bar has been lowered justifies the status quo: which, of course, is itself based on a tacit positive discrimination.

Furthermore, gender-segregated anthologies conveniently absolve the 'unconverted' from the need to consider the existence of bias. Damned if we do, damned if we do not. It is a conveniently insoluble problem. I too say 'no thanks' to a separate, girly sand-box to play in, thank you for the gift of this condescension. *The writing is all that should count.* To which I am tempted to reply to myself, and everyone: *in your dreams.*

In trying to shape a canon, anthology editors need to believe in their own vision and independence of thought, resistant to prevailing currents. In a review reprinted in his collection of essays *Poetry and the Age* (required reading), the poet/critic Randall Jarrell, blunts such ambitions with a characteristic wit:

> The typical anthologist is a sort of Gallup Poll with connections – often astonishing ones; it is hard to know whether he is printing a poem because he likes it, because his acquaintances tell him he ought to, or because he went to high school with the poet. But... he stares over his herd of poets like a patriarch, nodding or pointing with a large industrial air.[4]

Lacking the right body parts for the patriarch, I will point to the mostly patriarchal *Great Poets of the Twentieth Century*, a series of pamphlets published in spring 2008 by the *Guardian* newspaper in collaboration with Faber. These poets were deemed to be: Siegfried Sassoon, T.S. Eliot, W.H. Auden, Ted Hughes, Philip Larkin, Seamus Heaney and Sylvia Plath. In Britain at least, it is a truth universally acknowledged that Sylvia Plath and Elizabeth Bishop are the only women poets worthy of admission to the pantheon. Yet, such unanimity of thought in an otherwise divisive world is notable. (Indeed, throughout this Introduction, Plath is the ideal example to use in raising a number of issues: the lack of critical writing about her work – in the UK anyway – the nature of criticism about women poets more generally and during a later discussion about confessional poets.)

Gender issues aside, there is a strong case for replacing at least two writers on this list, chosen for reasons other than the writing. Surely, Sassoon is included to tick the box marked 'war poet'? He cannot be a plausible choice outside of this category. Regardless, this box is more acceptable than the one marked 'woman poet', which pertains to the so-called 'special interest' group comprising over half of this planet's population. Despite lip service to the contrary, criteria other than the writing are always applied, if selectively.

It seems hubris – or a calculated marketing strategy – to define such a small and select part of the canon while some of its authors live; if you dare to, surely knowledge and breadth of vision are prerequisites for the job. Identical and infallible good taste about Plath and Bishop aside, one wonders how many are *simply not familiar enough with major women poets' work to make an informed assessment of the hierarchy.* Who really knows the work of Louise Glück, Denise Levertov, Edna St.Vincent Millay, Kay

Ryan, Lorine Niedecker, Adrienne Rich and May Swenson, to name but a few (mostly) Americans? None of these are published by Faber, the *Guardian*'s partner for the series, but the lack of women on that list is further evidence of the problem. Broaching this subject brings a plague on your house. Several online discussions which did just this (including responses to a Guardian blog I wrote which forms the basis for this essay) elicited from contributors passionate views about the male-dominated literary world. Equally passionate, and telling, was the vitriol unleashed in response to these comments. It would be disingenuous to say I found it astonishing. Personal attacks, like rockets, whistled through the ether; launched under cover, the anonymous writers aired their opinions under an adopted – and often revealing – moniker. The issue was instantly hijacked into one about plausibility, women's experiences and their commentary on it dismissed as irrelevant, invalidated in one fell swoop. Statistics, demanded as proof superior to women's own experiences, were duly supplied. After more huffing and puffing, a nullifying silence fell, which further illustrated points of the argument. Here are some of these figures, mostly from volumes published in the enlightened post-1960s: *Penguin Book of Contemporary Verse* ed. Kenneth Allott – 5 women/90 men; *New Penguin Book of English Verse* ed. Paul Keegan – 16 women/81 men; *British Poetry Since 1945* ed. Edward Lucie-Smith – 7 women/90 men; *Oxford Book of Contemporary Verse* ed. D.J. Enright – 3 women/37 men; 101 *Sonnets* ed. Don Paterson – 13 women/87 men; *The New Poetry* ed. Al Alvarez – 2 women/26 men; *Poetry 1900-1965* ed. George Macbeth – 2 women/21 men; *New York Poets* ed. Mark Ford – no women; *New York Poets II* eds. Mark Ford & Trevor Winkfield – 2 women/9 men; *Forward Anthology of Poetry for the years 1993-2006* consistently features many more men than women; critical books are similarly lop-sided. *Ad nauseum*. I could bore us all to kingdom come.

The anthologies *The Firebox* ed. Sean O'Brien (34 women/91 men), *Emergency Kit* eds. Jo Shapcott & Matthew Sweeney (41 women/116 men) and *The Anthology of Twentieth Century British and Irish Poetry* ed. Keith Tuma (31 women/87 men), with the fairer acknowledgements these figures imply, nevertheless hit the proverbial glass ceiling, with women poets comprising roughly a third of the total, occasionally a smidgeon more; turning hopefully to Andrew Duncan's *Poetry Review* article on this last volume, we find that his thirty regretted omissions - poets from the 1950s-1990s - include not a single woman. The anthologies *Last Words* eds. Don Paterson & Jo Shapcott (33 women/55 men) and *The New Poetry* eds. David Kennedy, David Morley & Michael Hulse (17 women/38 men) all have a 'healthier' balance; Bloodaxe, the publisher of this latter, boasts a consistently better record when it comes to publishing women. Carol Ann Duffy's *Hand in Hand* and Adrienne Rich's *The Best American Poetry 1996* are the only two anthologies I could find comprised of more women than men. Here, it is worth quoting extensively Germaine Greer's perspective on the so-called 'arbitrary' nature of coincidences:

> It is not easy to imagine a male poet objecting to appearing in an anthology of men's poems, as most anthologies have been, though the fact is not highlighted in

their titles. The Amis anthology, to cite the most doggedly laddish, does not separate work by gender, but women would have been better served if it had; out of 242 poems, eight are by women. One, by Elizabeth Jennings, is included because Amis published it when he was at Oxford in 1949; another, by Felicia Hemans, because his class translated it into Latin hexameters when he was at school; one by Christina Rossetti is accompanied by a sneer, and another by the unknown Teresa Dooley is used to caricature all poetesses. Laura Riding was doubtless happy to be one of the select company of nine women poets represented in *The Rattle-Bag*, compiled by Seamus Heaney and Ted Hughes in 1982.[5]

She has more to say about the criteria for inclusion:

> ...the blokes like the girls best when they write like the blokes, and extra-specially when they write about girls the way the blokes do. It suits the male poet to believe that neither sex is specifically intended because it encourages him in his view that his specificity is actually universality. The woman poet who knowingly plays this game is not so much a ventriloquist as a ventriloquist's dummy.[6]

A snapshot of American anthologies shows us that *The Best American Poetry* anthologies (both 1989 & 2005), *The Best of the Best American Poetry: 1988-1997*, the *Oxford Book of American Poetry* ed. David Lehman (published in the UK but with an American editor) and the *Vintage Book of Contemporary World Poetry*, ed. J.D. McClatchy, adhering to our glass ceiling model, have somewhat better figures than the following: *British and Irish Poetry Since 1970* eds. Richard Caddel & Peter Quartermain – 10 women/45 men; *The New Naked Poetry* eds. Stephen Berg and Robert Mezey – 3 women/23 men; *New Lines* anthologies ed. Robert Conquest 1956 – 1 woman/8 men, and 1963 – 1 woman/23 men. The figures in the recent *Postmodern American Poetry: a Norton Anthology*, ed. P. Hoover (27 women/76 men) have improved since the *Norton Anthology of Modern Poetry* (1973), eds. Richard Elman and Robert O'Clair (19 women/132 men). Generally, the USA anthologies do seem more balanced. The figures quoted above for women editors speak for themselves.

Naturally, these anthologies reflect their editors' taste within the confines of what's available from publishers in the first place. These figures are themselves at odds with those from the 1960s onwards which show increasing numbers of women winning Gregory awards, this acknowledgement commonly regarded as a reliable and leading indicator of new (UK) talent. Women comprise two-thirds of the poetry-buying public and a majority of workshop attendees. More *ad nauseum*. I had not expected such appalling figures, but shouldn't be so shocked at others' lack of outrage.

Let us not get 'hysterical', though. Let us be 'reasonable', yes? Edna Longley, in choosing 10 women/49 men to represent *The Bloodaxe Book of Twentieth Century Poetry*, just prefers these poets. A talented writer herself, surely Dorothy Wordsworth was a reliable critic in being so scathing about women's poetry. In her book *Gendering Poetry*, Vicki Bertram notes how both Kathleen Raine and Laura Riding "had very firm views about the innate inferiority of female poets". (On cue come revelations about Riding's unacknowledged contributions to writing by her then partner, Robert Graves: a familiar tale.) So women also judge women on gender rather than merit.[7] In her *New York Times* article 'Of Women Writers and Writing About Women' (May 3, 1974), Barbara Probst Solomon refers to Elizabeth Hardwick's candid essay 'On Reading the Writings of Women' from the autumn 1959 issue of *Columbia Forum*, in which Hardwick examines her own responses to women writers: "...Toward the achievements of women I find my own attitudes expremely complicated by all sorts of vague emotions... As a writer I feel a nearly unaccountable attraction and hostility to the work of other women writers. Envy, competitiveness, scorn infect my judgments at times, and indifference is strangely hard to come by in this matter."

Our Modern Greats had hardly left the newsstands when, predictably, the *Guardian* commissioned a woman to justify their series' equally predictable lack of women: a well-worn, pre-emptive tactic employed by those defending a canon still being shorn of female talent. Also on cue, Erica Jong writes: "Women columnists still make their fortunes by attacking other women, as in the age of Clare Boothe Luce. It is, in fact, a time-honoured way to get a book contract or a political appointment. Trashing one's own gender remains a path to advancement." [8]

The poet and feminist Adrienne Rich admits that she had tried not to identify herself as a female poet until the late 1950s. She analyses the pressures which pit "woman against woman, woman against herself"[9]. Flattery and blandishments convince the chosen woman poet she is special. Separated from the herd of ordinary female poets, she is accorded the status of honorary man, and so a trustworthy critic, although she is exempt only within the terms of a system underwritten by masculine primacy:

> The token woman may come to believe that her personal solution has not been bought, but awarded her as a prize for her special qualities. And she may – indeed, must – have special qualities. But her personal solution has been bought at a political price; her 'liberation' becomes another small confirmation of the patriarchal order and its principle of division.[10]

Such 'fragmentation' is part of a sophisticated disposal system, crucial debate consigned to the 'women's pages' ghetto or women's anthologies, where indignation is safely stashed, available to the already-converted and otherwise largely ignored. Men rarely participate in such 'special interest' forums, except in reactionary guise.

It goes without saying our special poet is not a 'poetess', which demeaning term does not simply connote a female practitioner as some claim. In *Stealing the Language: The Emergence of Women's Poetry in America*, the poet and critic Alicia Ostriker states: "All of us know, or think we know, what a poetess is, and, to paraphrase Marianne Moore, we too dislike her". Meanwhile, back at the corral, writing about Sylvia Plath, James Fenton develops his theories:

> When Elizabeth Bishop and her college friends sat doubled up with laughter at Edna St. Vincent Millay's reading, with Millay wearing her long robe and clutching a curtain, what the girls were laughing at was a poetess, a woman imagining that a poetess must be something like a priestess.[11]

Regardless of this (to us) comic and ludicrous picture,[12] Fenton's conclusions are enlightening: "Women becoming priests – the Pagan-sounding Priestess - upsets the symbolism".[13] Such views accord with women's assigned role as defender of morality within "a Judaeo-Christian world view where a woman's value was above rubies and yet below that of men", as Sally Feldman describes it.[14] (Within the Judaic tradition – and others too I would guess – women's oppression is sometimes ennobled with the tag 'Queen of the Household', which phrase neatly denotes the limits of her realm.) She goes on to quote the Bishop of Rochester Michael Nazir-Ali's admiration for the historian Callum Brown who "notes particularly the part played by women in upholding piety and in passing on the faith in the home. It was the loss of this faith and piety among women which caused the steep decline in Christian observance in all sections of society".[15] What a heavy burden this is: to make a woman responsible for perceived failings in a hierarchy she's powerless to redefine or question.

The baggage attached to 'woman poet' – poetess or not – is more like a lead weight. Poet and critic Stanley Kunitz, in a review of Louise Bogan's *Land of Dust and Flame* quotes with dismay Allen Tate's reference to her as "the most accomplished woman poet of our time", and wonders if "to be perennially classified and reviewed as a 'woman poet', must prove discomfiting, at least to a poet... of superlative gifts and power",[16] and to anyone else, it is tempting to add, unless we are in an elitist mood. With a perception others sorely lack, Kunitz is disparaging about Stephen Spender's generalisation that:"when men write poetry they have their eyes fixed on several things at once, such as the form and effect of the poem, whereas women lose themselves in the subject-matter, the experience... and are careless of words themselves and rhythmic pattern".[17] Spender clearly had not read Plath, or many others, one is bound to say. And I had thought that women were meant to be the ultimate multi-taskers! But such clichés are always a moveable feast (sic).

James Fenton is "loathe to betray the spirit of Moore and Bishop by calling them women poets",[18] which term is commonly understood to be one of belittlement. It's hard to know how to take his comment that we can't know if Marianne Moore "achieved what she did only at the cost of the suppression of what might be taken as womanly",[19] which presumably would otherwise hinder her greatness. Sylvia Plath, doubtless fairer game than Moore or Bishop, is damned with faint praise (or praised with faint damning, I am not sure which): "...I was looking out for that particular tone of voice, the tone she acquires when she is not yelling (and most of the time she is not yelling)":[20] which final clause certainly begs the question of why he mentions "yelling" at all; in contrast, Linda W. Wagner's comments about how Helen Vendler "deals with the issue of Plath's confessional tendencies, pointing out that Plath is seldom out of control. Plath never rages."[21] Fenton utterly takes it for granted that women poets are subject to the conflicts between marriage and writing or career, which conflicts needn't pertain to men. Perhaps it's unfair (and naïve) to expect him to factor in or challenge this disparity or to ponder its consequences. Least of all would it occur to him to speculate how his male perspective on matters influences his own assessments of Plath's "conventional attitudes and shallow ambitions on the one hand, and (that) other self with its burning mysterious purpose",[22] thereby describing (but not objecting to) the necessary division of self and vocation not required of men.[23] Viewing with distaste Plath's unguarded elation at being the first woman poet Al Alvarez has taken seriously since Emily Dickinson, Fenton seizes the opportunity to express a predictable disparagement of female ambition. Plath's response to having nabbed one of the few seats at high-table reserved for women, while unseemly and gloating, is perhaps also understandable under such a weight of prejudice.

He later acknowledges with wonderful (dis-?)ingenuousness: "The invention of the woman poet as evil or threatening archetype, witch, harridan…was not Sylvia Plath's single-handed achievement".[24] To which I reply: quite. Indeed, one recognises in her writing precisely the audacity and rage of the powerful yet impotent woman and poet. Alicia Ostriker persuasively analyses Plath's 'bravado':

> That men do dread the avenging maenad Plath evokes… is unquestionable. At the same time, her incantation is hollow. She is impersonating a female Phoenix-fiend like a woman wearing a Halloween costume, or a child saying 'I'll kill you' to the grownups, or Lear bellowing 'I will do such things –/What they are yet I know/not, but they shall be/The terrors of the earth.' She is powerless, she knows it, she hates it.[25]

In missing the point – by not listening – Fenton provides clues to this very aspect of her work.[26] Though describing as 'courteous' Seamus Heaney's description of how she "rampages so permissively in the history of other people's sorrows"[27] he does acknowledge "a great deal of art is made from the history of other people's sorrows";[28] he also accords Plath credit, while explaining why her meaning and significance had failed to sink in on first reading, "The earliest English readers of Plath knew little about her, except perhaps that she was American and that she was sad, had died young. We thought of her, perhaps as the latest Faber poet… they were poems, not yet manifestos."[29] There are so many objectionable points here where do I begin? The judgement not of the writing but the life (ironic)? Conflating the writing with those terrible feminists' co-opting of it? With a tinge of condescending finality, and a smugness not unlike the tone he deplores in Plath, Fenton concludes: "like it or not, there was something masculine in the archetype of poet, with which it was difficult for a woman to come to terms".[30] In fact the real problem is this limited and limiting perspective from leading writers, especially within a volume widely set as required text. As Katha Pollitt says: "The very fact that Plath was a woman has dazed many a strong mind."[31]

The terms paying Plath's admission through the hallowed gates of the *Guardian* series are striking – and handed-down, one suspects. Margaret Drabble, the author of the Plath booklet rightly emphasises Plath's importance apart from her 'suicide' poems… by invoking the cliché of redemptive motherhood: "the vivid colours of giving birth, the pleasures of breast-feeding and the power and mystery of the maternal bond." Phew! It is a good thing she had kids. Otherwise what could be said about the work?! A contemporary of Plath's – which qualifies her in the pamphlet's words to be its author – Drabble describes her 'appalling' and 'exhilarating' poetry from the 'heart' rather than the head, thus minimising any formal dexterity and finesse (which needn't preclude the heart).[32] Apparently, it's radical to attribute her fame to the usual criteria: an exceptional feel for language, outstanding technical skills, a powerful vision and mastery of form. Apparently, it is naïve to expect ability and talent to be the king-makers' (sic) main criteria when it comes to women poets.

Double standards like this are rife, strengths turned to weaknesses undermining a poet's stature. Plath is misleadingly summed up and disparaged as 'confessional'; the term applied to Robert Lowell is never so negative. As we have seen from Fenton's remarks, critical writing about Plath typically eclipses the work itself by emphasising her fame as contingent on the sensationalist biographical events of her life and death, which issues are largely secondary in the writing about her husband, Ted Hughes. Sadly, this lack of critical engagement is characteristic of how most women poets are viewed – or are not viewed – as is more the case.

Alicia Ostriker examines how the critical lexicon varies to suit gender: "We seldom encounter, in praise of woman poets, terms like *great, powerful, forceful... large or true...*". Instead, she continues, "complimentary adjectives of choice... shift toward the diminutives: *graceful, subtle, elegant, delicate, cryptic* and, above all, *modest.*"[33] Repeatedly, women poets are admired for their retiring nature: "We know that Bishop was extremely cautious with the deployment of her private life and tenderest emotions in her poetry."[34] Having devoted a great part of his review to poems he doesn't like, Fenton does laud the "quiet, quizzical Plath".[35] Even Kunitz uses words like 'pretty' and 'elegance' to describe Bogan;[36] his essay on Marianne Moore begins in the following fashion: "Miss Moore is unique, and she never argues. Like peace she is indivisible".[37] According to W.H. Auden, Adrienne Rich's early poems are "neatly and modestly dressed, speak quietly but do not mumble...". (Here, the phrase 'eating of words' comes to mind.)

Ostriker dryly remarks: "Male poets engage in quests; women poets run errands".[38] The poetic material cited as proof of a male poet's depth and substance will, on the other hand, substantiate a woman poet's limited palette. Writing about partner or family, she is a 'domestic' poet; meanwhile, he is absorbed in the timeless themes of love and passion. Grappling with life and death issues, men are dragon-slayers; women embarked on such odysseys are rarely granted similarly heroic status. Instead, they're victims, a considerably less noble assignation which handily renders them vulnerable to criticism embedded with ulterior motives, and more susceptible to being undervalued and misunderstood, except in the context of their maternal role, or tragedy.

Rich refers to an "imaginative obsession with victimisation and death, unfair to Plath herself and her own struggle for survival",[39] which remark echoes my current preoccupation with a critical fetishisation of the damaged woman, as artist especially. Fenton takes pot-shots at living poets he thinks pale imitations of Plath, the very poet whose talent he had failed to recognise in the first place, while she lived; one wonders if he will be proven similarly wrong about these more recent targets. Dead, Plath becomes the conveniently passive subject of speculation, handily absent from the arena where power politics are played out.[40] Dead, she is protected and enhanced by virtue of this ultimate vulnerability.

For more temperate criticism of Plath's work (not to mention serious analysis about her technical flair which mitigates against more prevalent views bent on trashing confessional poets) we must turn mostly to books published in the USA: such as Anita Helle's *The Unraveling Archive: Essays on Sylvia Plath* or Linda W. Wagner's *Critical Essays on Sylvia Plath*, in which Peter Porter, comments on her technical flair by restating John Frederick Nims's comment: "[her] submerged iambics glisten like reefs under her expressionist surfaces", or perhaps turn to Sarah Hannah's scholarly monogram ' "Something Else Hauls Me Through Air": Sound and Structure in Four Late Poems by Sylvia Plath', in which she meticulously analyses how that poet's apprenticeship to craft led to a "precise manipulation of syntax, rhyme and structure to enact complex themes... even the simple sentence can serve as a hypnotic and expressive device in a poem". In fact, the recent death of the talented and young Sarah Hannah has me pondering the rescue of her work from these death-cult terms which routinely sidelines any critical analysis.

Similarly, Emily Dickinson's self-imposed purdah is both a virtue and symptom of the madness assumed to underpin her creativity, her retiring nature and oddball spinster status like a sandwich board which the artful strategist and vocational writer is forced to carry. Says Ostriker: "What we may call the 'accident' theory of female creativity persists in, among others, David Porter, whose *Dickinson: The Modern Idiom* argues that Dickinson's evasions of 'reality' inadvertently anticipate the radical gestures of postmodernism."[41] Maybe, to him all avant-gardism is an accident. A collation of routine not-so-subliminal 'forces' working against the writing woman provides the premise for Joanna Russo's book *How to Suppress Women's Writing* which, to rephrase slightly from the book jacket, goes something like this: *She didn't write it. She wrote it, but she shouldn't have. She wrote it, but she had help. She wrote it, but it isn't art. She wrote it, but she's an anomaly. She wrote it, but but but....*

Inevitably, an author's work is itself influenced and even compromised by the critical terms employed to describe it. Adrienne Rich notes the overexposure "in the schoolroom to Emily Dickinson's 'little-girl poems', her kittenish tones, as in 'I'm Nobody, Who are you' (a poem whose underlying anger translates itself into archness)[42], in contrast to poems more accurately attesting to that poet's power and depth.[43] After re-reading Virginia Woolf's *A Room of One's Own* for the first time in years, Rich exclaims:

> I was astonished at the sense of effort, of pains taken, of dogged tentativeness, in the tone of the essay. And I recognized that tone. I had heard it often enough, in myself and in other women. It is the tone of a woman determined not to appear angry, who is *willing* herself to be calm, detached, and even charming in a roomful of men where things have been said which are attacks on her very integrity.[44]

Accordingly, she observes her own development: "In those years formalism was part of the strategy – like asbestos gloves, it allowed me to handle materials I could-n't pick up bare-handed."[45] Rich – her poems in this volume illustrating two periods in her development – describes how she had regarded a poem as "an arrangement of ideas and feelings, pre-determined... [and saying] what I had already decided it should say"; which earlier 'absolutist' approach, she later realised, meant that she "suppressed, omitted, falsified even, certain disturbing elements, to gain that perfection of order": an aim some applaud quite regardless of the success of its effect. Rich goes on to describe her later writing: "Perhaps a simple way of putting it would be to say that instead of poems about experiences, I am getting poems that are experiences, that contribute to my knowledge and my emotional life even while they reflect and assimilate it."[46] Referring to Gayle Rubin's essay 'The Traffic in Women: Notes on the "Political Economy of Sex" ' (Second Wave: A Feminist Reader) and E.P. Thompson's The Making of the English Working Class, Carolyn Steedman comments on being an object within a patriarchal or capitalist exchange system: "We end up with fine insights into the minds of those who do the exchanging, but knowing next to nothing about the understanding of those, who like yams and shells, are the object of exchange."[47] Such a comment suggests precisely why poets might choose to abjure working in form, understanding its import and provenance. Although some feminists have rejcted traditional forms as oppressive, the subtle nuances of such gestures are handily and routinely oversimplified. In his essay 'Line Breaks and Back-Drafr: Not a Defence of Poem' (Poetry Review, Vol 85.4 Winter 05/06), John Kinsella comments: "...syntactical and rhetorical boundaries are prisons... [with] form... to be used pragmatically at times, but ultimately to ve tested at every opportunity... I don't want my poems to leisure or pleasure but I do want them to allow for a polymorphously perverse interaction with both myself and the reader. They are fetishes, but hopefully with adjustable appendages. It should go without saying that 'women poets' – like 'men poets' – make their aesthetic decisions based on the usual explorations and considerations that define the creative process.[48]

We could view in a wider context the dismal publishing figures and the tenor of critical writing about women. For example, the 2008 groundbreaking presidential nomination race in the US, by fielding a woman and a black candidate, flushed out an unpleasantly regressive zeitgeist...if one can call 'regressive' something that has never gone away. Websites boasting a merrily virulent misogyny proliferated. The predictable racist comments rightly provoked universal and unqualified outrage; in contrast, analogous sexist comments merited mild disapproval or uncomfortable laughs. A New York Times article's statistics showed that, consistently, people can overlook race more readily than gender, when it comes to asessing candidates for jobs. Nevertheless, the media carried on giving the lion's share of coverage to racism, as the major hurtle. Amy Wack reminds that the newly-minted platitude is: Feminism is a dirty word. In this context, we ponder a widespread ambivalence towards women's anthologies; in this context, we ponder not only the anger at the blatant under- and mis-representation of women poets, but the anger at this anger.

Consideration of such issues naturally come to mind while the choices for this book where made. I tend to agree that "[it] is a difficult task to marry the Muse happily to politics".[49] In fact, some editors prefer to exclude polemical poems perceived as endangering a book's aesthetic credentials: entrenched dogma answered with another kind of dogma. Such feeble gestures feed the very stereotypes we aim to overturn. Literary tradition is charged, informed and enhanced precisely by literature devised in part as a brave challenge to the personal attacks it will inevitably invite.

Nevertheless, to challenge the embedded biases of an entrenched status quo – itself intrinsically political of course – in this Introduction is to submit to an unwilling politicisation and to expose oneself to the negative connotations of the 'manifesto', which diverts attention away from the issue itself: in this case the writing. The fact that feminist poetry earns a specialist area of study in its own right becomes the excuse to regard it separately from other sub-groups which, however various their concerns, are nevertheless still assembled under the same literary umbrella. Furthermore, gender-segregated anthologies are commonly perceived to take gender politics as their main subject, critical books reinforcing such assumptions with "women... often grouped together in a chapter of their own".Vicki Bertram notes how Peter Childs, in his book *The Twentieth Century in Poetry: A Critical Survey*, "tries to avoid accusations of tokenism by having one chapter on 'recent male anthologies'; and another on 'recent anthologies by women' ", and she adds:"But while the first chapter covers a broad range of issues from Thatcherism to philosophy, the second takes feminism as its central theme".

Bertram posits "the dangers of an isolationist approach...[which] creates and sustains the impression that women poets' only subject is their woman-hood... (and) ensuring none of the men poets is explored with questions of sexual politics or gender in mind." She comments how "currently women poets' writing merits a separate chapter, an easily accommodated tributary, while the main river flows on undisturbed."[50] Although a thin trickle of women's voices – often the usual suspects – runs throughout mainstream anthologies, there's little value in an honour bestowed by editors (mostly male) who are *simply not familiar with enough women poets*. This book, in introducing this part of the canon and re-writing the list of 'essentials', throws down the gauntlet to future critics and editors in the hope they can better represent the true breadth and vitality of the tradition.

In the movie *Groundhog Day* a man is doomed to relive the same day repeatedly, until he can get it right. Then, Sonny and Cher will finally stop singing 'I Got You Babe', and everyone will rediscover Simone de Beauvoir's classic book *The Second Sex*, published over fifty years ago. Erica Jong, describing how her 1968 hope has evaporated, calls feminism "nameless again", but concludes: "Perhaps a new generation will discover it like the shard of an ancient cooking vessel. Perhaps someone will name it again. I'll be there."[51] Then we may not need women's anthologies to get the accurate measure of women's literary contributions, and won't need to devote this valuable space to saying what is commonly thought to be unsay-able. Many consider it passé – old hat – to bring up these subjects.What is really old hat is a societally sanctioned quashing of this important discussion. That both this book and its defence feel more necessary than ever suggests that some old hats should still be in vogue.

Now that the polemic is out of the way, and "we heathens have the town to ourselves",[52] this part of my Introduction offers up some tasters from the feast, and describes the book's format and editorial criteria for inclusion, in the context of a brief survey of the modern repertoire.

For several reasons, this collection is organised thematically, rather than geographically or chronologically – the usual strategies. Placed side-by-side, poems of different provenances further elucidate each other through the company they keep, these relationships and contrasts affording glimpses of a momentary synchronicity or a deeper parallel that casts new light all around. Fortuitous cross-currents – and such lateral jumps as characterise the creative process itself – prompted us to make a virtue of accidents with more conscious links. What inspires and surprises us hopefully does the same for the reader.

The titled chapters can themselves stand as slim volumes, with poems organised to highlight kinships. For example, Chapter One is book-ended thematically by two poems about weddings: Beth Ann Fennelly's 'Poem Not To Be Read At Your Wedding' (precisely intended for this purpose, of course) and Alice Oswald's sonnet, 'Wedding', with its incremental progression of imaginative simile and metaphor transcending artifice, to achieve an elevated tone that speaks truly of its subject. Chapter Two is similarly framed by Frances Cornford's 'Childhood' and Sharon Olds's 'I Go Back To May 1937', both based on an adult's view of the child's view of adults.

Elsewhere, thematic bridges arch between consecutive poems. Carol Ann Duffy's pithy sound-bite, 'Mrs. Darwin', disarmingly punctuates Hilary Llewellyn-Williams's 'Making Man', a variation on the Genesis story, and Duffy's 'Small Female Skull', with its tipsily elated curiosity, follows Anne Stevenson's 'The Spirit Is Too Blunt An Instrument': both meditations on the unlikely surprise of existence itself, expressed through an almost forensic description of a body's mortality. Dorianne Laux's 'The Shipfitter's Wife' and Jean Sprackland's 'The Apprentice' describe manual labour to convey intense eroticism. Situated side-by-side, two poems about paintings - Mary Ruefle's 'The Last Supper' and Vicki Feaver's 'Oi Yoi Yoi' – share theme and perspective, filling in missing parts of their respective pictures. Jane Kenyon's 'Otherwise' and Eavan Boland's 'An Elegy For My Mother In Which She Scarecely Appears', both about death, both 'tell it slant'; then comes Denise Levertov's 'Despair', its controlled diction describing others' uncontrollable grief, by which vicarious means the narrator eloquently expresses her own, from an effective dual stance of profound empathy and observational detachment.

Elsewhere, a single image may provide continuity: birds winging their way through several poems to alight finally in Margaret Danner's poem, transformed into a butterfly, which is 'The Painted Lady'. Adjoining poems may share a tonal quality; the music of the final lines of Pattiann Rogers's poem 'While You Watch Us Sleeping' – "Aren't you sorry? /Don't you love us" – prefigures the elegiac tone for the children who never existed in Gwendolyn Brooks's 'The Mother'. Sometimes, the development of an idea can be traced from poem to poem. The implicitly political yet lyrical 'Family Secrets', by Toi Derricotte, puts a different slant on the previous poem, Freda Downie's 'Great Grandfather'. The beauty of an artefact is the conduit to war's horrors in Naomi Shihab Nye's 'The Small Vases Of Hebron', which subject subtly suggests it may well be 'A Bad Time For The Sublime', written in Kay Ryan's characteristically slim-line pattern and wryly opaque tone.

In 'Mock Orange' by Louise Glück, the intoxicating scent of a flower – not to mention its very name – is metaphor for our susceptibility to the vicissitudes of love, a more jaded appraisal overtaken by a soaring, ravishing lyricism: "How can I be content/when there is still/that odor in the world?" By the time we reach Katherine Pierpoint's 'This Dead Relationship', any residual cynicism has been filtered into a tone both deliciously dry and devastatingly accurate too:

> I carry a dead relationship around everywhere with me.
> It's my hobby.
> How lucky to have a job that's also my hobby.

As part of our canny plot to light up the paths between poems, we've employed another organising principle: another game of parallels and kinships. 'War Poetry' by Kate Clanchy, an elegantly suggestive sonnet, and Katha Pollitt's 'Trying To Write A Poem Against The War' – this latter's colloquial and self-conscious humility earning a difficult subject – are printed near to each other. However, in between, we pause to take in 'After Great Pain' by Emily Dickinson; her work is dotted throughout the book, as touchstones for other poems, all juxtaposed in mutually referential ways.

From an earlier generation than most poets here, yet Dickinson does not strike one as such, her conventional four-square hymn structures disrupted by an idiosyncratic typography which famously prompted bemused early editors to normalise her punctuation. Germaine Greer describes this unique style: "[her] dashes and exclamation points crack across the page like rifle shots."[53] One of the two great American innovators of her time – with Walt Whitman – Dickinson remains of primary importance. In a letter to her mother, Sylvia Plath jokes about her own writing: "any resemblance to Emily Dickinson is purely intentional."[54] The typographical explorations – stylistic allusions and direct references – in Alice Fulton's work all pay homage to a poet about whom Fulton says elsewhere: "Favorite poets come and go throughout one's life, but (Dickinson) is one whose work deepened for me as years went by."

In book form, we've arranged a long enfilade of mirrors, fashioning our own somewhat idiosyncratic and hopefully enlightening format. In this refraction of time and place, poets face each other, or we face ourselves, sometimes through others. So much the better if we throw a few spanners into the works. Certainly, it is high time to shatter the surprisingly persistent stereotype of what is meant to constitute 'women's subjects': present a new status quo instead of just a reactionary response to the old one.

The 'Work' in our title primary signifies 'opus'. Our revised – and not so radical – agenda takes it for granted that women poets engage with a range of themes as varied as their lives.[55] For example, they are as interested as men – or not – in babies, family and housework, which last subject is here presented contextually, with other kinds of work, such as Molly Peacock's "woman in her workpants smelling of/gasoline and cut grass", or U.A. Fanthorpe's witty job advertisement for 'The Poet's Companion' (which this editor not only seconds, but places here in hopes of a reply!). From many chapters and angles, one may look back over one's shoulder at that 'Work' of the title: for example, clocking Joan Murray's distinctive cadences:

> You talk of art, of work, of books.
> Have you ever sat down, thought all that's to do? [56]

We are stopped in our tracks by the hauntingly ambiguous and evocative Lorine Niedecker:[57] "What horror to awake at night/and in the dimness see the light". The poem continues:

> I'm pillowed and padded, pale and puffing
> lifting household stuffing
> carpets, dishes, benches, fishes,
> I've spent my life on nothing.

I'm with Elizabeth Bishop and Robert Lowell who "shared a resistance to abstract or codified theory",[58] and with Groucho Marx who would not belong to any club that would have him as a member. Depending on who you ask – and at what time of day – the poetry world is either enriched by, or fractured into, Movements or Schools, like sports teams with stadiums of cheering or jeering fans. A poet's presumed attachment to a particular team can prejudice, in advance of actually reading the work. That's show business, as they say: hearsay, and the weight of a critic's word. While many poets don't categorise themselves, nor write to exemplify theory, nevertheless it needs to be acknowledged how poets contribute in these terms: however unwittingly, or in an iconoclastic spirit. A Jewish poet with Catholic tastes, I've cast the net wide, hauling in all varieties of idioms and aesthetics, including poems from these Schools which seem to quantify the original spirit of exploration rather than a soulless attachment to orthodoxy.

Although many readers may be familiar already with the history of poetry in the twentieth century, we will run through a potted history of modernism, partly so as to mention poets included here. To begin at the turn of the twentieth century, and moving forward – in a somewhat stuttering chronological way – Modernism is commonly understood to have been seeded in the run-up to World War One which then accelerated its growth. "By the war's end in 1918, the centuries-old European domination of the world had ended and the 'American Century' had begun."[59] Marianne Moore was a leading poet during this post-war innovatory period, instrumental in establishing the modern voice.[60] "Cubism, Construc-tivism, Futurism, Acmeism, and Imagism were among the most influential banners under which new artists grouped themselves."[61] This last subgroup, represented here by H.D. and Amy Lowell – themselves influenced by the Symbolists – then later influenced or were succeeded by the San Francisco Renaissance, the Objectivists

(Lorine Niedecker),[62] the New York School [63] and the Black Mountain Poets and the Beats: all part of the New American Poets rubric.

The battle against social conformity and literary tradition was central to the work of the Beats"[64] in the 1950s; 'Women Beats' almost seems a contradiction of terms, but you'll find Diane Wakoski and Anne Waldman in these pages.[65] Tacking across the ocean to Britain during this same period we find the English movement called... The Movement. This school, wishing to avoid romantic excess, defined its ethos – as some schools do – in terms of what it was *not*. Most sources, albeit clearly inadequate, list Elizabeth Jennings as the only woman in this group. Just as the Liverpool Poets in the 1960s (Adrian Henri, Roger McGough, Brian Patten) were influenced by the Beats, The British Poetry Revival (Elaine Feinstein), a looser description of the 1960s and 70s modernist-inspired reaction to The Movement's more conservative approach, forged more links with the American vernacular and scene. As a woman and from a family of Jewish immigrants, Feinstein was "looking for a tradition that could accommodate the voice of an outsider", and she explains how the "cautious, ironic tone of the new Movement did not excite me. It was so smugly self-protective, so determined not to expose the indignities of feeling."[66]

Schools of thought can result simply from poets, who may be quite different from each other, residing in geographical proximity to each other, as was the case at the fabled Black Mountain College. The Black Mountain Poets shared with the New York Poets avant-garde principles practised by a swathe of artists from different disciplines, including the composer John Cage and abstract expressionists Willem and Elaine de Kooning during the latter part of its heyday, which encompassed the 1930s-1950s and culminated in Charles Olson's seminal essay on the 'Projectivists', as these poets were also known. In this, he posits an aesthetic theory calling for a poetry of 'open field' composition; primary importance is placed on the 'breath' and spontaneity is valued above much else, with process emphasised over product.

A main legacy of this movement was an experimental ethos which reiterated the importance of the creative arts as an area of study. Ironically, it is the institutionalisation of this creative art which has been blamed for its decline in cultural importance, the subject of Dana Gioia's essay 'Can Poetry Matter?', in which he cites Joseph Epstein's "mordant 1988 critique 'Who Killed Poetry'", first published in *Commentary*: "Epstein indicted the poets themselves and the institutions they had helped create especially creative-writing programs"[67] (of which, more later). Denise Levertov is one of the few Black Mountain woman poets; the fact that her name crops up in Confessional discussions too indicates a degree of fluidity between categories, and presumably the fluidity of creative thought itself.

Arising firstly from a period of experimentation, literary theory is often only solidified as such latterly, for historical convenience and textbooks: its premises subjugated in service of a containable, teachable methodology which doesn't always best serve the health of a creative writing 'industry', it has to be said; the daughter of invention is the institutionalisation of the creative arts. As with the Beats, challenges to a previous orthodoxy help define the New, defined at least in part in terms of a renunciation of the Old, which often it seems imperative to render obsolete.

Several later branches of modernism, such as the New York Poets, developed partly as a direct challenge to the perceived prevalence of the Confessionals in the 1960s, which fact precisely reiterates the importance of a group some poets like Louise Bogan thought self-indulgent. (Interestingly, in light of such views, although Bogan adhered to strict lyrical forms, within these she "maintained a high emotional pitch", her poems particularly focused on the "perpetual disparity of heart and mind."[68]) It is in England where we seem to find the most widespread and persistent aversion to the confessional aesthetic as it is understood, which often it is not. Critics willy-nilly use this word, first used by M.L. Rosenthal to describe Robert Lowell's work, to encompass a multitude of sins; such misappropriations may be contrasted to Philip Larkin's comment about our exemplar Sylvia Plath, that: "it was hard to see how she was labelled confessional".[69]

In her Introduction to *Critical Essays on Sylvia Plath*, Linda W. Wagner notes how "by the end of the 1970s the confessional term had become almost completely pejorative", in being applied to any mention of Sylvia Plath, Anne Sexton and John Berryman, who all committed suicide.[70] Elsewhere Wagner remarks: "(The) range of critical reaction – and the heat that reaction has generated – suggests that Plath's poetry is more important to contemporary poets than some critics would have us believe"; indeed, this comment might equally apply more generally to the confessionals. Do away with the poets mining this seam and we lose Marie Howe's bold and fearless 'Death, The Last Visit', and Sharon Olds's 'I Go Back to May 1937' which poem's final line – "Do what you are going to do, and I will tell about it." – is bravura underlined with vulnerability, of exactly the kind previously discussed with reference to Plath. This poem raises uncomfortable questions about catharsis – the need to chronicle pain to render it less harmful – and, indeed, the writer's vocation in this context: whether it's a duty to reveal hidden histories or truths, or a betrayal, which issues are clearly relevant to the ongoing controversy about the confessional idiom itself. In fact, poets such as Denise Levertov and Adrienne Rich, in placing the personal in a socio-political context, exemplify how confessional poets encompass a much broader territory than likes to be acknowledged by fiercer critics of this transgressive crew.

We'll need to backtrack to the first half of the twentieth century, to trace another strand in the rope. Like the later San Francisco Renaissance, the Harlem Renaissance (Angelina Weld Grimke) was more a collage of individuals and communities encompassing a diversity of genres – poetry and music especially – rather than a single ideological movement.[71] It describes a major artistic flowering from the first black generation free from slavery which was yet within living memory. Racial pride was a unifying ethic, although some artists were criticised for adopting flavours from caucasian artists, from which tradition a distance was sought, for obvious reasons. All movements branch into sub-groups, perhaps distinguished from each other by no more than minute gradations of perspective. For example, the Negritude movement, (to use the name of its period) led by French-speaking writers and intellectuals was inspired by the Harlem Renaissance. Its ideology provoked the Nigerian writer Wole Soyinka to say: "un tigre ne proclâme pas sa tigritude, il saute sur sa proie"(A tiger doesn't proclaim its tiger-ness; it jumps on its prey).[72]

This artistic flowering set the stage for the Black Arts Movement of the 1960s and 70s (Gwendolyn Brooks, Nikki Giovanni) which arose alongside the Black Power movement; its crucial legacy includes the creation of numerous publishing forums and the establishment of university programs specialising in African American literature which impelled a slow revision of the canon as represented in mainstream anthologies (expedited latterly by affirmative action policies) and led to a more routine inclusion of poets such as June Jordan, Maya Angelou, Margaret Walker, Lucile Clifton, Josephine Miles, Alice Dunbar Nelson[73] and Margaret Danner.

Addison Gayle Jr., editor of *The Forerunners: Black Poets in America* regards Danner as an important transitional writer in African American literature: a 'bridge' from the Harlem Renaissance to a more distinctively modern black voice. Her use of implicit political metaphor couched in a more poetic rhetoric finds echoes in a later poem like 'The Shoes Of Dead Comrades' by Jackie Kay (in contrast to the more explicit polemic of Valerie Bloom's epigrammatic 'Yuh Hear 'bout...?') and in poetry from other traditions which also integrates politics more at a slant: "The music is coming from the engine, seven centuries old,/And the words of it say love has changed everything" ('Novocaine' by Mary Baine Campbell).[74] In Thylias Moss's poem, 'The Warmth Of Hot Chocolate', a sprawling free-association riff on perceptions of identity, we perceive how the 'American voice' (what is commonly recognised as such, and not just in black writers) has absorbed tone, timbre and rhythm from jazz music – a wholly American invention connected to the Harlem Renaissance – and from a literature which, grown largely from African roots, is so intertwined with American culture as to be a profoundly important part of its development, despite the views of ethnic traditions as separate from the mainstream – just as women's poetry, of majority interest, is sidelined as a 'minority' one. In the UK, for historical and imperialistic reasons, the black tradition (Bernardine Evaristo, Grace Nichols) is often more Caribbean-based though not exclusively so (Jackie Kay, Patience Agbabi). Only recently has England formally acknowledged its role in the slave trade, righting a tacit presumption that this was confined to American soil.

Not only did the Black Arts movement help encourage and formulate an ethos of activism in other areas too, but the fervour to redress an imbalance (a subject of interest here) attracted more attention to diversity in general – to other overlooked cultures (Kimiko Hahn, Mimi Khalvati, Choman Hardi, Sujata Bhatt, Moniza Alvi) including Asian voices in the UK, and those descended from the American Indians (Diane Glancy, Louise Erdrich, Joy Harjo, Linda Hogan and Dorianne Laux). This last culture has been intertwined with black history at times, through the usual intermarriage between disenfranchised groups and an analogous relationship with the ruling classes. Those from outside the USA do not always realise the extent to which there still exists a native Indian tradition, despite the nineteenth century massacres and a wholesale theft of land: contracts broken by governmentally-sanctioned trickery. In the poem 'Columbus' ("We think he god from skie.Yup.Yup. Wedu") and in 'Kemo Sabe', Diane Glancy bends language itself, to suggest the usurper of power and culture. This latter poem takes as its premise a startling revisionism – "In my dream I take the white man" – and then continues:

I put other words into his mouth,
words he doesn't understand
like spoonfuls of smashed lima beans
until his cheeks bulge.
Chew now, dear, I say.
I flick his throat until he swallows.

All these voices challenge the dominant white discourse from different angles; the stories of immigration and hardship, or those from a buried or sidelined history, tell the story of the very foundation of America as a country (in contrast to clichés that prevail elsewhere) and the story of the ongoing multi-ethnic diversity of the western world. Celtic cultures in the UK and Ireland have been similarly nurtured and revived in the latter part of the twentieth century. The structure of Nuala Ní Dhomhnaill's poem 'The Language Issue' is an extended metaphor, based on the Moses story:[75]

I place my hope on the water
in this little boat
of the language

Gwyneth Lewis has the following to say about her first tongue: "...[the Welsh language has], against all the odds, found itself in the modern world, coining words for 'television' and 'fast reactor fuel rods'. Half a million speakers, numbers in decline – it's an 'all hands on deck' situation".[76]

Writers cursed and blessed by a birthright at the intersections of identity harvest a good creative crop out of the often difficult job of straddling borders, and are likely to have insights into analogous kinds of disenfranchisement. Perhaps this situation provides the impetus to write in the first place, for many other writers too. Fleur Adcock, originally from New Zealand, lives in England, as does Anne Stevenson who was nevertheless raised in the US; Molly Peacock resides in Canada, with its stunningly strong literary tradition sometimes not distinguished as it should be from the USA one. In fact, despite the etymological richness and diversity of vocabulary, dialects and slang all contributing to the language (hence English as a great success story), there exists rivalry and unease between linguistic siblings: for example, in the USA/UK relationship:[77] two places "divided by a common language", to use the popular phrase.

Here, you'll find poets known perhaps on home territory (USA, Canada, Australia, New Zealand, UK and Ireland) but who have not crossed oceans: those mentioned elsewhere in this Introduction and others such as: Anna Wickham, Gwen Harwood, P.K. Page, Amy Gerstler, Mary Ruefle, Rommi Smith, Lauris Edmond, Marie Ponsot, Lorna Crozier, Colette Inez, Marilyn Nelson, Colette Bryce and Vona Groarke. Certainly, living in the internet age – the global village, it seems time to cross international boundaries in a studied, more comprehensive way, as we do here: to break the anthologist's habit of favouring the home team, which is done often out of expediency rather than in honour of nationality. We'd prefer issues of nationality not to trump the appealing communality implied by this book as both its pleasure and duty. Our organising principle resists racial and nationalistic categorisation; poets from various nationalities and ethnicities are scattered throughout the book not primarily as representatives of any culture, but as another strand of the modern tradition, constantly in flux and contingent on its current practitioners.

It is not mandatory to write about one's culture, or not exclusively, however much one may believe that poetry should not be isolated from the society that produces it; you will also find in this volume poems engendered by exactly such isolation, and poets such as Selima Hill "working with some kind of Truth, but one which is aesthetic or even spiritual rather than moral. With an ethic which is inclusive, expansive and celebratory rather than exclusive or proscriptive".[78] In his essay 'Poetry After Modernism'[79] Dick Allen quotes Wordsworth – "The world is too much with us; late and soon, /Getting and spending, we lay waste our powers" – and then goes on to comment how these lines "[have] has never been more true". He continues: "We suspect we could write our lyric poetry better if we had no television, airplanes, telephones, vast highways systems, shopping malls – oh, to live in a cabin in the dark woods and watch the butterflies in the morning and the moths at night." One can identify with this sentiment and we hope that among the variety of work here – inward and outward poems, corporeal and spiritual poems, free verse and formal poems... all kinds of poems – everyone will find something with which they can identify.

Following the Black Mountain Poets and New York Poets, Language or L=A=N=G=U=A=G=E poetry (Susan Howe, Lyn J. Hejinian, Fanny Howe,)[80] developed in the 1960s and 1970s, and is still being defined... and decried." Seeking to change the reader's relationship with the text – involving the reader with the creation of meaning, as it's described – this movement includes many women practitioners, in part because Gertrude Stein is one of its leading lights. Of her iconic "a rose is a rose is a rose", Stein says that it was no longer the case as it was "with Chaucer and Homer – [that] the poet could use the name of a thing and the thing was really there," this comment perhaps a starting-point for an explanation of a model of writing which subordinates meaning to technique. Of her textually innovative book, *Tender Buttons*, published in 1914 the following has been said: "Simultaneously considered to be a masterpiece of verbal Cubism, a modernist triumph, a spectacular failure, a collection of confusing gibberish, and an intentional hoax, the book is perhaps more often written about than actually read."[81]

Stein's defiance of conventional syntax and grammar continues to inspire later generations of experimental avant-garde poets, especially prose-poem writers, as the book was itself meant to be read as one long prose-poem. Carolyn Forché's poem 'The Colonel', appears here (although it should be said she doesn't usually write in this form). While many prose poems tend to avoid conventional narratives, this one is nearly plain reportage in how it utterly eschews rhetorical contrivance out of respect for its horrifying subject, with one notable example:"He spilled many human ears on the table. They were like dried peach halves. There is no other way to say this." Here, we return to the essay 'Line Breaks and Back-Draft: Not a Defence of Poem' (*Poetry Review* - Vol 95.4, 2005/06), in which John Kinsella remarks: "For me, the measure of a poem is the word, not the line". Using his own poem as an example, he unpicks the usual notion of the "one-unit-of-thought-per-line" not to oppose the lineation but to enlarge our understanding of this convention to which Alice Fulton professes attachment: "Poets are so lucky to have the line as a way of making meaning. I think its why I've never been interested in writing 'prose poetry.' I don't want to give up the possibilities of the line."[82]

Marianne Moore writes: "...we would do well not to forget that it is an expedient for making one's self understood and that what is said should at least have the air of having meant something to the person who wrote it — as is the case with Gertrude Stein and James Joyce."[83] Although Anne Stevenson believes "...it does harm... to make either the writing or the understanding of poetry easy" yet she goes on to say, with reference to post-modern developments, that "the notion that art 'progresses' in the way science does has led to hideously destructive misunderstandings."[84] Indeed, it is hard not to suspect that sometimes a wilful obscurity for its own sake is conflated with ostensible ideology. Eavan Boland persuasively describes the damage done with this alienation of the reader in her essay 'The Wrong Way'. Apparently going 'boldly' where few are willing to go, she begins by saying: "I am writing this to propose that twentieth century poetry took a wrong turning; that the living proof of this is that the dialect and vernacular have not only separated, but that they were in fact — with hindsight and understanding — deliberately sundered." Boland goes on to say that the aim "to remake, not the poem... but the reader of the poem" was nothing less than "catastrophic", and asserts that in "[retraining] the poetry reader away from the old joys of memory and sentiment and song, the secondary modernist project cut deep into the root and sap of the art." She eloquently expresses anguish at losses she views as "incalculable... a centuries-old, bright partnership between poet and reader has been injured. An ancient trust has been hurt." This response, not simply a superficial, reactionary resistance to the 'new', accords with others', especially in its perception that the universities have been complicit in these alarming developments: "... almost by stealth, a new set of pieties was moving into place. Almost without noticing or understanding it, a new way of configuring both the poem and the idea of the poet — we now call it high modernism — had become the mainstream culture of poetry... not simply a moment in poetry. It had become, as if by mandate, its manifest destiny."[85]

Dana Gioia's essay 'Can Poetry Matter?' tackles the seeming paradox — a "Zen riddle of cultural sociology" — whereby a specialist audience increases, to the tune of a general decline in general readership:

> ...the poetry boom has been a distressingly confined phenomenon. Decades of public and private funding have created a large professional class for the production and reception of new poetry comprising legions of teachers, graduate students, editors, publishers and administrators. [86]

Based mostly in universities, these groups have gradually become the main audience for contemporary verse. Because bureaucracies are ill-equipped to measure "something as intangible as literary quality", the criteria for academic success have become "primarily quantitative", encouraging poets to churn out poems as if on an assembly line. The proliferation of journals is less proof of the vigour of poetry, more a symptom of the problem. Many publish only verse "[addressed] to an insular audience of literary professionals", instead of within the context of a broader cultural agenda.[87] Gioia describes the bulk production:

> ...page after page of freshly minted poems. The heart sinks to see so many poems crammed so tightly together like downcast immigrants in steerage. One can easily miss a radiant poem amid the many lacklustre ones.[88]

In 'Poetry and the University', Bruce Bawer analyses how academia has nurtured a hierarchy based on false principles:

> We live in an era when the poetic act – in America at least – is increasingly performed on assignment and negotiated in committee under the auspices of a bureaucracy... all too frequently the quality of the verse that a contemporary poet has written seems a far less reliable index of his relative importance than the grants and fellowships he has received, the writing colonies he has attended, the universities at which he as studied, taught, or given readings, and the number of books he has written."[89]

As Gioia puts it: "The slow maturation of genuine creativity looks like laziness to a committee."[90]

Gioia further looks at the issue in economic terms, observing "Like subsidized farming that grows food no one wants, a poetry industry has been created to serve the interests of the producers and not the consumers."[91] Elsewhere he comments how "...most contemporary poets have been alienated from their original cultural function. As Marx maintained and few economists have disputed, changes in a class's economic function eventually transform its values and behaviour."[92] However, he also acknowledges that these problems come during a "period of genuine achievement", particularly as regards the richness of émigré poetry in America. Yet with humour and vigour Gioia quotes Cyril Connolly's bitter comment: "Poets arguing about modern poetry: jackals snarling over a dried-up well."

If questions of accessibility factor largely in debates about post-modernism, on the other side of the equation and equally controversial is the perceived over-accessibility of populist poets. Certain poets are often perceived as popular in a way that underestimates them, as with the sharp and technically nimble Wendy Cope and Sophie Hannah, both serious and funny, not to mention seriously funny. These two latter poets illustrate the cross-over territory between the so-called 'page' and 'performance' poets.[93] Although some poets mumble from behind a lectern into the gutter of their book, many 'page' poets adopt not exactly a theatrical style, but one more akin to a conversational intimacy, embellished with some kind of *spiel* – to entertain and let each poem settle – these elements contributing to an illusory spontaneity integeral to the performative trick.

One of the most visible and popular manifestations of the oral traditions, the

Slam, originally from Chicago,[94] urges a democratisation of the art form, with the audience judging readers on content and delivery, which format is not amenable to all. (At one Anti-Slam, all forms of expression were given a six-minute set and all participants are given a perfect ten by the judges!) Voices drawing on hip-hop, rap, Dub poetry and the West Indian tradition, are markedly in evidence at UK slams.[95] In a *Paris Review* interview the critic Harold Bloom calls the movement "the death of art", which one hopes is alarmist. In response to him, Victor D. Infante wrote in *OC Weekly*[96]: "[The death of art] is a big onus to place on anybody…". Infante continues in inflammatory manner: "…but Bloom has always had a propensity for (reactionary) generalizations and burying his bigotries beneath 'aesthetics,' insisting – as he did in his prologue to the anthology *Best of the Best of American Poetry* – the 'art' of poetry is being debased by politics." The proliferation of spoken word events may have helped make all poetry more visible, and helped set a precedent for more mixed-arts events – poetry presented in a broader context, as espoused by Gioia – but there exists an irritating segregation with performance venues perpetuating exactly the exclusionary ethos, assumed to exist among the 'page' poets, who are often not invited to the party. In his new Preface, Dana Gioia says:

> In the decade since 'Can Poetry Matter?' was first published, the state of American poetry has changed radically – often in ways suggested by the title essay. Although the university writing programs critiqued in the book remain largely the same, they have lost their monopoly on contemporary poetry because the literary culture around them has experienced a vast renewal by reconnecting poetry with a broader audience. There are now countless poetry festivals, book fairs, reading series, discussion groups, and conferences based in the community rather than the academy." [97]

One wonders what Mr. Bloom would think of Cowboy Poetry, which strand of the populist oral tradition uses ballad and song forms, not unlike country music lyrics, which themselves hearken back to an American folk tradition derived from and heavily influenced by Irish and Celtic culture. As one might expect, Cowboy themes "derive from the American West: horses, cattle, fire, prairie storms, mythic figures of cowboys and ranchers, and the sublime wilderness."[98] While the Slam has migrated successfully to the UK, and further afield, it has proven more difficult to transport the horses and cattle (not to mention the cowboys themselves). "Writing about Jazz poetry is, as they say, like dancing about architecture."[99] So too, there are limits to how an oral tradition can be represented in book form. If a poem is itself the best expression of what it needs to say, – or, indeed what it is – without the performance, much is lost from poems primarily devised to be performed."[100] In this late mention of the New Formalists one might interpret a strong predilection either for or against them. The numbers tell the story: A.E. Stallings, Phillis Levin[101], Molly Peacock, Marilyn Hacker and many more. A widespread ideological rejection and distrust of form – still evident in America especially – could be ascribed partly to the Black Mountain ideology, which perspective is just as surprising and irritating as the UK aversion to any whiff of the confessional. Bruce Bawer acerbically blames what he sees as a wholesale rubbishing of heritage on the Beats, who:

in a grotesque reaction to high modernism… encouraged young people to think of poetry as something that requires not craft or intelligence or talent so much as sincerity. Just write what you feel, the idea goes, and you have a poem.[102]

It does seem the case that many perceive the traditional elements of verse to be mere historical anachronism: unearthed ancient artefacts of interest perhaps to the archaeologist.

Robert McPhillips remarks: "For [some] poets a return to form provided a fresh angle from which to convey personal experiences as well as to escape from the obsessively private concerns of the confessional free verse poem". They were reacting to those poets for whom writing in traditional forms "….had become ideologically as well as aesthetically unfashionable".[103] This last group thus responds to perceived dogma with more kind of dogma, and not of the literary kind; some critics even claim that to write in traditional forms is 'un-American', thus "automatically [equating] politics with aesthetics and [arguing] from political rather than from aesthetic grounds, reducing the revival of meter and rhyme in all of its diverse manifestations to mere reflections of a reactionary political ideology."[104] Inadequate criticism of the New Formalists often "[fails] to… provide an overview of the movement and to make distinctions among the numerous poets writing in form",[105] although it's quick to acknowledge the indisputable pitfalls, the danger in "[overvaluing the form]…at the expense of a poem's emotional impact."[106] As with the Confessionals, the responses from "fervid champions of free verse suggest the [New Formalist] movement's potency."[107] I recall now, as I headed out to the airport, MFA degree in hand, pre New Formalist days, fellow Columbia students warned me about those dastardly English metricists, mobsters in trenchcoats, under which are hidden fearsome scansion rulers! (They had not even seen the lousy sonnets I was guiltlessly writing in the privacy of my own home!)

No apologies are made for the numerous sonnets here: the eloquent 'Cassetta Frame'; by Sarah Hannah, Edna St. Vincent Millay's biting 'Sonnet', in which she upends the conventions of the form itself, and Marilyn Hacker's 'Mythology' (and also her lyrically evocative 'Square Du Temple II', with its perfectly realised portrait of the writer as detached observer nevertheless integral to the world around her). Other commonly used forms are represented: the sestinas 'First Time: 1950' by Honor Moore and 'Elementary' by Linda France, the ghazal 'The Servant' by Mimi Khalvati, etc. (We regret particularly the omission of Elizabeth Bishop's famous villanelle 'One Art'.)

You will find here unjustly overlooked poems which may enlarge on strengths less visible in an author's more commonly reproduced poems, many of which we also publish here. Jorie Graham's poem, 'Wanting a Child', is different from the more abstract work for which she is known. An early poem of Adrienne Rich's, 'The Insusceptibles' appears along with the classic 'Diving into the Wreck', in which allegory poetically articulates polemic. Plath's 'bleakly wonderful' poem 'Sheep in Fog'[108] illustrates a deft and nuanced technique, irrespective of the more sensationalistic aspects of her work. However, you will also find here 'Lady Lazarus', about which Peter Porter writes, in his review of Crossing the Water: "It is the miracle of [this poem] that though it seems a wild and incoherent outpouring of terror and self-hatred, it also has the true control of art", which assessment can be contrasted to more handed-down responses already discussed: clichés about hysterical women, thinly disguised as rhetorical sophistry.

You will find here Anne Rouse's slyly muted allusion to creative angst, conveyed through an homage to a natural landscape; Denise Duhamel's explicit, wittily raucous social comment; Jane Hirshfield's lucid philosophical speculations. Naturally, we claim editorial neutrality, while admitting a bias for poems with wit, passion and vitality (Heather McHugh, Louise Erdrich, Margaret Atwood). Poems were chosen for their originality (Fanny Howe, Ann Lauterbach); their musicality, and linguistic and tonal richness (Amy Clampitt, Sarah Arvio); their intelligence and complexity (Sandra McPherson, Melanie Challenger, Brigit Pegeen Kelley); their conscience and emotional authenticity (Elizabeth Macklin, Ruth Stone, Penelope Shuttle). We chose poems because they have many of these qualities all at once.

We look again to Randall Jarrell for his enunciation of the anthologist's dilemma regarding our inclusion of some poems not to our personal taste:

> Disliking what is bad is only the other face of liking what is good; but what a dark, dank, grudging, graceless face, one endeared neither to gods nor men! And the good in poetry, is always a white blackbird, an abnormal and unlikely excellence."[109]

Yet, we are no more qualified than posterity to alter its pronouncements; Christina Rossetti's devotional mode may not be the 'cat's pyjamas' (sic), yet how many realise that she wrote 'In the Bleak Midwinter' later famously set as a Christmas carol by the composer Gustav Holst and others? Many know the almost generic lines on the Statue of Liberty "...Give me your tired, your poor, / Your huddled masses yearning to breathe free" but how many know they are taken from a poem by the Portuguese Sephardic Jewish poet Emma Lazarus, who corresponded with Ralph Waldo Emerson?

How many can name a female war poet (Lynette Roberts)? Adelaide Crapsey, before she died prematurely, invented a variation on the *cinquin* or *quintain*, a five-line form of twenty-two syllables influenced by the Japanese haiku and tanka. It is not widely known that Sylvia Townsend Warner, who contributed short stories to *The New Yorker* for forty years, was also a poet; Janet Frame is more acclaimed for her memoir *An Angel at My Table*. Charlotte Mew's unique radicalism couched in conventional form – at first sight – heralded a modernist sensibility, and yet she too is little known, especially outside the UK. In her Introduction to a newer selection of Mew's poems Eavan Boland describes her own 1953 selection of that poet's work, how "within its rosy, tattered dust jacket and sturdy covers burns and lives the music of dissidence". Here, we take pleasure in unearthing hidden histories like these, re-drawing the canon to include oversights and unfairly sidelined poets.

We need to explain some omissions. Famously, Elizabeth Bishop declined to be in a women-only anthologies, remarking to George Starbuck: "I didn't think about it very seriously, but I felt it was a lot of nonsense, separating the sexes. I suppose this feeling came from feminist principles stronger than I was aware of."[110] (The second portion of this quote is routinely overlooked, in service of handy oversimplification.) Sheenagh Pugh and Gjertrud Schnackenberg are absent due to their principled stands; others similarly inclined, were convinced otherwise. Some poets were reluctantly omitted if estate or publisher fees entailed dropping too many others. Anne Carson, Nina Cassian and May Swenson are particularly regretted omissions, the latter unjustly neglected and little known in the UK.[111]

Inevitably, the first choices were personal: poems carried around for years in my head and heart: by Emily Dickinson, Sylvia Plath and Elizabeth Bishop.[112] Carolyn Kizer and Patricia Goedicke were influential teachers, at Columbia University and Sarah Lawrence College. Kizer's outspokenness and outgoing generosity of spirit were memorable. I recall being awakened to the power of metaphor, reading for the first time Jorie Graham's 'Wanting a Child'; she and Stanley Kunitz were also teachers at Columbia. In fact, Marie Howe brought her poem 'Death, the Last Visit' to Kunitz's workshop, which we both attended. Awed by its clever and shocking conceit – its drive and fearlessness – I'd carried around the yellowed copy of that poem ever since, waiting to place it in this book.

Around this period, I recklessly attended a class in ancient Greek at the New School with the as yet unpublished Amy Clampitt. Unlikely to master the language in just two terms, I had gone along for the etymological ride; from her subsequently published work perhaps Clampitt had too. Carol Ann Duffy was the first poet I knew and read after moving to Britain, her mix of the demotic and lyrical another revelation. I may have been one of the first people in the Uk to review Sharon Olds, for Poetry Review, and did so guessing at the furore she would be bound to provoke until her fame would supersede such antipathy. Reading such daring work gave me a real jolt, as if I had been sleepwalking, lulled into submission by poems impersonating poems. It occurred to me that the failures resulting from such risk-taking were deeply relevant to the purpose of poetry, more than any more cosseted if crafted mediocrity. Vital poems seem revelations, however uncomfortable; infused with passion, they make you think and question, and of course they make you want to write.

With "one long hoot of adieu", I will hop onboard Nina Bogin's train, for the familiar view in her poem 'Going Up the Hudson River, After Twenty Years'; after twenty years living in the UK, this view is still vivid in my mind, accompanied by the nostalgia Bogin so perfectly captures. Going home, I can also pay last respects to Patricia Goedicke, this book's secondary dedicatee and an inspirational teacher who died while this volume was being compiled; it will be an enduring regret that that I never got to thank her properly.

Last and far from least, this book's main dedicatee, the poet Sarah Hannah, was my student at Wesleyan Writer Conference and, within moment of our meeting, a close friend and kindred spirit. From the word 'Go' we talked pell-mell–sometimes within the space of five minutes – about form, family, teaching, nature, the cynical and lyrical heart, pain and evil, dogs and lizards, sex and rock n' roll, "the odd and genuine"[113] and everything else on the planet and off the planet too, which vast spectrum describes concerns of the writers you'll find here. I would like for this book to invoke her memory, and remind us all what we are for.

Notes

1. Unless otherwise noted, all the women poets cited in this Introduction have poems in this anthology.
2. Germaine Greer, 'A Biodegradable Art', *Times Literary Supplement*, June 30, 1995.
3. A few potential contributors to this book needed to be reassured that the writing was the only criteria for inclusion; that this collection grew from an aesthetic not a political root.
4. Dana Gioia points out how in less affluent times people depended on anthologies for their reading. More recent ones have a short shelf-life and more 'clubby' feeling, "compiled in the spirit of congenial opportunism: *The 1983 Morrow Anthology of Younger American Poets...* [which] is not so much a selective literary collection as a comprehensive directory of creative-writing teachers (it even offers a photo of each author)." – Dana Gioia, 'Can Poetry Matter?', *Can Poetry Matter?* (Graywolf Press), essay first published in Atlantic Monthly, 1991).
5. Germaine Greer, op. cit.
6. Ibid
7. Elizabeth Bishop, in befriending the poet May Swenson in letters, was also just a little condescending; she tried to make Swenson's poems less vulgar and with less attention to the body, which sensibility may shed light on both Bishop's wide acceptance and Swenson's relative obscurity within the UK.
8. Erica Jong, 'Don't forget the F-word', *Guardian*, April 12, 2008.
9. Adrienne Rich, 'The Antifeminist Woman', *On Lies, Secrets and Silence: Selected Prose 1966-78* (Norton, 1995).
10. Ibid
11. James Fenton, 'Lady Lazarus', *The Strength of Poetry: Oxford Lectures* (Oxford University Press, 2001).
12. Deryn Rees-Jones offers more contextual and rhetorically objective views about Edith Sitwell's not dissimilar sartorial sense and theatricality in *Consorting with Angels: Essays on Modern Women Poets* (Bloodaxe, 2005).
13. Priestess is another diminutive of course. Perhaps his view was helped along by Stephen Spender's assessment of her as "a priestess cultivating her hysteria". Contrast this discomfort with Marjorie Perloff's literary analysis: "hers is an 'oracular poetry' in the tradition of such later eighteenth-century poets as Smart, Cowper, Collins and Blake, the poets of what Northrop Frye has called 'the Age of Sensibility'." ('Angst and Animism in the Poetry of Sylvia Plath', *Critical Essays on Sylvia Plath*, ed. Linda W. Wagner, (G.K. Hall & Co., 1984).
14. Sally Feldman, 'Gender Traitors', *New Humanist*, July/August 2008.
15. Ibid
16. Stanley Kunitz, 'Land of Dust and Flame', *A Kind of Order, A Kind of Folly: Essays and Conversations* (Little, Brown & Co., 1975).
17. Ibid
18. James Fenton, 'Lady Lazarus', op. cit.
19. Ibid
20. Ibid
21. Linda W. Wagner, 'Introduction', op.cit.
22. James Fenton, 'Lady Lazarus', op. cit.
23. Says Eavan Boland: "I stumbled, almost without knowing it, into the life of a woman. I married. I moved to a suburb. ('The Wrong Way', *Strong Words: Modern Poets on Modern Poetry*, eds. W.N. Herbert & Matthew Hollis, [Bloodaxe, 2001]). Here is the 17-year-old Plath on her seemingly inescapable appointment with destiny: "I am afraid of getting married. Spare me from cooking three meals a day – spare me from the relentless cage of routine and rote. I want to be free…" (Sandra M. Gilbert, 'In Yeats's House: The Death and Resurrection of Sylvia Plath', Wagner, op. cit.)
24. James Fenton, 'Lady Lazarus', op. cit.
25. Alicia Ostriker, 'The Americanization of Sylvia', Wagner, op. cit.
26. A comment by Stevie Smith springs to mind, even if her intent is different: "My Muse is like the painting of the Court Poet and His Muse in the National Gallery; she is also howling into an indifferent ear." – *Me Again: Uncollected Writings*, eds. Jack Barbera & William McBrien - from *Strong Words: Modern Poets on Modern Poetry*, eds. W.N. Herbert & Matthew Hollis, (Bloodaxe, 2001).
27. Seamus Heaney, *The Government of the Tongue: Selected Prose 1978-1987* (Faber & Faber, 1989).
28. James Fenton, 'Lady Lazarus', op. cit.
29. Ibid
30. Ibid
31. Katha Pollitt, 'Note of Triumph [The Collected Poems]', Wagner, op. cit.

32. One wonders if Drabble has read Plath's comments on her own poem, 'Point Shirley' in which she weighs up her chosen techniques, thus giving the measure of her skills and intent: "Oddly powerful and moving to me in spite of rigid formal structure". In the esaay 'An Interesting Minor Poet', the title of which is taken from Irving Howe's limited judgement of her work precisely in order to dispute it, William Pritchard adds: "If we may correct Sylvia Plath, it moves us not in spite of but partly because of its 'rigid formal structure' ". (Wagner, op. cit.)

33. Alicia Suskin Ostriker, *Stealing the Language: The Emergence of Women's Poetry in America* (Beacon Press, 1987).

34. James Fenton, 'Lady Lazarus', op. cit.

35. Ibid

36. Stanley Kunitz, 'Land of Dust and Flame', op. cit.

37. Stanley Kunitz, 'Pangolin of Poets', op. cit.

38. Alicia Ostriker, op. cit.

39. Adrienne Rich, 'Anne Sexton: 1928-1974', op. cit.

40. Fiona Sampson, editor of *Poetry Review*, comments that "the often low standard of critical practice in combination with power-broking" affects how women poets are perceived and treated. She continues: "This power-politics works on every level, starting with simple matters of credit or attribution."

41. Alicia Ostriker, op. cit.

42. Adrienne Rich, 'Vesuvius at Home: the Power of Emily Dickinson', op. cit.

43. Randall Jarrell, making the same contrast, notes the "arch and silly and terrible poems", by a writer he also calls "one of the most individual writers who ever lived, one of those best able to express experience at its most absolute". ('The Year in Poetry', *Harper's*, October 1955 and also *Kipling, Auden & Co: Essays and Reviews 1935-64* (Farrar, Straus, Giroux, 1980)

44. Adrienne Rich, 'When We Dead Awaken: Writing as Revision', *Arts of the Possible: Essays and Conversations* (Norton, 2002).

45 Ibid

46. 'Poetry and Experience: Statement at a Poetry Reading', *Adrienne Rich's Poetry: Texts of the poems, The Poet on her Work, Reviews & Criticism*, ed. Barbara Charlesworth and here reprinted from *Strong Words: Modern Poets on Modern Poetry*, eds. Herbert & Hollis, op. cit. With regard of these same points, and in this same volume (20 women/57 men), see also Selima Hill's description of her own creative process.

47. Carolyn Steedman, *Landscape for a Good Woman: a Story* (Rutgers University Press, 1987).

48. One can find just such subtle nuances, discussed and analysed at length in Vicki Bertram's *Gendering Poetry*.

49 Dana Gioia, 'Can Poetry Matter?', op. cit.

50. Vicki Bertram, *Gendering Poetry: Contemporary Women and Men Poets* (Pandora Press, 2005).

51 Erica Jong, 'Don't forget the F-word', op. cit.

52. 'A Non-Christian On Sunday' by Amy Gerstler, page 250.

53. Germaine Greer, 'A Biodegradable Art', op. cit.

54. Sandra M. Gilbert, 'In Yeats's House: The Death and Resurrection of Sylvia Plath', Wagner, op. cit.

55. The poet Dorianne Laux has worked as a housecleaner, gas station manager, *TV Guide* salesperson, cook in a sanatorium, and doughnut-holer. Elizabeth Bartlett was a medical receptionist for the British National Health Service. Anne Rouse, a nurse, was a director of a mental health charity for many years. Marilyn Hacker has been an antiquarian bookseller. Working in academia for only a year, Sylvia Plath found it sapped her creatively; at various times she was an au pair, waitress, spinach-picker and of course a typist for Ted Hughes. Poets Hilary Menos and Gillian Clarke are farmers. Here is Colette Inez on her Resume: "(I've) read letters for a nickel to illiterate women near 105th and St. Clair... (and) as a Gal Friday: switchboard operator, secretary... including at the America Cyanamid company..." – Poetry Society of America, http://www.poetry-society.org/inez.-html.

56. A virtually forgotten poet these days, Joan Murray died young, leaving behind a small oeuvre which testifies to a striking talent.

57. Lorine Niedecker cared for her deaf mother for years, a situation which perhaps influenced her work, stylistically. Her other jobs included librarian, cleaner and stenographer – all traditionally female occupations. Stevie Smith was a secretary, as were many others (often for writer partners!). Even now, women's primary value is understood in terms of such badly-paid or unpaid contributions: in their role as wife and mother.

58. Eds. Thomas Travisano with Saskia Hamilton, *Words in Air: The Complete Correspondence between Elizabeth Bishop and Robert Lowell*, (Farrar, Straus, Giroux, 2008).

59. Academy of American Poets, Poets http://www.poets.org/viewmedia. php/prmMID/5664

60. Ibid. "What was new in Marianne Moore was her brilliant and utterly original use of quotations in her poet-

ry, and her surpassing attention to the poetic image." Many a poet – and editor – delights in mischievously quoting "I too dislike it", the now famous first lines from her poem 'Poetry', included in this volume (page 163).

61. Ibid
62. Niedecker was also influenced in her early work by the Imagists, before developing her own highly original style with its "austere yet vivid imagery". – Academy of American Poets, http://www.poets.org/poet.php/prmPID/729
63. Mark Ford's second volume of New York Poets (Carcanet, 2006) finally locates Barbara Guest and Alice Notley.
64. Academy of American Poets, http://www.poets.org/viewmedia.php/prmMID/5646
65. Carolyn Cassady's memoir Off the Road (Penguin, 1991) provides a woman's prose perspective on this scene.
66. Elaine Feinstein, 'A Question of Voice', Strong Voices, eds. Herbert and Hollis, op. cit.
67. Dana Gioia, op. cit.
68. Academy of American Poets, http://www.poets.org/poet.php/prmPID/77
69. Linda Wagner, 'Introduction', op. cit.
70. Ibid
71. Singers such as Billie Holiday, Ella Fitzgerald, James Brown and many others launched their careers at the famous Apollo Theatre in Harlem, NYC, which is still in operation.
72. Academy of American Poets, http://www.poets.org/viewmedia.php/prmMID/5666
73. Alice Dunbar Nelson is the only poet mentioned here who is not included in this volume.
74. We might mention at this juncture, Donna Kate Rushin's 'The Bridge' and Nikki Giovanni's, 'Nikki Rosa', placed either side of the aptly named 'Fragment' by Angelina Weld Grimke; an anthem of selfhood slotted between two anti-manifesto manifesto poems, with their challenges to stereotypical assumptions about race.
75. The remit of this book was poems written in English. After much thought, an exception was made to include this poem, written in Irish and translated by Paul Muldoon.
76. Gwyneth Lewis, 'Whose Coat is this Jacket? Whose Hat is that Cap?', (eds. Herbert & Hollis, op. cit.) In fact, as Amy Wack points out: "according to the last census the Welsh language is declining in the old 'heartlands' of north and west Wales, but increasing in Cardiff and in the southeast due to the proliferation of Welsh Language medium education, (all classes taught in Welsh)."
77. "Almost from the beginning of the colonial experience it has been a common assumption in Britain that a word or turn of phrase is inferior simply by dint of its being American-bred. In dismissing the 'vile and barbarous word talented' Samuel Taylor Coleridge observed 'most of these pieces of slang come from American'. That clearly was ground enough to detest them... A reviewer of Thomas Jefferson's Notes on the State of Virginia entreated Jefferson to say what he would about the British character, but 'O spare, we beseech you, our mother-tongue.' Another, noting his use of the word belittle, remarked: 'It may be an elegant [word] in Virginia, and even perfectly intelligible, but for our part all we can do is guess at its meaning. For shame, Mr. Jefferson!' Jefferson also coined the word Anglophobia. No wonder." – Bill Bryson, Mother Tongue: English and how it got that way (Harper Perennial, 1991).
78. Selima Hill, 'Racoons – or, can Art Be Evil?', eds. Herbert & Hollis, op. cit.
79. Ed. Robert McDowell, Poetry After Modernism (Story Line Press 1998).
80. Among other recent postmodernists, Denise Riley is one of the first woman poets to combine feminist concerns with experimental poetic practise.
81. http://www.poets.org/viewmedia.php/prmMID/5951
82. Folio, http://www.american.edu/cas/lit/folio/spring2005inter.html
83. Although 'Idiosyncrasy and Technique' is originally from A Marianne Moore Reader, I took this from Modern Poets on Modern Poetry, ed. James Scully (Collins, 1970). This is the only essay by a woman, among a total of sixteen.
84. Anne Stevenson, 'A Few Words for the New Century', eds. Herbert & Hollis, op. cit. Although Frederick Turner has admitted some changes since the publication in the 1970s of his essay 'Of Mighty Poets In Their Misery Dead; A Polemic on the Contemporary Poetry Scene', many of his points hold true: "...part of our contemporary image of poetry is that it has no canons and that it is essentially 'innovative' and 'experimental', that in contemporary poetry we have outgrown the myopic standards of the past and that our poetry is, must be, revolutionary." , Poetry After Modernism, ed. Robert McDowell, op. cit.
85. Eavan Boland, 'The Wrong Way', eds. Herbert & Hollis, op. cit.
86. Dana Gioia, 'Can Poetry Matter?' from Can Poetry Matter?, New Edition, (Graywolf Press, 2002).
87. Ibid. On the other hand, a magazine like The New Yorker, publishes fiction, non-fiction and, famously, cartoons.
88. Ibid

89. Bruce Bawer, 'Poetry in the University', ed Robert McDowell, op. cit.

90. Dana Gioia, op. cit.

91. Ibid

92. Ibid

93. Geraldine Monk, a post-modern poet associated with the north of England, mines some of the same territory as Denise Riley; her dual allegiance to page and performance foretells a current blurring of these boundaries.

94. Bob Holman, a poetry activist and former slam master of the Nuyorican Poets Café, a leading venue in NYC, describes a "spoken word revolution...led by a lot of women and by poets of color. It gives a depth to the nation's dialogue that you don't hear on the floor of Congress. I want a floor of Congress to look more like a National Poetry Slam. That would make me happy." http://enwikipedia.org/wiki/Poetry_slam

95. The Liverpool Poets had a strong allegiance to pop music, with readings mostly taking place in pubs and clubs.

96. A political west coast alternative and progressive free paper, much like the *Village Voice* in NYC.

97. Dana Gioia, 'Preface', op. cit.

98. Academy of American Poets, http://www.poets.org/viewmedia.php/prm-MID/5651, "The National Cowboy Poetry Gathering, a program of the Western Folklife Centre, is a yearly 'jubilee of conversation, singing, dancing, great hats and boots, stories...big steaks [and] incessant rhymes...' "

99. 'A Brief Guide To Jazz Poetry', www.poetrs.org "Jazz poetry can be seen as a thread that runs through the Harlem Renaissance, the Beat Movement, and the Black Arts Movement – and it is still vibrant today."

100. On the other hand, "were one to hear a piece of concrete poetry read aloud, a substantial amount of its effect would be lost. Commonly understood to describe poems typographically laid out in the shape of the object which is the poem's theme, a broader understanding of this movement from the 1950s explains how: "...works of concrete poetry are as much pieces of visual art made with words as they are poems. – Academy of American Poets, http://www.poets.org/viewmedia.php/-prmMID/5649.

101. Levin is also the editor of *Penguin Book of the Sonnet*.

102. Bruce Bawer, 'Poetry and the University', ed. MacDowell, op. cit.

103. Robert McPhillips, 'Reading the New Formalists', ed. McDowell, op. cit.

104. Ibid

105. Alice Fulton explains her interest in mathematical elements of poetry: in logic, calibration and fractals: "The essay Of Formal, Free, and Fractal Verse: Singing the Body Eclectic' was written in the mid-eighties... (when) the 'form wars' were raging; some poets were questioning the validity of free verse and calling for a return to traditional meter and rhyme... I happened upon an article (explaining how) fractals allowed us to perceive form in shapes previously regarded as amorphous. And it occurred to me that fractal form would be a good analogue for free verse, with its irregular metrics and eccentric characteristics. So my first essay suggests fractals as a way to think about the hidden structures of free verse." – Folio, http://www.american.edu/cas/lit/folio/spring2005inter.html

106. Robert McPhillips, 'Reading the New Formalists', ed. Robert McDowell, op. cit.

107. Ibid.

108. William Pritchard, 'An Interesting Minor Poet?', Wagner, op. cit.

109. Randall Jarrell, 'Recent Poetry', *Kipling, Auden & Co*, op. cit.

110. Permission was granted for the use of Bishop's work in the excellent *Faber Book of Twentieth Century Women's Poetry*, ed. Fleur Adcock. We failed to get to the bottom of how Faber managed this sleight of hand.

111. Spanish is virtually a second language in the USA; the length and breadth of this tradition has meant it's impossible to cover it here. Other regretted omissions include: Cynthia MacDonald, Mary Jo Salter, Jane Cooper, Audre Lorde, Alice Walker, Alice Dunbar-Nelson and Dorothy Molloy.

112. I'd include as crucial Elizabeth Bishop's poems 'In The Waiting Room', 'One Art', 'The Fish', and 'The Fishhouses'.

113. Eds. Travisano and Hamilton, 'Introduction: What a Block of Life', op. cit.

Acknowledgements and Thanks

To the poets who appear in this book, for the poems and much else besides: Alicia Suskin Ostriker, Fiona Sampson, Elizabeth Macklin, Mary Baine Campbell, Phillis Levin, Ruth Fainlight, Molly Peacock, Jane Hirshfield, Rhian Gallagher, Jane Holland, Annie Finch, Deborah Garrison, Margaret Atwood, Adrienne Rich, and to all who stayed for the long haul, and to my co-editor, Amy Wack, for all the heated discussions and for taking on this epic task with great surety and enthusiasm, or it wouldn't have happened."

To friends and family for incalculably valuable support, suggestions, epic patience and friendship during trying times: Zarina Maiwandi, Charlotte Purton, Stephanie Dawn Cross, Karin Randolph & Bob Sullivan (and kitties Luna Fish, et al.), Jules Mann, Nathan Goldstein, Harriet Fishman, the Howell/Brookner clan for Providence (and doggies Dalben and Maia).

To other friends, writers and editors, for being first and close readers: John Kinsella, Vicki Bertram, Jane Holland and Sian Williams. And for suggestions, advice and keeping me on the ball: Dana Gioia, Ciaran Carson, Greg Delanty, Kadija George, Robert Vas Dias, Mick Felton, Chris McCabe, Chris Hamilton, Emery Jack and Adele Foley, Michael Schmidt, Neil Astley, Stephen Pain, Edmund Hardy, Steven Waling, Katy Evans-Bush, David Kennedy, Roddy Lumsden, Angel Dahouk, Martin Kelly (somebody's gotta know computers, and also for the Salsa dance).

To the Wompo List for the lively conversations and knowledge, especially; Amanda Surkont, Kate Bernadette Benedict, Barbara Crooker, Pat Fargnoli, Janet McAdams, Peggy Shumaker, Pit Pinegar, Amy Newman, Felice Aull, Nina Lara Davies, Allison Hedge Coke, Janet Holmes.

To teachers present, past and absent, especially: Patricia Goedicke, Carolyn Kizer, Elizabeth Hardwick, C.K. Williams, Josef Skvorecky, Stephen Dunn, Stephen Sandy, Ben Belitt, Thomas Lux, Derek Walcott, Joseph Brodsky, Jorie Graham, Stanley Kunitz and Frank McCourt for lighting the way.

Eva Salzman

Introduction: Amy Wack

"Feminism" I once heard Margaret Atwood say on the radio, in her marvellously laconic drawl, "is the new 'F' word". This neatly encapsulates how certain terms get co-opted and consigned to stereotype. The other dirty word is "liberal", which I've always associated with the adjective "progressive" but is now spit like an insult by right-wing talk show demagogues and denotes someone of the hopelessly wet left, steeped in political correctness and devoid of moral boundaries. And yet, as our capacious anthology suggests, surely we are post-backlash now? What was once radicalism is now culture and women have an 'access all areas' pass, hence our ability to dedicate chapters to themes that are not strictly 'feminine' but profoundly human.

And yet, I write on the day that the first woman ever to be a serious contender for president of the United States had to graciously bow out. And, I'm old enough to remember the hard-fought battles of the sixties, some of the rhetoric of pioneers like Germaine Greer and Betty Friedan, of Gloria Steinem's witty reply, when asked why she didn't "just get married and have children?": "I don't like to breed in captivity." I still recall the searing impact Sylvia Plath's *Ariel* had on my generation of women poets. The quieter, thoughtful 'feminist light' posturing of recent times, such as in the books by Naomi Woolf, have brought some of these ideas to new generations, however 'Girl Power' via girl bands while persuasively anthemic for the young, also often seems just another hard-sell, a commodification of female flesh. The statistics about unequal pay-scales and the dearth of women at boardroom level in business and the arts and in government still make worrying reading.

It is also human nature to take hard fought advantages for granted. The iconoclast British tabloid columnist, Julie Burchill, once suggested a new reality TV show called 'I'm not a feminist, but...' where women who say this are then subjected to having one of their so-called rights removed from them a day at a time: Today: no job, tomorrow: no driving, the next day: no buying your own clothes, etc. She surmised that quite soon, feminist sentiments would rise to the surface of the hitherto apolitical. Rapid globalization also makes it hard to forget that we are talking about advantages for women in the comparatively rich Western nations covered in this book.

What we must note as well is that poets of either sex mostly resist being conscripted to anyone's agenda and tend, like explorers, to seek out the forbidden zones. One of the many things I learned while working on this book was how successive generations of women poets have influenced each other, using the multifarious resources of the English language to evolve a feminine culture as richly layered as complex sedimentary rock.

It is also worthwhile to point out that putting together such an anthology does not mean we hate men, indeed, on a personal level we share our lives with them and on the professional one, we admire their poems just as fervently. The impetus for this book arises from the knowledge that the late twentieth and early twenty-first centuries have been and are particularly ripe times for the rise of women poets, a fact not always represented in general anthologies.

Quite notable in our author biographical section, is the role of universities, particularly in the USA, as training ground, source of employment and haven for poets. In the UK, we have the Arts Council, and specifically here in Wales, we have the Welsh Books Council, a body that over the years has supported Seren in this, as in many publishing ventures. We salute their enlightened patronage. I also must quote a line sent to me by one of the older contributors to this book. Before there was anything like a career structure via the universities, "Many of us had whole other lives before we could devote ourselves to what we really wanted to do: Write."

In my nearly two-decades career as an editor, in my lifetime as a reader, I've been privileged to witness the development of confident, technically astute, inspirational women poets of all ages. It is worthwhile to remind ourselves that these poems are the flowers that grew on battlefields.

Amy Wack
Cardiff, Wales
2008

Acknowledgements and Thanks

Thanks are due to first of all, to the many fine poets who are featured here, for their patience with our proofs and enquiries, particularly Diane Wakoski, Phillis Levin, Alice Fulton, Martha Kapos, Olive Senior, Pascale Petit, Carol Rumens and my amazing co-Editor, Eva Salzman who had to endure a blizzard of e-mails in turbulent times.

Secondly, I must thank some of the large number of people in the publishing world (agents, assistants, permissions people, editors and estates) who helped with the permissions process, starting with Suzanne Fairless-Aitken at Bloodaxe and Pam Heaton at Carcanet and Suzanna Tamminen at Weslyan and including: Bob Arnold, Kate Auseman, Margie Bachman, R.V. Bailey, Hannah Bannister, Faith Freeman Barbato, Elizabeth Barnett, Jean Barry, Jill Bialosky, Tom Booth, Mellisa Brandt, Mary Branley, Rick Campbell, Harry Chambers, Chris and Jen at Salt, Clare at Eddison Pearson, Frederick T. Courtright, Elizabeth Clementson, Jane Cramb, Angela Crocombe, Jennifer Dellava, Jennie Doling, Frances Edmond, Sherri Feldman, Mary Fox, Gabriel Fried, Deborah Garrison, Leslie Gillilan, Bette Graber, Joanna Green, Michelle Griffin, John Harwood, Ron Hussey, Tim and Elke Inkster, Jessie Lendennie, Candide Jones, Jill Jones, Jane Jordan, Andrea Joyce, Ken at Reality Street, Joanne King, Kathleen Kornell, Mary Krienke, Cynthia Lamb, Deborah Llanglois, Lori Anne Larson, Katy Loffman, Hamish MacGibbon, John McSpaydyen, Meredith McKinney, Rebecca Myers, Steph Opitz, Martha Rhodes, Angharad Rhys, Zoe Ross, Peter Sansom and Janet Fisher, Sheila E. Sharpe, Nichole Shields, Morgan Grady-Smith, Stephen Stewart-Smith, Jeffrey Shotts and Rolph Blythe, Becky Thomas, Stephanie Thwaite, Tony Ward, Sarah Webster, Gabriel White, and Carol Wilson.

Thanks are due as well to tireless Seren staff: Mick Felton, Simon Hicks, Jennifer Campbell, Penny Thomas, Clancy Pegg, Tori Kirwan-Taylor, and Robin Grossmann; our London Publicist, Sian Williams; as well as past and present Seren Board members Cary Archard, Patrick McGuiness and Dannie Abse.

Also, to my family, husband Kevin and daughter, Siobhán, and to my wonderful mother, Rita, exemplar of flair and determination.

Amy Wack

1. How Love Works

Love, Lust, (hopefully both at the same time), Marriage

Beth Ann Fennelly

Poem Not To Be Read At Your Wedding

You ask me for a poem about love
in place of a wedding present, trying to save me
money. For three nights I've lain
under the glow-in-the-dark-stars I've stuck to the ceiling
over my bed. I've listened to the songs
of the galaxy. Well, Carmen, I would rather
give you your third set of steak knives
than tell you what I know. Let me find you
some other, store-bought present. Don't
make me warn you of stars, how they see us
from that distance as miniature and breakable
from the bride who tops the wedding cake
to the Mary on Pinto dashboards
holding her ripe, red heart in her hands.

Molly Peacock

Why I Am Not A Buddhist

I love desire, the state of want and thought
of how to get; building a kingdom in a soul
requires desire. I love the things I've sought – you
in your beltless bathrobe, tongues of cash that loll
from my billfold – and love what I want: clothes,
houses, redemption. Can a new mauve suit
equal God? Oh no, desire is ranked. To lose
a loved pen is not like losing faith. Acute
desire for nut gateau is driven out by death,
but the cake on its plate has meaning,
even when love is endangered and nothing matters.
For my mother, health; for my sister, bereft,
wholeness. But why is desire suffering?
Because want leaves a world in tatters?
How else but in tatters should a world be?
A columned porch set high above a lake.
Here, take my money. A loved face in agony,
the spirit gone. Here, use my rags of love.

Alice Fulton

My Diamond Stud

He'll be a former cat burglar
because I have baubles
to lose. I'll know him
by the black
carnation he's tossing:
heads, he takes me,
stems, the same. Yes,
he'll be a hitchhiker at this
roller-rink I frequent, my diamond
stud who'll wheel up shedding
sparks & say *Ecoutez*
bé-bé. I'm a member
of a famous folded trapeze act.
My agility is legend, etc."
keeping his jeweler's eye on
my gold fillings. He'll know
what I really want: whipping
me with flowers, his finger's grosgrain
sanded smooth, raw
to my every move. For our tryst
we'll go to travel-folder heaven
& buff-puff each other's
calluses in valentine tubs.
He'll swindle the black heart
between my thighs
dress me up in ultra-
suede sheaths, himself
in Naugahyde. No,
leather. He'd never
let anything touch him
that wasn't once alive.

Dorianne Laux

The Shipfitter's Wife

I loved him most
when he came home from work,
his fingers still curled from fitting pipe,
his denim shirt ringed with sweat,
smelling of salt, the drying weeds
of the ocean. I'd go to where he sat
on the edge of the bed, his forehead
anointed with grease, his cracked hands
jammed between his thighs, and unlace
the steel-toed boots, stroke his ankles
and calves, the pads and bones of his feet.
Then I'd open his clothes and take
the whole day inside me – the ship's
gray sides, the miles of copper pipe,
the voice of the foreman clanging
off the hull's silver ribs. Spark of lead
kissing metal. The clamp, the winch,
the white fire of the torch, the whistle,
and the long drive home.

Jean Sprackland

The Apprentice

I married a big man with clumsy hands,
whose touch left me fingerprinted with bruises.
I had to keep him from my bed
till he learned some delicacy.
I wanted him dextrous

so I trained him on nimble tasks. First time
hanging out washing, he snapped a dozen pegs,
let underwear fall in the wet grass.

Then I had him sowing lettuces,
pricking out the seedlings, growing them on.
He was close to tears with the smallness of the work.

I schooled him in needle and thread,
a hard apprenticeship in gentleness.
He fumbled the button, knocked the licked end of thread
against the stubborn eye of the needle,
stabbed his fingertip. Blood on his white shirt.

One night, after dinner, the final test:
unfastening my silver necklace.
When I felt those skilful fingers
lift my hair and charm the tiny clasp apart,
I stood astonished, sheened in desire. I turned
and took his hands, set them free.

Anna Wickham

The Fired Pot

In our town, people live in rows.
The only irregular thing in a street is the steeple;
And where that points to God only knows,
And not the poor disciplined people!

And I have watched the women growing old,
Passionate about pins, and pence, and soap,
Till the heart within my wedded breast grew cold,
And I lost hope.

But a young soldier came to our town,
He spoke his mind most candidly.
He asked me quickly to lie down,
And that was very good for me.

For though I gave him no embrace –
Remembering my duty –
He altered the expression of my face,
And gave me back my beauty.

Leland Bardwell

How My True Love and I Lay Without Touching

How my true love and I lay without touching
How my hand journeyed to the drumlin of his hip
my pelvis aching
Just like two saints or priests or nuns
my true love and I lay without touching.

How I would long for the brush of a kiss
to travel my cheek or the cheek of my groin
my heart aching
But just like two saints or priests or nuns
my true love and I lay without touching.

Last night in my dreams I spoke with his wife
his true love who had left him surely as they lay without touching
my heart for her was aching
For like two saints or priests or nuns
the two loves once lay without touching.

But the dream of her faded before concentrating
each to each in our innocent mutual hating
her hand aching
to blind me with bullets to prevent herself from pining
for a once love she longed for and lay without touching.

Now my true love lies in the mutton of madness
"I was always troubled by sex," he says, with great sadness
his wife and I aching
in our cold single beds with many seas dividing
as we think of the years that we spent without touching.

Elizabeth Barrett Browning
Sonnet 43

How do I love thee? Let me count the ways.
I love thee to the depth and breadth and height
My soul can reach, when feeling out of sight
For the ends of Being and ideal Grace.
I love thee to the level of every day's
Most quiet need, by sun and candle-light.
I love thee freely, as men strive for Right;
I love thee purely, as they turn from Praise.
I love thee with the passion put to use
In my old griefs, and with my childhood's faith.
I love thee with a love I seemed to lose
With my lost saints, I love thee with the breath,
Smiles, tears, of all my life! and, if God choose,
I shall but love thee better after death.

Ruth Herschberger
The Huron

I swam the Huron of love, and am not ashamed,
It was many saw me do it, scoffing, scoffing,
They said it was foolish, winter and all,
But I dove in, greaselike, and swam,
And came up where Erie verges.
I would say for the expenditure of love,
And the atrophy of longing, there is no cure
So swift, so sleek, so fine, so draining
As a swim through the Huron in the wintertime.

A. V. Christie

Evermay-on-the-Delaware

You sleep in the sharp Adirondack chair,
surrounded by a still cloud of larkspur
and I am in the long shadows of lupine
which almost reach you in late afternoon.
I'm remembering the night of our wedding,
how rain throbbed on the windshield, each drop
a shadow blooming somewhere on the map.
I wanted you to know the way along
roads blurred by a fury of rain. I yearned
for you to reinvent yourself as lightning
spread its repertoire, its variations.
But love is each repetition, each small return;
night after night love is the way you gather
the birds, lifting their cage like a lantern.

Deryn Rees-Jones

I know Exactly the Sort of Woman I'd Like to Fall in Love With

If I were a man.

And she would not be me, but
Older and graver and sadder.
And her eyes would be kinder;
And her breasts would be fuller;
The subtle movements
Of her plum-coloured skirts
Would be the spillings of a childhood summer.

She would speak six languages, none of them my own.

And I? I would not be a demanding lover.
My long fingers, with her permission
Would unravel her plaited hair;
And I'd ask her to dance for me, occasionally,
Half-dressed on the moon-pitted stairs.

Selima Hill

Please Can I Have A Man

Please can I have a man who wears corduroy.
Please can I have a man
who knows the names of 100 different roses;
who doesn't mind my absent-minded rabbits
wandering in and out
as if they own the place,
who makes me creamy curries from fresh lemon-grass,
who walks like Belmondo in *A Bout de Souffle*;
who sticks all my carefully-selected postcards –
sent from exotic cities
he doesn't expect to come with me to,
but would if I asked, which I will do –
with nobody else's, up on his bedroom wall,
starting with Ivy, the Famous Diving Pig,
whose picture, in action, I bought ten copies of;
who talks like Belmondo too, with lips as smooth
and tightly-packed as chocolate-coated
(melting chocolate) peony buds;
who knows that piling himself stubbornly on top of me
like a duvet stuffed with library books and shopping-bags
is all too easy: please can I have a man
who is not prepared to do that.
Who is not prepared to say I'm 'pretty' either.
Who, when I come trotting in from the bathroom
like a squealing freshly-scrubbed piglet
that likes nothing better than a binge
of being affectionate and undisciplined and uncomplicated,
opens his arms like a trough for me to dive into.

Eva Salzman

Alex, Tiffany, Meg

rode fast convertibles, rose up like the Furies
blazing scarves and halters in a fire-trail.
The local boys, at first no more than curious,
went mad for the sting in their beautiful tails.

Such kindly girls; they deftly wound my hair
with strange accessories. Naked, like stone,
I bore the slender fingers and thundery stares
as they ripped and ripped away at my bikini-line.

Not ugly, nor evil, they were taken so seriously
their shadows slip beneath each lover, the Fates
re-grouping nightly, featured in the crumpled sheets
or the legacy of silk, my abandoned freight.
Pursued or in pursuit, I find your street
and fly into your bed. Calm this fury, please.

Denise Duhamel

Lawless Pantoum

Men are legally allowed to have sex with animals,
as long as the animals are female.
Having sexual relations with a male animal
is taboo and punishable by death.

As long as the fish are female
saleswomen in tropical fish stores are allowed to go topless.
Adultery is punishable by death
as long as the betrayed woman uses her bare hands to kill her husband.

Saleswomen in tropical fish stores are allowed to go topless,
but the gynecologist must only look at a woman's genitals in a mirror.
The woman uses her bare hands to kill her husband,
then his dead genitals must be covered with a brick.

The gynecologist must only look at a woman's genitals in a mirror
and never look at the genitals of a corpse –
these genitals must be covered with a brick.
The penalty for masturbation is decapitation.

A look at the genitals of a corpse
will confirm that not much happens in that region after death.
The penalty for masturbation is decapitation.
It is illegal to have sex with a mother and her daughter at the same time.

To confirm what happens during sex,
a woman's mother must be in the room to witness her daughter's
                                                    deflowering,
though it is illegal to have sex with a mother and her daughter at the
                                                    same time.
It is legal to sell condoms from vending machines as long as

a woman's mother is in the room to witness her daughter's deflowering.
Men are legally allowed to have sex with animals –
why it's even legal to sell condoms from vending machines, as long as
everyone's having sexual relations with a male animal.

Denise Duhamel

Sex With a Famous Poet

I had sex with a famous poet last night
and when I rolled over and found myself beside him I shuddered
because I was married to someone else,
because I wasn't supposed to have been drinking,
because I was in a fancy hotel room
I didn't recognize. I would have told you
right off this was a dream, but recently
a friend told me, *write about a dream,*
lose a reader and I didn't want to lose you
right away. I wanted you to hear
that I didn't even like the poet in the dream, that he has
four kids, the youngest one my age, and I find him
rather unattractive, that I only met him once,
that is, in real life, and that was in a large group
in which I barely spoke up. He disgusted me
with his disparaging remarks about women.

He even used the word 'Jap'
which I took as a direct insult to my husband who's Asian.
When we were first dating, I told him
"You were talking in your sleep last night
and I listened, just to make sure you didn't
call out anyone else's name." My future-husband said
that he couldn't be held responsible for his subconscious,
which worried me, which made me think his dreams
were full of blond vixens in rabbit-fur bikinis,
but he said no, he dreamt mostly about boulders
and the ocean and volcanoes, dangerous weather
he witnessed but could do nothing to stop.
And I said, "I dream only of you,"
which was romantic and silly and untrue.
But I never thought I'd dream of another man –
my husband and I hadn't even had a fight,
my head tucked sweetly in his armpit, my arm
around his belly, which lifted up and down
all night, gently like water in a lake.
If I passed that famous poet on the street,
he would walk by, famous in his sunglasses
and blazer with the suede patches at the elbows,
without so much as a glance in my direction.
I know you're probably curious about who the poet is,
so I should tell you the clues I've left aren't
accurate, that I've disguised his identity,
that you shouldn't guess *I bet it's him...*
because you'll never guess correctly
and even if you do, I won't tell you that you have.
I wouldn't want to embarrass a stranger
who is, after all, probably a nice person,
who was probably just having a bad day when I met him,
who is probably growing a little tired of his fame –
which my husband and I perceive as enormous,
but how much fame can an American poet
really have, let's say, compared to a rock star
or film director of equal talent? Not that much,
and the famous poet knows it, knows that he's not
truly given his due. Knows that many
of these young poets tugging on his sleeve
are only pretending to have read all his books.
But he smiles anyway, tries to be helpful.
I mean, this poet has to have some redeeming qualities, right?
For instance, he writes a mean iambic.
Otherwise, what was I doing in his arms.

Kim Addonizio

"What Do Women Want?"

I want a red dress.
I want it flimsy and cheap,
I want it too tight, I want to wear it
until someone tears it off me.
I want it sleeveless and backless,
this dress, so no one has to guess
what's underneath. I want to walk down
the street past Thrifty's and the hardware store
with all those keys glittering in the window,
past Mr. and Mrs. Wong selling day-old
donuts in their café, past the Guerra brothers
slinging pigs from the truck and onto the dolly,
hoisting the slick snouts over their shoulders.
I want to walk like I'm the only
woman on earth and I can have my pick.
I want that red dress bad.
I want it to confirm
your worst fears about me,
to show you how little I care about you
or anything except what
I want. When I find it, I'll pull that garment
from its hanger like I'm choosing a body
to carry me into this world, through
the birth-cries and the love-cries too,
and I'll wear it like bones, like skin,
it'll be the goddamned
dress they bury me in.

Louise Glück

Anniversary

I said you could snuggle. That doesn't mean
your cold feet all over my dick.

Someone should teach you how to act in bed.
What I think is you should
keep your extremities to yourself.

Look what you did –
you made the cat move.

But I didn't want your hand there.
I wanted your hand here.

You should pay attention to my feet.
You should picture them
the next time you see a hot fifteen year old.
Because there's a lot more where those feet come from.

Rita Ann Higgins

The Did-You-Come-Yets of the Western World

When he says to you:
You look so beautiful
you smell so nice -
how I've missed you -
and did you come yet?

It means nothing,
and he is smaller,
than a mouse's fart.

Don't listen to him....
Go to Annaghdown Pier
with your father's rod.

Don't necessarily hold out
for the biggest one;
oftentimes the biggest ones
are the smallest in the end.

Bring them all home,
but not together.
One by one is the trick;
avoid red herrings and scandal.

Maybe you could take two
on the shortest day of the year.
Time is the cheater here
not you, so don't worry.

Many will bite the usual bait:
They will talk their slippery way
through fine clothes and expensive perfume,
fishing up your independence.

These are,
The did-you-come-yets of the western world,
the feather and fin rufflers.
Pity for them they have no wisdom.

Others will bite at any bait.
Maggot, suspender, or dead worm.
Throw them to the sharks.

In time one will crawl
out from under thigh-land.
Although drowning he will say,

"Woman I am terrified, why is the house shaking?"
And you'll know he's the one.

Bernardine Evaristo

Amo Amas Amat

Prologue to 'The Emperor's Babe', a novel in verse

Who do you love? Who *do* you love?
When the man you married goes off

for months on end, quelling rebellions
at the frontiers, or playing hot-shot senator in Rome;

his flashy villa on the Palatine Hill, home
to another woman, I hear,

one who has borne him offspring.
My days are spent roaming this house,

its vast mosaic walls full of the scenes on Olympus,
for my husband loves melodrama.

They say his mistress is an actress,
a flaxen-fraulein type, from Germania Superior.

Oh everyone envied me, *Illa Bella Negreeta!*
born in the back of a shop on Gracechurch Street,

who got hitched to a Roman nobleman,
whose parents sailed out of Khartoum on a barge,

no burnished throne, no poop of beaten gold
but packed with vomiting brats,

and cows releasing warm turds
onto their bare feet. Thus perfumed,

they made it to Londinium on a donkey,
with only a thin purse and a fat dream.

Here in the drizzle of this wild west town
Dad wandered the streets looking for work,

but there was no room at the inn
so he set up shop on the kerb

and sold sweet cakes which Mum made.
(He's told me this story a *mille* times.)

Now he owns several shops, selling everything
from vino to shoes, veggies to tools,

and he employs all sorts to work in them,
a Syrian, Libyan, Jew, Persian,

hopefuls just off the olive barge from Gaul,
in fact anyone who'll work for pebbles.

When Felix came after me, Dad was in ecstasy
Father-in-law to Lucius Aurelius Felix, no less.

I was spotted at the baths of Cheapside,
just budding, and my fate was sealed,

to a man thrice my age, and thrice my girth –
all at sweet eleven, even then Dad

thought I was getting past it.
Then I was sent off to a snooty Roman bitch

called Clarissa for decorum classes,
learnt how to talk, eat and fart,

how to get my amo amas amat right, and ditch
my second generation plebby creole.

Zuleika accepta est.
Zuleika delicata est.
Zuleika bloody goody-two shoes est.

But I dreamt of creating mosaics,
of remaking my town with bright stones and glass.

But no! Numquam! It's not allowed.
Sure, Felix brings me presents, when he deigns

to come west. I've had Chinese silk, a marble
figurine from Turkey, gold earrings

shaped like dolphins and I have the deepest
fondness for my husband, of course,

sort of, though he spills over me like dough
and I'm tempted to call cook mid-coitus

to come trim his sides so that he fits me.
Then it's puff and *Ciao Baby!*

Solitudoh, solitudee, solitudargh!

Sophie Cabot Black

Interrogation

When you have me as I'm standing
Against a wall, my sex becomes
Suddenly agnostic; strange new words
Slip out, your name mentioned twice.

This is not a careful time.
These bodies that have collected love,
That have closely followed the goals
Of line or curve, are becoming

Sentimental. We wander in and out
Of each other's mouths. I keep thinking
You're asking me something. Light
Pours in, hangs like a valuable stone above us.

I lose words remembering to speak.
You press into my skin for veins, finger
By finger, your eyes blank and glazed.
My eyes start to empty too, become

Exactly like yours, until all there is
Is a heart, each beat rendering the last silent.

Barbara Guest

Parachutes My Love, Could Carry Us Higher

I just said I didn't know
And now you are holding me
In your arms,
How kind.
Parachutes, my love, could carry us higher.
Yet around the net I am floating
Pink and pale blue fish are caught in it,
They are beautiful,
But they are not good for eating.
Parachutes, my love, could carry us higher
Than this mid-air in which we tremble,

Having exercised our arms in swimming,
Now the suspension, you say,
Is exquisite. I do not know.
There is coral below the surface,
There is sand, and berries
Like pomegranates grow.
This wide net, I am treading water
Near it, bubbles are rising and salt
Drying on my lashes, yet I am no nearer
Air than water. I am closer to you
Than land and I am in a stranger ocean
Than I wished.

Menna Elfyn

Couplings

Life is a house in ruins. And we mean to fix it up
and make it snug. With our hands we knock it into shape

to the very top. Till beneath this we fasten a roofbeam
that will watch the coming and going of our skyless life,

two crooked segments. They are fitted together,
timbers in concord. Smooth beams, and wide.

Two in touch. That's the craft we nurture in folding
doubled flesh on a frame. Conjoining the smooth couplings

that sometimes arch into one. Aslant above a cold world,
hollow wood wafting passion. Then stock still for a time.

And how clear-cut the roof, creaking love at times,
as it chides the worm to keep off and await its turn.

translated from the Welsh by Joseph Clancy

Emily Dickinson

249

Wild Nights – Wild Nights!
Were I with thee
Wild Nights should be
Our luxury!

Futile – the Winds –
To a Heart in port –
Done with the Compass –
Done with the Chart!

Rowing in Eden –
Ah, the Sea!
Might I but moor – Tonight –
In Thee!

Helen Dunmore

Safe Period

Your dry voice from the centre of the bed
asks "Is it safe?"

and I answer for the days as if I owned them.
Practised at counting, I rock
the two halves of the month like a cradle.

The days slip over their stile
and expect nothing. They are just days,

and we're at it again, thwarting
souls from the bodies they crave.

They'd love to get into this room
under the yellow counterpane
we've torn to make a child's cuddly,

they'd love to slide into the sheets
between soft, much-washed
flannelette fleece,

they'd love to be here in the moulded spaces
between us, where there is no room,

but we don't let them. They fly about gustily,
noisy as our own children.

Edna St. Vincent Millay

Sonnet

I, being born a woman and distressed
By all the needs and notions of my kind,
Am urged by your propinquity to find
Your person fair, and feel a certain zest
To bear your body's weight upon my breast:
So subtly is the fume of life designed,
To clarify the pulse and cloud the mind,
And leave me once again undone, possessed.
Think not for this, however, the poor treason
Of my stout blood against my staggering brain,
I shall remember you with love, or season
My scorn with pity, – let me make it plain:
I find this frenzy insufficient reason
For conversation when we meet again.

Adrienne Rich

The Insusceptibles

Then the long sunlight lying on the sea
Fell, folded gold on gold; and slowly we
Took up our decks of cards, our parasols,
The picnic hamper and the sandblown shawls
And climbed the dunes in silence. There were two
Who lagged behind as loves sometimes do.
And took a different road. For us the night
Was final, and by artificial light
We came indoors to sleep. No envy there
Of those who might be watching anywhere
The lustres of the summer dark, to trace
Some vagrant splinter blazing out of space.
No thought of them, save in a lower room
To leave a light for them when they should come.

Alice Fulton

What I Like

Friend – the face I wallow toward
through a scrimmage of shut faces.
Arms like towropes to haul me home, aide-
memoire, my lost childhood docks, a bottled ark
in harbor. *Friend* – I can't forget
how even the word contains an *end*.
We circle each other in a scared bolero,
imagining stratagems: postures and imposters.
Cold convictions keep us solo. I ahem
and hedge my affections. Who'll blow the first kiss,
land it like the lifeforces we feel
tickling at each wrist? It should be easy
easy to take your hand, whisper down this distance
labeled hers or his: what I like about you is

Deborah Landau

August in West Hollywood

All day I watch the neighbor's boy
paint the side of his house.

He seems to rest so easily on the ladder rungs,
shirtless, lanky-limbed, hips tilting in the sun.

In the morning, I am the house, blueing beneath his brushstrokes,
each rib a shingle, my breasts, windowpanes, my waist,

the broad wood planks flattening beneath his brushstrokes,
my shoulders, shutters, lips and eyelashes fluttering eaves.

By four, I'm the roller brush,
turned and turning in his working hands.

Come dusk, I'm the open pail of paint
beside him on the grass – wide-mouthed, emptied.

The neighbor's house breathes in its new skin beneath the streetlamp.
It puts its face to the darkness and does not recognize itself.

Pascale Petit

The Second Husband

After what feels like two thousand years
        I find you under the permafrost.
I dig and dig until your twelve frozen horses
        spring up in their red felt masks and ibex horns.
You must have ridden each one to heaven

        in your high headdress with its gold foil frieze
                of Celestial Mountains, your crest
        of winged snow leopards and antlered wolves
                with eagle tines. When you ask me to stay
        I know this is the afterlife.

Alice Oswald

Wedding

From time to time our love is like a sail
and when the sail begins to alternate
from tack to tack, it's like a swallowtail
and when the swallow flies it's like a coat;
and if the coat is yours, it has a tear
like a wide mouth and when the mouth begins
to draw the wind, it's like a trumpeter
and when the trumpet blows, it blows like millions...
and this, my love, when millions come and go
beyond the need of us, is like a trick;
and when the trick begins, it's like a toe
tiptoeing on a rope, which is like luck;
and when the luck begins, it's like a wedding,
which is like love, which is like everything.

2. Love Not Working

Loss, Adultery, Betrayal, Divorce

Louise Glück

Mock Orange

It is not the moon, I tell you.
It is these flowers
lighting the yard.

I hate them.
I hate them as I hate sex,
the man's mouth
sealing my mouth, the man's
paralyzing body –

and the cry that always escapes,
the low, humiliating
premise of union –

In my mind tonight
I hear the question and pursuing answer
fused in one sound
that mounts and mounts and then
is split into the old selves,
the tired antagonisms. Do you see?
We were made fools of.
And the scent of mock orange
drifts through the window.

How can I rest?
How can I be content
when there is still
that odor in the world?

Katherine Pierpoint
This Dead Relationship

I carry a dead relationship around everywhere with me.
It's my hobby.
How lucky to have a job that's also my hobby,
To do it all the time.

A few people notice, and ask if they can help carry this thing.
But, like an alcoholic scared they will hear the clink of glass in the bag,
I refuse – scared they'll smell rottenness,
Scared of something under their touch
That will cave in, a skin over brown foam on a bad apple.
I cram this thing over the threshold
Into the cold and speechless house,
Lean against the front door for a moment to breathe in the dark
Then start the slow haul to the kitchen.
Steel knives catch the moonlight on white tiles.

This dead relationship.

Or not yet dead.

Or dead and half-eaten,
One eye and one flank open, like a sheep under a hedge.

Or dead but still farting like the bodies in the trenches,
Exploding with their own gas. Hair and nails still growing.

It has the pins and needles of returning feeling in a deadness.
It is a reptile in my hand, quick and small and cool;
The flip of life in a dry, cold bag of loose skin.
A pressure without warmth of small claws and horn moving on my palm.

At night it slips slow but purposeful across the floor towards the bed.
Next thing it's looking out of my eyes in the morning –
And in the mirror, though my eyes are not my own,
My mouth shows surprise that I am still there at all.

Oh, a sickness that can make you so ill,
Yet doesn't have the decency to kill you.

A mad free-fall that never hits the ground,
Never knows even the relief of sudden shock;
Just endless medium-rare shock, half-firm, half-bloody all the time.
A long, slow learning curve.
The overheating that can strip an engine badly,
Strain it far worse than a racing rally.
The fear that you will slow to a stop
Then start a soft, thick, slow-gathering roll backwards.

I want something that is familiar but not.
To feel in someone else's pocket for a key
While they lean away, laughing, their arms up,
Hands in the air covered in grease or dough or paint or clay.

I have to carry it around.
A weeping mother brings a baby to hospital,
Late-night emergency.
The tired doctor smooths the hand-made lace back from its face.
He sees it was stillborn weeks ago, has been dead for weeks.
He looks at her, there is no air in the room...

This dead relationship. This dead and sinking ship.
Bulbs lie, unplanted, on a plate of dust.
Dry and puckered pouches, only slightly mouldy;
Embalmed little stomachs but with hairy, twisted fingers,
Waiting for something to happen without needing to know what it is.
When it happens everything else in the universe can start.

This dead relationship.

I am this thing's twin.
One of us is dead
And we don't know which, we are so close.

Carolyn Kizer

Bitch

Now, when he and I meet, after all these years,
I say to the bitch inside me, don't start growling.
He isn't a trespasser anymore,
Just an old acquaintance tipping his hat.
My voice says, "Nice to see you,"
As the bitch starts to bark hysterically.
He isn't an enemy now,
Where are your manners, I say, as I say,
"How are the children? They must be growing up."
At a kind word from him, a look like the old days,
The bitch changes her tone: she begins to whimper.
She wants to snuggle up to him, to cringe.
Down, girl! Keep your distance
Or I'll give you a taste of the choke-chain.
"Fine, I'm just fine," I tell him.
She slobbers and grovels.
After all, I am her mistress. She is basically loyal.
It's just that she remembers how she came running
Each evening, when she heard his step;
How she lay at his feet and looked up adoringly
Though he was absorbed in his paper;
Or, bored with her devotion, ordered her to the kitchen
Until he was ready to play.
But the small careless kindnesses
When he'd had a good day, or a couple of drinks,
Come back to her now, seem more important
Than the casual cruelties, the ultimate dismissal.
"It's nice to know you are doing so well," I say.
He couldn't have taken you with him;
You were too demonstrative, too clumsy,
Not like the well-groomed pets of his new friends.
"Give my regards to your wife," I say. You gag
As I drag you off by the scruff,
Saying, "Good-bye! Good-bye! Nice to have seen you again."

Eleanor Brown

Terrible Sonnet

(from 50 Sonnets)

Not if you crawled from there to here, you hear?
Not if you beg me, on your bleeding knees.
Not if you lay exhausted at my door,
and pleaded with me for a second chance.
Not if you wept (am I making this clear?)
or found a thousand different words for "Please",
ten thousand for "I'm sorry"; I'd ignore
you so sublimely; every new advance
would meet with such complete indifference.
Not if you promised me fidelity.
Not if you meant it! What impertinence,
then, is this voice that murmurs, "What if he
didn't?" That isn't his line of attack.
What if he simply grinned, and said, "I'm back?"

Sara Teasdale

The Look

Strephon kissed me in the spring,
    Robin in the fall,
But Colin only looked at me
    And never kissed at all.

Strephon's kiss was lost in jest,
    Robin's lost in play,
But the kiss in Colin's eyes
    Haunts me night and day.

Deborah Randall

Ballygrand Widow

So, you have gone my erstwhile glad boy,
Whose body, I remember, stained my big cream bed,
And didn't we mix the day and the night in our play,
We never got up for a week.

If I must set my alarm again,
And feed the hungry hens in the yard,
And draw the milk from my cow on time,
And skulk my shame down Ballygrand Street
To get a drink,
It'll not be for you I think,
But my next husband,
A fine cock he shall be.

So, you are no more in this town
My lovely schoolboy, and how the floss
Of your chin tickled mine.
And you swam your hands all over,
You shouted for joy, the first time.
Ah, my darling!

I wear your mother's spit on my shoes,
The black crow priest has been to beat me.
But you gave me a bellyful, the best,
And they shan't take it.
The days are unkind after you, they are empty.
I lie in the sheets, the very same sheets;
You smelled sweeter than meadow hay.
My beautiful boy you have killed me.

Connie Bensley

Politeness

They walked awkwardly along the towpath
bumping together, because his arm
was round her shoulder. He was saying:
I shall always remember this walk.
I'll never forget last night.
I'll never forget you. Oh God.

After a pause, she made a short
non-committal noise. The morning had turned
wet and dark. She felt dilapidated by the rain
and of course had forgotten her umbrella
due to the unexpected turn of events.
Trust me, he said, *you will, won't you?*

Trust him to what, she wondered.
Which men could one trust? Any man
carrying a musical instrument, perhaps?
Any man walking along reading a book?
Most doctors – with reservations about those
wearing bow ties. *Trust you to what?* she asked.

To never let you down, he said,
splitting the infinitive, crushing her
against his wet tweeds. She fought
for breath as he loomed over her.
Little one, I can't let you go.
I'll be back on Thursday. Expect me.

So many imperatives. The situation
had become unwieldy. She longed
for buttered toast, looked furtively
at her watch. *I know, I know, we have*
so little time. The suffocating squeeze
into the spongy lapels.

I've never felt like this before
Have you ever felt like this before?
Fatigue and embarrassment were
all too familiar to her. She stirred the leaves
with the toe of her boot *No* she said
politely. *Not exactly like this.*

Dorothy Parker

Unfortunate Coincidence

By the time you swear you're his,
Shivering and sighing,
And he vows his passion is
Infinite, undying –
Lady, make a note of this:
One of you is lying.

Shirley Kaufman

Jealousy

He is sulking again because whatever she does
it's the wrong thing or she's talking to somebody else
and he can't stand it. But he won't tell her about it
oh no he walks away from the museum shop and she can't
find him and even up in the galleries it starts, she
wants to tell him about the Botticelli in room number nine
and he is already ahead in number eleven. And out
in the street the others are drinking capuccino at a table
on the sidewalk and they have their arms around each other
lightly and she has to ask if they've seen him and there
he is dragging his feet in the distance, studying the windows,
spending the rest of the day attached to somebody else.
And she runs after him and asks why did you leave me,
and he says he wanted to look at Bergamo or Inverness or
Jaipur and she was too busy buying postcards, and that
isn't it at all, that's never it. And what can she do
but eat lamb's testicles or crawl on her belly
through the long night or fall in the lake
with her clothes on or throw herself from the parapet.
Until he is sorry and she is sorry and they are both
sorry until the next time which is in Santorini.

Sarah's Laughter

Sarah's laughter's sudden, like a hurdle, like an old loud crow
that comes out of the blue.

The graceful men at the makeshift table –
there, in the shade of the tree, in the heat of the day, in Bethel –

look up from the all too tender veal,
the buttermilk, the three small

cakes of meal she's made them. For her husband
Abraham, she's sifted, shaped them in her old dry hand.

Good Lord, no. Laugh? Not I. For Sarah's suddenly afraid.
She did what she could

when she sent him in to that Hagar, handmaid, then,
yes, then dealt hardly with her, only then

let her bide with the lad
Ishmael. A sturdy lad.

It's hidden, the hurt, like a hard little bird in the tent
of her heart. She's tended it.

Cleopatra Mathis

Getting Out

That year we hardly slept, waking like inmates
who beat the walls. Every night
another refusal, the silent work
of tightening the heart.
Exhausted, we gave up; escaped
to the apartment pool, swimming those laps
until the first light relieved us.
Days were different: FM and full-blast
blues, hours of guitar "you gonna miss me
when I'm gone." Think how you tried
to pack up and go, for weeks stumbling
over piles of clothing, the unstrung tennis rackets.
Finally locked into blame, we paced
that short hall, heaving words like furniture.
I have the last unshredded pictures
of our matching eyes and hair. We've kept
to separate sides of the map,
still I'm startled by men who look like you.
And in the yearly letter, you're sure to say
you're happy now. Yet I think of the lawyer's bewilderment
when we cried, the last day. Taking hands
we walked apart, until our arms stretched
between us. We held on tight, and let go.

Sarah Maguire

Spilt Milk

Two soluble aspirins spore in this glass, their mycelia
fruiting the water, which I twist into milkiness.
The whole world seems to slide into the drain by my window.

It has rained and rained since you left, the streets black
and muscled with water. Out of pain and exhaustion you came
into my mouth, covering my tongue with your good and bitter milk.

Now I find you have cashed that cheque. I imagine you
slipping the paper under steel and glass. I sit here in a circle
of lamplight, studying women of nine hundred years past.

My hand moves into darkness as I write, *The adulterous woman
lost her nose and ears; the man was fined.* I drain the glass.
I still want to return to that hotel room by the station

to hear all night the goods trains coming and leaving.

Gwyneth Lewis

Advice On Adultery

(from: Welsh Espionage)

The first rule is to pacify the wives
if you're presented as the golden hope
at the office party. You're pure of heart,
but know the value of your youthful looks.
Someone comments on your lovely back.
Talk to the women, and avoid the men.

In work they treat you like one of the men
and soon you're bored with the talk of the wives
who confide in you about this husband's back,
or that husband's ulcer. They sincerely hope
you'll never have children... it ruins your looks.
And did you know David has a dicky heart?

You go to parties with a beating heart,
start an affair with one of the men.
The fact you've been taking good care of your looks
doesn't escape the observant wives
who stare at you sourly. Cross your fingers and hope
that no one's been talking behind your back.

A trip to the Ladies. On your way back
one of them stops you for a heart to heart.
She hesitates, then expresses the hope
that you won't take offence, but men will be men,
and a young girl like you, with such striking looks...
She's heard nasty rumours from some of the wives.

She knows you're innocent, but the wives,
well, jump to conclusions from the way it looks...
In a rage, you resolve she won't get him back,
despite the pressure from the other wives.
They don't understand... you'll stick with the men,
only they are *au fait* with affairs of the heart.

You put it to him that you're living in hope.
He grants that you're beautiful, but looks
aren't everything. He's told the men,
who smirk and wink. So now you're back
to square one, but with a broken heart.
You make your peace with the patient wives.

Don't give up hope at the knowing looks.
Get your own back, have a change of heart:
Ignore the men, start sleeping with the wives.

Wendy Cope

Men and Their Boring Arguments

One man on his own can be quite good fun
But don't go drinking with two –
They'll probably have an argument
And take no notice of you.

What makes men so tedious
Is the need to show off and compete.
They'll bore you to death for hours and hours
Before they'll admit defeat.

It often happens at dinner-parties
Where brother disputes with brother
And we can't even talk among ourselves
Because we're not next to each other.

Some men like to argue with women –
Don't give them a chance to begin.
You won't be allowed to change the subject
Until you have given in.

A man with the bit between his teeth
Will keep you up half the night
And the only way to get some sleep
Is to say, "I expect you're right."

I expect you're right, my dearest love.
I expect you're right, my friend.
These boring arguments make no difference
To anything in the end.

Maura Dooley

History

It's only a week but already you are slipping
down the cold black chute of history. Postcards.
Phonecalls. It's like never having seen the Wall,
except in pieces on the dusty shelves of friends.

Once I queued for hours to see the moon in a box
inside a museum, so wild it should have been kept
in a zoo at least but there it was, unremarkable,
a pile of dirt some god had shaken down.

I wait for your letters now: a fleet of strange cargo
with news of changing borders, a heart's small
journeys. They're like the relics of a saint.
Opening the dry white papers is kissing a bone.

Linda Gregg

Marriage and Midsummer's Night

It has been a long time now
since I stood in our dark room looking
across the court at my husband in her apartment,
watched them make love.
She was perhaps more beautiful
from where I stood than to him.
I can say it now: She was like a vase
lit the way milky glass is lighted.
He looked more beautiful there
than I remember him the times
he entered my bed with the light behind.
It has been ten years since I sat
at the open window, my legs over the edge
and the knife close like a discarded idea.
Looked up at the Danish night,
that pale, pale sky where the birds that fly
at dawn flew on those days all night long,
black with the light behind. They were caught
by their instincts, unable to end their flight.

Anne Rouse

Sum

Let's not revert to lovers' algebra:
if she, if you, if then, if I, if we.
You're hers, and that's the sum of it,
and I've held to a unique geometry
whereby the self's augmented, not diminished,
fitting its dramas to this little square,
and if no figure's perfect there,
it isn't for the want of application – and, like you,
I've risked a passionate miscalculation.

Honor Moore

First Time: 1950

In the back bedroom, laughing when you pull
something fawn-colored from your black
tight pants, the unzipped chino slit.
I keep myself looking at the big belt
buckled right at my eyes, feel the hand
ruffle my hair: You are called Mouse, baby-

sitter trusted Wednesdays with my baby
brother. With me. I still see you pull
that huge bunch of keys from a pocket, hand
them to my brother, hear squeaking out back –
Mrs. Fitz's clothesline – as you unbelt,
turn me to you, my face to the open slit.

It's your skin, this thing, head, its tiny slit
like the closed eye of a still-forming baby.
As you stroke, it stiffens like a new belt –
your face gets almost sick. I want to pull
away, but you grip my arm. I see by your black
eyes you won't let go. With your left hand

you take my chin. With your other hand
you guide it, head reddening, into my slit,
my five-year-old mouth. In the tight black
quiet of my shut eyes, I hear my baby
brother shaking the keys. You lurch, pull
at my hair. I don't breathe, feel buckle, belt,

pant. It tastes lemons, musty as a belt
after a day of sweat. Mouth hurts, my hands
push at your hips. I gag. You let me pull
free. I open my eyes, see the strange slits
yours are; you don't look at me. "Babe, babee –"
You are moaning, almost crying. The black

makes your chin clam-white now, your jewel-black
eyes blacker. You buckle up the thick belt.
When you take back the keys, my baby
brother cries. You extend a shaking hand
you make kind. In daylight though a wide slit,
an open shade leaves, I see her pull.

Mrs. Fitz pulling in her rusty, soot-black
line. Framed by a slit, her window, her large hands
flash, sort belts, dresses, shirts, baby clothes.

Valeria Melchioretto

The Girl With The Shoe Fetish

The slippers she will make from the soft skin of your penis
will fit her as perfectly as you fitted her and I will do nothing
but watch as if reading religiously an ancient text on rejection.

She will rip your balls off and sew them to the slippers as pompoms.
You won't recognise me as I will take on the shape of a cormorant
sitting on the fifth branch of the world tree where pity won't reach me.

The slippers will be made according to a pattern to match her collection.
She will polish the shoes with pigs' fat, put them on and dance
digging her heels into your chest until the vultures will come for you.

Like a shaman she will hit the shoe carton with your funny bone
making a sound so eerie; it will shake the world tree at its roots,
but by then your ears will be deaf to your own helpless prayers.

I will repeat the past after myself and bless your eyes that won't see
the mist fall nor the rain nor darkness itself. I will do this until I lose
my voice,
until I move up a branch on the tree or fly into a wide open sky.

Alicia Ostriker

Liking It

Some men like it if the woman can't tell
Whether it's a gun she has in her mouth
Or a prick.

Some women believe the shallow razor slashes
Their lovers make on their necks
(Underneath the long

Elliptically tangled hair) and chest
Are like a secret engagement dramatized by a real
Diamond, to be proud of

But not reveal. He's her high school
Mathematics teacher, and she does it to him, too,
Because after the vodka comes the need to punish

Their sinful bodies, she thinks about it all week,
Bright red released in lines like devil's writing coming out,
The sharing of blood, the licking, the cleansing

Of wounds, and how perfectly painful that is,
Cuts even hiss from the alcohol swab, it's like acid,
And the candles in the livingroom dance like they're alive,

Like hellfire, you can't imagine
The discipline required. The purity
Of self-loathing needed to cut the man

You love – what do her parents understand about love,
She wonders, her poor parents not guessing
What her arms look like under her sleeves:

White nicks, white nicks, white crucifixes,
Sharp little mouse tracks up and down. Some men
Like you to wear a religious medal

When you fuck, some women
Like the man to cry and beg forgiveness.

Sophie Hannah

The End of Love

The end of love should be a big event.
It should involve the hiring of a hall.
Why the hell not? It happens to us all.
Why should it pass without acknowledgement?

Suits should be dry-cleaned, invitations sent.
Whatever form it takes – a tiff, a brawl –
The end of love should be a big event.
It should involve the hiring of a hall.

Better than the unquestioning descent
Into the trap of silence, than the crawl
From visible to hidden, door to wall.

Get the announcements made, the money spent.
The end of love should be a big event.
It should involve the hiring of a hall.

Rachel Wetzsteon

Young Love

After their first electric conversation
she bolted to her room, and he to his;
colorful sparks and shapely images
brightened their thoughts with new illumination –

cursing her appetite, whose lustful motive
gobbled up all her efforts to be proper,
blessing her stubborn tendency to stopper
sentiment with dry wit, she set up votive

candles in her own honor. He in his turn
blazed with the brilliant role he had created;
scholarly, stern, but dying to be dated
when the right moment came, he let a flame burn

until it looked like ardor. Both had groundless
reasons for love, although they called it boundless.

Night hurried off with what the day had woven,
dreams showed the happy pair where they were heading.
In a deserted valley he lay bleeding
while a repulsive animal with cloven

hooves and familiar features leapt around
in a balletic swoon, then fired an arrow
(which had been dipped in sugar) at a sparrow
who faltered, then fell, lifeless, to the ground.

That this was heaven there was no mistaking,
but a long wait revealed her residence
as a cloud to whose lofty eminence
nobody traveled. Both awoke and, shaking,

pondered a painful quandary: should love
settle for hell below, or hell above?

Menacing shadows colored their next meeting,
although the scene was passionate enough,
made up primarily of harmless fluff:
she called him "heaven sent", he called her "sweeting".

But before long, she dropped the fatal bombshell:
wouldn't a loving merger cost too much?
Two lines so similar could never touch,
two restless yolks would squirm inside one eggshell.

Moved, he agreed: why meddle with perfection?
She was his angel and he was her savior.
Sully their love with bestial behavior
and the spoiled egg would barely pass inspection.

He was in tears, and she was broken-hearted.
Hastily, and with relief, they parted.

Barbara Bentley

Fax

(from: Telephone Sonnets)

The faxed post slithers through a desktop chink.
FOA The Manager from his wife.
You bastard, it reads. Did you really think
I'd swallow that guff on the phone last night?
Tied up, you said. Too bloody right. Tied up
at some meeting in an en suite, no doubt –
all expenses paid while you're shacked up
with your Personal Assistant. I want out.

The kids send their love. They're strapped in the car.
I should be going. But I'm hanging on
for a phoned through telegram. If you care,
fax us. Fax, damn you. Or we're leaving home.
The document's in a tray marked Urgent,
FAO the boss, who's out with a client.

Emily Dickinson

303

The Soul selects her own Society –
Then – shuts the Door –
To her divine Majority –
Present no more –

Unmoved – she notes the Chariots – pausing –
At her low Gate –
Unmoved – an Emperor be kneeling
Upon her Mat –

I've known her – from an ample nation –
Choose One –
Then – close the Valves of her attention –
Like Stone –

Vona Groarke

Call Waiting

Three times I call, three times you're engaged.
You know I am incoming, according to the voice:
my call heralds itself with two round pips,
beads on a chain of intimate, dead air
coiled like the flex around your index finger now
as you stand in the kitchen of the house where I am not
and where, upstairs, is the ring he gave her,
that she gave to me and his dovetailed dress-jacket
she begged me not to wear but I did anyway,
sixteen, blue-haired, all my plans laid out as parallels
marked with a ruler and measured for space
claimed as gracelessly as those black squares
we inked on our fingernails. I must have been nine
when I learned to split a circle three-ways
from just above the centre out, like the Pye sign
in the country town we drove through yesterday.
The boy who told my fortune in Greece
said I had too many lines: they threw him
every which way and he couldn't tell my heart
from head or how the life would span,
but he was right about the indoor garden
I planted with ivy and the little gate that opens
on nothing but its own three arduous notes.
There's a leaf of copper beech in my hand now
and the voice is telling me to hold for a connection.
I tear along the veins and find I am left
with one trefoil that splays like any fish spine
or the crow's feet that have settled round my eyes.
My call is brushing up against yours now
like a ten cent coin between two fifties in my pocket
or a marble with three colours curled
to skim the arc of two others in its path.
Or like the way your breath on the back of my hand
had three things to say, and none of them got said.

Kathryn Maris

The Boatman
for M.R.

Ruddy rower of the boat called Merry Man, merry
man of the dark marsh, host of the party barge.

His arms are like a farmer's: slight but hard
from the drag and the drag of a task –

the oars that lap the flat of the black bog
until the reedmace sways its kinky heads.

I see the boat from the land where I stand.
I can see the greasy distance, and the boatman's grin.

He likes his drink. His myopia is a droll trick.
When he snakes into the far-off, his focus goes vague

and he's known to mistake a quarrel for a dance,
an embrace for containment, ardor for arduousness.

I am the same. I see what I want when he is far,
when love goes distant. I can see him and then I can't

and then I can and, when I can, I see the merry man,
the merry man is really just the ferryman.

3. Family Trees

Kin & Kith, Birth, Children, Childhood

Frances Cornford

Childhood

I used to think that grown-up people chose
To have stiff backs and wrinkles round their nose,
And veins like small fat snakes on either hand,
On purpose to be grand.
Till through the banisters I watched one day
My great-aunt Etty's friend who was going away,
And how her onyx beads had come unstrung.
I saw her grope to find them as they rolled;
And then I knew that she was helplessly old,
As I was helplessly young.

Jorie Graham

Wanting a Child

How hard it is for the river here to re-enter
the sea, though it's most beautiful, of course, in the waste
of time where it's almost
turned back. Then
it's yoked, trussed... The river
has been everywhere, dividing, discerning,
cutting deep into the parent rock,
scouring and scouring
its own bed.
Nothing is whole
where it has been. Nothing
remains unsaid.
Sometimes I'll come this far from home
merely to dip my fingers in this glittering, archaic
sea that renders everything
identical, flesh
where mind and body
blur. The seagulls squeak, ill-fitting
hinges, the beach is thick
with shells. The tide
is always pulsing upward, inland,
into the river's rapid
argument, pushing
with its insistent tragic waves – the living echo,
says my book, of some great storm far out at sea, too far
to be recalled by us
but transferred
whole onto this shore by waves, so that erosion
is its very face.

Carolyn Kizer

Parent's Pantoum

Where did these enormous children come from,
More ladylike than we have ever been?
Some of ours look older than we feel.
How did they appear in their long dresses

More ladylike than we have ever been?
But they moan about their aging more than we do,
In their fragile heels and long black dresses.
They say they admire our youthful spontaneity.

They moan about their aging more than we do,
A somber group – why don't they brighten up?
Though they say they admire our youthful spontaneity
They beg us to be dignified like them

As they ignore our pleas to brighten up.
Someday perhaps we'll capture their attention
Then we won't try to be dignified like them
Nor they to be so gently patronizing.

Someday perhaps we'll capture their attention.
Don't they know that we're supposed to be the stars?
Instead they are so gently patronizing.
It makes us feel like children – second-childish?

Perhaps we're too accustomed to be stars.
The famous flowers glowing in the garden,
So now we pout like children. Second-childish?
Quaint fragments of forgotten history?

Our daughters stroll together in the garden,
Chatting of news we've chosen to ignore,
Pausing to toss us morsels of their history,
Not questions to which only we know answers.

Eyes closed to news we've chosen to ignore,
We'd rather excavate old memories,
Disdaining age, ignoring pain, avoiding mirrors.
Why do they never listen to our stories?

Because they hate to excavate old memories
They don't believe our stories have an end.
They don't ask questions because they dread the answers.
They don't see that we've become their mirrors,
We offspring of our enormous children.

Elizabeth Bartlett

Birth

When they gave you to me you were redolent
Of acrid badly-made soap and blood,
And indeed you were covered with a waxy layer,
Like rice-paper on a macaroon, or cottage cheese.
You had obviously done some very heavy laundry
In the womb, using soda, wringing your hands,
Purple and sodden like a washer-woman,
Whose feeble fingers have mandarin's nails
With which you scratched your face, adding
To the general air of wear and tear and age.
And yet you were so young, a few minutes,
And the placenta not yet flowering in the bowl,
Your doll's clothes still airing, your air-way
Choked with mucus. All night we drained
You like a boiled potato, tipping you up
And, newly-washed we looked upon your great
High forehead, and your thin crop of hair,
And marvelled that you had travelled so far
Through such a small tunnel, no cuts,
No stitches, no forceps, just a long journey
And a small body, like a fish, sliding neatly
Into a quiet house, and an old bed,
Where no other child had been born before.
You cried a little, and then, exhausted, fell
Into the deepest sleep there is, apart
From death, and I lay flat and empty
Awake all night, tired beyond sleep,
Fearing and hoping beyond all bounds
That you would not live to curse your birth
As many have done before you,
And will do again.

Kathleen Jamie

from: Ultrasound

(for Duncan)

I
Ultrasound
Oh whistle and I'll come to ye,
my lad, my wee shilpit ghost
summoned from tomorrow.

Second sight,
a seer's mothy flicker,
an inner sprite:

this is what I see
with eyes closed,
a keek-about among secrets.

If Pandora
could have scanned
her dark box,

and kept it locked –
this ghoul's skull, punched eyes
is tiny Hope's,
hauled silver-quick
in a net of sound,
then, for pity's sake, lowered.

VII
Prayer
Our baby's heart, on the sixteen-week scan
was a fluttering bird, held in cupped hands.

I thought of St. Kevin, hands opened in prayer
and a bird of the hedgerow nesting there,

and how he'd borne it, until the young had flown
– and I prayed: this new heart must outlive my own.

Sara Berkeley

The Call

The Fall winds covered my bed with a sheet of leaves;
drought in much of the country, fires already.
I was dry in my skeleton, old bones
crackling in their sleep beneath the duck down,
dreams like teasing sheep's wool through a dark hole.

I thought I was a member of ordinary time,
two Sundays after the Ascension, or was it the Assumption?
But then she was here, new under the sun;
she examined every leaf, one by one by one;
she rolled on the bed laughing, and I joined in.

Hail to her, and sunlight, and spirit songs.
She bends the back of the wind and lets it go
so it springs forward with a shower of bright stars.
I touch her tiny shoulder blades as a gentle reminder –
she'll be my flown one; I will call after her

and my call will go higher and higher
till it's just air and only dolphins hear it.

Helen Farish

Newly Born Twins

In separate incubators one of the twins was dying.
Against doctor's orders, a nurse put them together.

The strong twin, the one with nothing
pulling her back, she slung
her newly born arm over
the one who was wanting to leave,
and stabilised her heartbeat, made everything
regular in the body of the one who'd already
had enough.

The strong one, she will think
she is God, that she can pull back
life from where it was going.
It will be harder for her
than for the one who already knows
about separation, loneliness, where
they can make you want to go.

Joy Katz

The Family, One Week Old

The parents, as if clubbed between the eyes
But with no memory of it, regard the infant
Who has no self-regard and none for them.
It gazes into the world and shits:
It will not be so independent again
Until old age. Where did the baby come from?
La la, mother sings.
Father has it on his forearm, king;
Baby swims, no fear of falling.
Self-forgetfulness means one has a self to forget
Grown big and bruised as a pear. What joy
When it disappears!

Linda France

Elementary
(for Rufus)

I ask my son what he knows of earth,
of properties of metal,
the rings in the heart of wood,
what shapes he can trace in air,
how deep is the blue of water;
remind him to take care with fire.
He has a dangerous fondness for fire,
my son, learning the lessons of earth;
knows magnets are science, metal,
observes their attraction through water.
He's aware that a kite, and he, needs air,
the paper he'd miss so much is wood.

We scramble hand in hand through the wood
near our house, feeling the damp earth
spring under our feet, the lapping of water
in the silence. The cold air
makes him cough so we go home to the fire,
welcomed by kettle's singing metal.

His toys are plastic; mine were metal,
with sharp corners. They rusted in water.
Now the fashion's back for wood,
carved and painted trains, trucks and fire engines.
Things have changed. This earth
I thought I knew, and love, is mutable as air.

My son was four the year the air
blew from the east, poisoned by fire,
a fire kindled with no wood.
The smell of my sweat was metal.
We couldn't trust rain, milk or earth,
were afraid to drink the water.

He loves to play in water,
and I to watch him, in the tenuous air
of summers. I lean against knotted wood,
by the river glinting metal.
As certain as flames in fire
we're held in the breath of earth.

I pray to the gods of air, goddesses of wood
and water, that he'll be saved from fire,
and save, like precious metal, all he knows of earth.

Naomi Shihab Nye

Making a Fist

For the first time, on the road north of Tampico,

I felt the life sliding out of me,

a drum in the desert, harder and harder to hear.

I was seven, I lay in the car

watching palm trees swirl a sickening pattern past the glass.

My stomach was a melon split wide inside my skin.

"How do you know if you are going to die?"

I begged my mother.

We had been traveling for days.

With strange confidence she answered,

"When you can no longer make a fist."

Years later I smile to think of that journey,

the borders we must cross separately,

stamped with our unanswerable woes.

I who did not die, who am still living,

still lying in the backseat behind all my questions,

clenching and opening one small hand.

Rachel Hadas

The Red Hat

It started before Christmas. Now our son
Officially walks to school alone.
Semi-alone, it's accurate to say:
I or his father track him on the way.
He walks up on the east side of West End,
we on the west side. Glances can extend
(and do) across the street; not eye contact.
Already ties are feeling and not fact.
Straus Park is where these parallel paths part;
he goes alone from there. The watcher's heart
stretches, elastic in its love and fear,
toward him as we see him disappear,
striding briskly. Where two weeks ago,
holding a hand, he'd dawdle, dreamy, slow,
he now is hustled forward by the pull
of something far more powerful than school.
The mornings we turn back to are no more
than forty minutes longer than before,
but they feel vastly different – flimsy, strange,
wavering in the eddies of this change,
empty, unanchored, perilously light
since the red hat vanished from our sight.

Rita Dove

After Reading *Mickey in the Night Kitchen* for the Third Time Before Bed

I'm in the milk and the milk's in me!.. I'm Mickey!

My daughter spreads her legs
to find her vagina:
hairless, this mistaken
bit of nomenclature
is what a stranger cannot touch
without her yelling. She demands
to see mine and momentarily
we're a lopsided star
among the spilled toys,
my prodigious scallops
exposed to her neat cameo.

And yet the same glazed
tunnel, layered sequences.
She is three; that makes this
innocent. *We're pink!*
she shrieks, and bounds off.

Every month she wants
to know where it hurts
and what the wrinkled string means
between my legs. *This is good blood*
I say, but that's wrong, too.
How to tell her that it's what makes us –
black mother, cream child.
That we're in the pink
and the pink's in us.

Julia Darling

My Complicated Daughter

What can I do for my complicated daughter,
my terror, my dark heart, so lost in this house?
Where can we meet? On the stairs, on the landing?
At night as we dream? In the bold brass of the day?
If only I could make her a cagoule of rescue,
heal all her scars, wrap her sore life in silk,
or bury her pain at the end of the garden
with my bare hands. I'd give her a sack full of wishes.
But she will not hear me, and I cannot see her.
We collide in the bathroom, by the terrible mirror,
so apart, so unable to give or receive.

Catherine Phil MacCarthy

Rag Doll

Straw-haired. Patchworked. I am
the rag doll you threaten to lose.
Each time, you push me

into the dark under the bed
to see if I'll be lost
when you turn blindly groping

cobwebs. Sometimes you slap me
on the face and warn
that I have to be good. Once,

you even tried to strangle me,
the vice grip of your small fingers
on my throat so fierce, tears

dripped from your eyes. At night
I sleep next to you on the pillow.
Your eyelashes brush my cheek.

Soon I'll be gone forever.
Neither of us will know
exactly how it happened.

Eavan Boland

The Black Lace Fan My Mother Gave Me

It was the first gift he ever gave her,
buying it for five francs in the Galeries
in pre-war Paris. It was stifling.
A starless drought made the nights stormy.

They stayed in the city for the summer.
They met in cafés. She was always early.
He was late. That evening he was later.
They wrapped the fan. He looked at his watch.

She looked down the Boulevard des Capucines.
She ordered more coffee. She stood up.
The streets were emptying. The heat was killing.
She thought the distance smelled of rain and lightning.

These are wild roses, appliqued on silk by hand,
darkly picked, stitched boldly, quickly.
The rest is tortoiseshell and has the reticent,
clear patience of its element. It is

A worn-out, underwater bullion and it keeps,
even now, an inference of its violation.
The lace is overcast as if the weather
it opened for and offset had entered it.

The past is an empty café terrace.
An airless dusk before thunder. A man running.
And no way now to know what happened then –
none at all – unless, of course, you improvise:

The blackbird on this first sultry morning,
in summer, finding buds, worms, fruit,
feels the heat. Suddenly she puts out her wing –
the whole, full, flirtatious span of it.

Lynn Emanuel

Frying Trout While Drunk

Mother is drinking to forget a man
Who could fill the woods with invitations:
Come with me he whispered and she went
In his Nash Rambler, its dash
Where her knees turned green
In the radium dials of the 50s.
When I drink it is always 1953,
Bacon wilting in the pan on Cook Street
And mother, wrist deep in red water,
Laying a trail from the sink
To a glass of gin and back.
She is a beautiful, unlucky woman
In love with a man of lechery so solid
You could build a table on it
And when you did the blues would come to visit.
I remember all of us awkwardly at dinner,
The dark slung across the porch,
And then mother's dress falling to the floor,
Buttons ticking like seeds spit on a plate.
When I drink I am too much like her –
The knife in one hand and in the other
The trout with a belly white as my wrist.
I have loved you all my life
She told him and it was true
In the same way that all her life
She drank, dedicated to the act itself,
She stood at this stove
And with the care of the very drunk
Handed him the plate.

Pascale Petit

My Mother's Perfume

Strange how her perfume used to arrive long before she did,
    a jade cloud that sent me hurrying
first to the loo, then to an upstairs window to watch for her taxi.
    I'd prepare myself
by trying to remember her face, without feeling afraid. As she drew
    nearer I'd get braver
until her scent got so strong I could taste the coins in the bottom
    of her handbag.
And here I am forty years on, still half-expecting her. Though now
    I just have to open
the stopper of an expensive French bottle, daring only a whiff of
    Shalimar
which Jacques Guerlain created from the vanilla orchid vine.
    Her ghostly face
might shiver like Christ's on Veronica's veil - a green-gold blossom
    that sends me back
to the first day of the school holidays, the way I used to practise
    kissing her cheek
by kissing the glass. My eyes scanned the long road for a speck
    while the air turned amber.
Even now, the scent of vanilla stings like a cane. But I can also smell
    roses and jasmine
in the bottle's top notes, my legs wading through the fragrant path
    to the gloved hand emerging
from a black taxi at the gate of Grandmother's garden. And for a
    moment I think I am safe.
Then Maman turns to me with a smile like a dropped
    perfume bottle, her essence spilt.

Pauline Stainer

The White Shell

No headstone –
just your ashes
scattered on white flowers
for the dead take up
too much inconsolable space.

Candour was your quality,
as in that Japanese print
where the shell is unseen
but everything whitens
with its referred radiance
the way snow accumulates silence.

Melanie Challenger

Mother

*Sprinkle on them waters of atonement; they have caused
A razor to pass over all their flesh.*
Unguessed in the hotbed, awaiting discovery,
The ghost-lives of children breathing their intentions
Inside me like mist, I prayed for thee.
I prayed for thee, O mother, accouche
Accouche to blessed consanguinity
Your daughter to the headwaters.

Imparting my sum and substance as a fait accompli
Upon the earthweight, laid open to the historicity
Of this hour, this life, how I prayed for thee.
How I begged for thee, O mother, accouche
Accouche your only daughter
To the atoning waters of our sorority.

Elizabeth Alexander

My Grandmother's New York Apartment

1. Apartment
Everything pulled out or folded away:
sofa into a bed, tray tables that disappear
behind a door, everything
trasmutable, alchemy in small
spaces, even my grandmother tiny
and changeable: a housecoat and rollers
which vanish and become an Irish
tweed suit, a tilted chapeau, a Hello
in the elevator just like, as she
would say, the Queen of Denmark.

2. Bathroom
Cuticle cream and orange sticks, bath oil pearls,
cotton wisps, boxed perfume in a lower
drawer, wire rollers, seaweedy stockings
drying on a rod, white garter belts,

white cotton gloves and vaseline at night,
nail lacquer, tweezers, red lipsticks.
Push against your front teeth so they don't
go buck. Grease elbows, hair-ends, kneecaps, lips.

Grandmother smoked on the toilet at night.
Stop chewing your nails, stop picking your face.
Here is a diamond-dust fingernail file.
Your brand new rain-bonnet lost already?

Julia Copus

The Back Seat of My Mother's Car

We left before I had time
to comfort you, to tell you that we nearly touched
hands in that vacuous half-dark. I wanted
to stem the burning waters running over me like tiny
rivers down my face and legs, but at the same time I was reaching out
for the slit in the window where the sky streamed in,
cold as ether, and I could see your fat mole-fingers grasping
the dusty August air. I pressed my face to the glass;
I was calling to you – *Daddy!* – as we screeched away into
the distance, my own hand tingling like an amputation.
You were mouthing something I still remember, the noiseless words
piercing me like that catgut shriek that flew up, furious as a sunset
pouring itself out against the sky. The ensuing silence
was the one clear thing I could decipher –
the roar of the engine drowning your voice,
with the cool slick glass between us.

With the cool slick glass between us.
the roar of the engine drowning, your voice
was the one clear thing I could decipher –
pouring itself out against the sky, the ensuing silence
piercing me like that catgut shriek that flew up, furious as a sunset.
You were mouthing something: I still remember the noiseless words
the distance, my own hand tingling like an amputation.
I was calling to you, Daddy, as we screeched away into
the dusty August air. I pressed my face to the glass,
cold as ether, and I could see your fat mole-fingers grasping
for the slit in the window where the sky streamed in
rivers down my face and legs, but at the same time I was reaching out
to stem the burning waters running over me like tiny
hands in that vacuous half-dark. I wanted
to comfort you, to tell you that we nearly touched.
We left before I had time.

Jackie Kay

The Shoes of Dead Comrades

On my father's feet are the shoes of dead comrades.
Gifts from the comrades' sad red widows.
My father would never see good shoes go to waste.
Good brown leather, black leather, leather soles.
Doesn't matter if they are a size too big, small.

On my father's feet are the shoes of dead comrades.
The marches they marched against Polaris. UCS.
Everything they ever believed tied up with laces.
A cobbler has replaced the sole, heel.
Brand new, my father says, look, feel.

On my father's feet are the shoes of dead comrades.
These are in good nick. These were pricey.
Italian leather. See that. Lovely.
He always was a classy dresser was Arthur.
Ever see Wullie dance? Wullie was a wonderful waltzer.

On my father's feet are the shoes of dead comrades.
It scares me half to death to consider
that one day it won't be Wullie or Jimmy or Arthur,
that one day someone will wear the shoes of my father,
the brown and black leather of all the dead comrades.

Jackie Kay

I Am The Child

I am the child who is about to be born.
I already know I won't live long.
I will be lucky if I live until I am three.
My mother won't be able to help
Passing down to me
A strange fruit from the family tree.

I am the child who has lost her mother.
There are no grownups living here.
I have to be mother to my sister.
I need a bathroom tap and water,
But mostly I want somebody to tuck us up at night,
Somebody to sing us to sleep, hold us tight.

I am the child who is about to die.
There are too many children like me.
Every hour, every day, every year
Death will keep us company.
Imagine all the children
Imagine all the children
Imagine all the children
Exactly like me

Jill Bialosky

Fathers In The Snow

After father died
the love was all through the house
untamed and sometimes violent.
When the dates came we went up to our rooms
and mother entertained.
Frank Sinatra's 'Strangers in the Night',
the smell of Chanel No.5 in her hair and the laughter.
We sat crouched at the top of the stairs.
In the morning we found mother asleep on the couch
her hair messed, and the smell
of stale liquor in the room.
We knelt on the floor before her,
one by one touched our fingers
over the red flush in her face.
The chipped sunlight through the shutters.
It was a dark continent
we and mother shared;
it was sweet and lonesome,
the wake men left in our house.

Mary Baine Campbell

The Wake

The child is holding the hand
Of another child he does not care for
But cares for now, now that the taker
Of care is in the ground,
Like the mother of the child
Who is caring for the child he
May not love.
                    The dead
Are not only dead to us
But to each other. Where they go
Is very dark, not even a place.
No one is ever there to talk to
Or hold on to. We the living
Are lucky – the child holds on
To the child and I hold on
To them as though they were their mothers
Or my own, who also went
Where she could not be touched
Or spoken to.
                    You'd think
The living would hold on
More tightly to each other
But they've learned
A light touch, death
Is everywhere now, teaching
That touch, showing you
How not to leave tracks
In the endless snow.

Death is everywhere now. The living
Stand in circles within circles, teaching
Each other the light touch, touching
Each other lightly – "Time to go."

Death is everywhere now. It's like a flame
That touches every head, even
The heads of those who can't imagine it,
Or couldn't. Now they can.

Peg Boyers

Tobacco

To rid yourself of envy and sin
mix honey with tobacco.
          – *Cuban folksong*

Tabaco, tu boca,
tus bocas – your mouths,
sweet island uncles, your lips

fragrant with Cuban *puros*, and you
lifting me
in a cloud of smoke

for a good-night kiss, passing me,
one to one,
with your dark burly arms,

hugging me close so that
my hair, my nightie, take back the smell
to linger over in bed under the mosquito net.

The cousins asleep in rows of cots on the veranda,
ocean breeze billowing the netting
so it scratches my cheek – the lightest of stings.

Little huddles of white, snug as tobacco hills
swathed in gauze, baking the blonde inner leaves
to wrap, ring with bands and burn.

The sound of Mamita and her sisters singing
– *Quando salí de l'Habana válgame dios* –
Habana puro.

My shallow smoker's breath,
asthmatic, subverts the soul's infant desire,
but the memory of pleasure persists.

Tabaco, tu boca,
tus bocas – Lelén, Pili, Pancho,
and the priest, Benjamín, all the *tíos*

in starched *guayaveras,*
pleats pressed over their stout middles:
tobacco musk of men,

chiefs in a circle, smoking
the weed
like the first *caciques*

Columbus found when he waded to shore
at *Puerto de Mares,* Port of Seas,
Port of Surfs,

Port of Sorrows.
Tabaco. Tu boca –
No se toca.

Tío Cheo, you weren't like the rest. Your
arms were smooth and pink and fine.
And your breath

smelled of *guarapo* when you leaned over
and sang to us
in your pitch perfect voice

American show tunes you'd picked up in college
before the seminary, before
the priesthood, before Uncle Ben

nailed you, took off your frock
and drove you
to Bellevue

where drugs and shock-treatment
dulled away desire.
Too mad now

even for the Franciscans, banished
from their monastery, your habit
repossessed,

you phone from the asylum, asking
for cigarettes: still, at eighty,
craving, unrequited.

Freda Downie

Great-Grandfather

Great-grandfather would sit in the back parlour
For hours listening to the gramophone.
I have no photograph of him doing this,
So the picture I see of him sitting alone

With his head inclined towards the trumpeting
Green lily is colourful and unfaded.
The handkerchief, with which he blots the tears
Schubert serenades from him, is distinctly red

And the gramophone's tin horn grows steadily
More greenly lily-like and rare,
Grows into antiquity – and soon will be found
Surviving only behind glass in conditioned air.

Great-grandfather knows nothing of this, but
Such an instrument will be treasured as though
It were a silver trumpet once discovered
Lying in the tomb of some young Egyptian Pharaoh;

And only on certain occasions will it be taken
From its case and played with careful ceremony –
When thinnest sound will summon the ready armies
Of imagination to salute the music lovers of history.

And great-grandfather will be one of those.

Toi Derricotte

Family Secrets

They told my cousin Rowena not to marry
Calvin – she was too young, just eighteen,
& he was too dark, too too dark, as if he
had been washed in what we wanted
to wipe off our hands. Besides, he didn't come
from a good family. He said he was going
to be a lawyer, but we didn't quite believe.
The night they eloped to the Gotham Hotel,
the whole house whispered – as if we were ashamed
to tell it to ourselves. My aunt and uncle
rushed down to the Gotham to plead –
we couldn't imagine his hands on her!
Families are conceived in many ways.
The night my cousin Calvin lay
down on her, that idol with its gold skin
broke, & many of the gods we loved
in secret were freed.

Gwen Harwood

In The Park

She sits in the park. Her clothes are out of date.
Two children whine and bicker, tug her skirt.
A third draws aimless patterns in the dirt.
Someone she loved once passes by – too late

to feign indifference to that casual nod.
"How nice," et cetera. "Time holds great surprises."
From his neat head unquestionably rises
a small balloon... "but for the grace of God..."

They stand a while in flickering light, rehearsing
the children's names and birthdays. "It's so sweet
to hear their chatter, watch them grow and thrive,"
she says to his departing smile. Then, nursing
the youngest child, sits staring at her feet.
To the wind she says, "They have eaten me alive."

Sharon Olds

I Go Back To May 1937

I see them standing at the formal gates of their colleges,
I see my father strolling out
under the ochre sandstone arch, the
red tiles glinting like bent
plates of blood behind his head, I
see my mother with a few light books at her hip
standing at the pillar made of tiny bricks,
the wrought-iron gate still open behind her, its
sword tips aglow in the May air,
they are about to graduate, they are about to get married,
they are kids, they are dumb, all they know is they are
innocent, they would never hurt anybody,
I want to go up to them and say Stop,
don't do it – she's the wrong woman,
he's the wrong man, you are going to do things
you cannot imagine you would ever do,
you are going to do bad things to children,
you are going to suffer in ways you have not heard of,
you are going to want to die. I want to go
up to them there in the late May sunlight and say it,
her hungry pretty face turning to me,
her pitiful beautiful untouched body,
his arrogant handsome face turning to me,
his pitiful beautiful untouched body,
but I don't do it. I want to live. I
take them up like the male and female
paper dolls and bang them together
at the hips, like chips of flint, as if to
strike sparks from them, I say
Do what you are going to do, and I will tell about it.

4. Heroines & Rebels

Famous, Infamous, Not so Famous

Muriel Rukeyser

Myth

Long afterward, Oedipus, old and blinded walked the
roads.   He smelled a familiar smell.   It was
the Sphinx.   Oedipus said, "I want to ask one question.
Why didn't I recognise my mother?"   "You gave the
wrong answer," said the Sphinx.   "But that was what
made everything possible," said Oedipus.   "No", she said.
"When I asked, What walks on four legs in the morning,
two at noon, and three in the evening, you answered,
Man.   You didn't say anything about woman."
"When you say Man," said Oedipus, "you include women
too. Everyone knows that."   She said, "That's what
you think."

Sylvia Plath

Lady Lazarus

I have done it again.
One year in every ten
I manage it –

A sort of walking miracle, my skin
Bright as a Nazi lampshade,
My right foot

A paperweight,
My face a featureless, fine
Jew linen.

Peel off the napkin
0 my enemy.
Do I terrify? –

The nose, the eye pits, the full set of teeth?
The sour breath
Will vanish in a day.

Soon, soon the flesh
The grave cave ate will be
At home on me

And I a smiling woman.
I am only thirty.
And like the cat I have nine times to die.

This is Number Three.
What a trash
To annihilate each decade.

What a million filaments.
The peanut-crunching crowd
Shoves in to see

Them unwrap me hand and foot –
The big strip tease.
Gentlemen, ladies

These are my hands
My knees.
I may be skin and bone,

Nevertheless, I am the same, identical woman.
The first time it happened I was ten.
It was an accident.

The second time I meant
To last it out and not come back at all.
I rocked shut

As a seashell.
They had to call and call
And pick the worms off me like sticky pearls.

Dying
Is an art, like everything else,
I do it exceptionally well.

I do it so it feels like hell.
I do it so it feels real.
I guess you could say I've a call.

It's easy enough to do it in a cell.
It's easy enough to do it and stay put.
It's the theatrical

Comeback in broad day
To the same place, the same face, the same brute
Amused shout:

'A miracle!'
That knocks me out.
There is a charge

For the eyeing of my scars, there is a charge
For the hearing of my heart –
It really goes.

And there is a charge, a very large charge
For a word or a touch
Or a bit of blood

Or a piece of my hair or my clothes.
So, so, Herr Doktor.
So, Herr Enemy.

I am your opus,
I am your valuable,
The pure gold baby

That melts to a shriek.
I turn and burn.
Do not think I underestimate your great concern.

Ash, ash –
You poke and stir.
Flesh, bone, there is nothing there –

A cake of soap,
A wedding ring,
A gold filling.

Herr God, Herr Lucifer
Beware
Beware.

Out of the ash
I rise with my red hair
And I eat men like air.

Catherine Bowman

1-800-HOT-RIBS

My brother sent me ribs for my birthday.
He sent me two six-pound, heavily scented,
slow-smoked slabs, Federal Express,
in a customized cardboard box, no bigger
than a baby coffin or a bulrush ark.

Swaddled tight in sheaves of foam and dry ice,
those ribs rested in the hold of some jetliner
and were carried high, over the Yellowhammer State
and the Magnolia State and the Brown Thrasher State,
over Kentucky coffee trees and Sitka spruce

and live oak and wild oak and lowland plains
and deep-water harbors, over catfish farms
and single-crib barns and Holiness sects
and strip-malls and mill towns and lumber
towns and coal camps and chemical plants

to my table on this island on a cold night
with no moon where I eat those ribs and am made
full from what must have been a young animal,
small-boned and tender, having just
the right ratio of meat to fat.

Tonight outside, men and women enrobed
in blankets fare forth from shipping crates.
A bloodhound lunges against its choke
to sniff the corpse of a big rat and heaps
of drippings and grounds that steam

outside the diner as an ashen woman deep
in a doorway presses a finger to her lips.
A matted teddy bear impaled on a spike
looms over a vacant lot where a line of men
wreathe in fellowship around a blazing garbage can.

Tonight in a dream they gather
all night to labor over the unadorned
beds they have dug into the ground and filled
with hardwood coals that glow like remote stars.
Their faces molten and ignited in the damp,

they know to turn the meat infrequently,
they know to keep the flame slow and the fire
cool. From a vat of spirits subacid and brackish,
they know to baste only occasionally. So that
by sunrise vapor will continue to collect, as usual,

forming, as it should, three types of clouds,
that the rainfall from the clouds, it is certain,
will not exceed the capacity of the river,
that the river will still flow, as always,
sweet brother, on course.

Alice Oswald

The Thing In The Gap-Stone Stile

I took the giant's walk on top of the world,
peak-striding, each step a viaduct.

I dropped hankies, cut from a cloth of hills,
and beat gold under fields
for the sun to pick out a patch.

I never absolutely told
the curl-horned cows to line up their gaze.
But it happened, so I let it be.

And Annual Meadow Grass, quite of her own accord,
between the dry-stone spread out emerald.

(I was delighted by her initiative
and praised the dry-stone for being contrary.)

What I did do (I am a gap)
was lean these elbows on a wall
and sat on my hunkers pervading the boulders.

My pose became the pass across two kingdoms,
before behind antiphonal, my cavity the chord.

And I certainly intended
anyone to be almost
abstracted on a gap-stone between fields.

Dorothy Parker

Oscar Wilde

If, with the literate, I am
Impelled to try an epigram,
I never seek to take the credit;
We all assume that Oscar said it.

Lynn Emanuel

Blonde Bombshell

Love is boring and passé, all the old baggage,
the bloody bric-a-brac, the bad, the gothic,
retrograde, obscurantist hum and drum of it
needs to be swept away. So, night after night,
we sit in the dark of the Roxy beside grandmothers
with their shanks tied up in the tourniquets
of rolled stockings and open ourselves, like earth
to rain, to the blue fire of the movie screen
where love surrenders suddenly to gangsters
and their cuties. There in the narrow,
mote-filled finger of light, is a blonde
so blond, so blinding, she is a blizzard, a huge
spook, and lights up like the sun the audience
in its galoshes. She bulges like a deuce coupé.
When we see her we say good-bye to Kansas.
She is everything spare, cool, and clean,
like a gas station on a dark night or the cold
dependable light of rage coming in on schedule like a bus.

Amy Wack

Tooth Fairy

Not Titania or Tinkerbell, not minute
with dragonfly wings and a dimple,
but fleshly and glamorous, her hair,
a blonde waterfall, her breath, a mint
chill. She moves like Ginger Rogers
in that white feather dress she wore to
dance with Fred Astaire in *Top Hat*.
Perfume sizzles on her skin, she eats
candyfloss and drinks gin with a twist
poured over diamond-shards of ice.
She's uncanny as seraphim or aliens,
and strangely craven, this apparition,
colour of the cloud's bright lining.

But to a small child she is an angel,
almost a mother, an aura, an air,
her song higher than the mosquito,
her touch invisible, benificent, pure.
Her coins glitter as they fall to the pillow.
She fingers each small tooth like a jewel,
puts it in a silken sack that she slings
over her wings as she dissapates like mist.

What does she do with them all?
They warm her throat like pearls,
they fasten her dress, stud her shoes,
spark in circlets on her wrists and gleam
in the spikes of her tiara like a smile.
Somewhere there must be a white throne
in a white palace, in a white city,
– all a vast unholy mosaic of milk-teeth.
She waits there for her lover to finish
his equally vast and punishing shift.
She calls to him softly, "Hey, Sandman".

H.D.

Helen

All Greece hates
the still eyes in the white face,
the lustre as of olives
where she stands,
and the white hands.

All Greece reviles
the wan face when she smiles,
hating it deeper still
when it grows wan and white,
remembering past enchantments
and past ills.

Greece sees unmoved,
God's daughter, born of love,
the beauty of cool feet
and slenderest knees,
could love indeed the maid,
only if she were laid,
white ash amid funereal cypresses.

Marilyn Hacker

Mythology

Penelope as a garçon manqué.
weaves sonnets on a barstool among sailors,
tapping her iambs out on the brass rail. Ours
is not the high-school text. Persephone
a.k.a. Telemaque-who-tagged-along,
sleeps off her lunch on an Italian train
headed for Paris, while Ulysse-Maman
plugs into the Shirelles singing her song
('What Does a Girl Do?'). What does a girl do
but walk across the world, her kid in tow,
stopping at stations on the way, with friends
to tie her to the mast when she gets too
close to the edge? And when the voyage ends,
what does a girl do? Girl, that's up to you.

Kathryn Gray

Friend,

when we find ourselves once more on the floor
of Indian restaurant, public house or pushed back
to cigarette-scarred polyprop seats of taxi rank,
loud and right for the drink we've sunk,
each wrestled down to her quick for past wrongs:
the birthday missed, the boyfriend shared,
skirt returned, but torn, never to be worn again...

when they pull us apart and threaten the police,
and we walk out to a pavement loose with rain,
slivers of kebab meat and our bared toes brace
against the stipples that come heavier, and we are
not together, one a yard ahead of the other, arms

crossed, miles from morning doorsteps, two women
on an A-road and we stop to explain to one another...
please be quiet, come nearer and let our cupped hands
pool the languages of loose change, mascara, fiver.

Eiléan Ní Chuilleanáin

Translation
(for the reburial of the Magdalenes)

The soil frayed and sifted evens the score –
There are women here from every county,
Just as there were in the laundry.

White light blinded and bleached out
The high relief of a glance, where steam danced
Around stone drains and giggled and slipped across water.

Assist them now, ridges under the veil, shifting,
Searching for their parents, their names,
The edges of words grinding against nature,

As if, when water sank between the rotten teeth
Of soap, and every grasp seemed melted, one voice
Had begun, rising above the shuffle and hum

Until every pocket in her skull blared with the note –
Allow us now to hear it, sharp as an infant's cry
While the grass takes root, while the steam rises:

Washed clean of idiom : the baked crust
Of words that made my temporary name
A parasite that grew in me : that spell
Lifted : I lie in earth sifted to dust
Let the bunched keys I bore slacken and fall
I rise and forget : cloud over my time.

Louise Bogan

Cassandra

To me, one silly task is like another.
I bare the shambling tricks of lust and pride.
This flesh will never give a child its mother, –
Song, like a wing, tears through my breast, my side,
And madness chooses out my voice again,
Again. I am the chosen no hand saves:
The shrieking heaven lifted over men,
Not the dumb earth, wherein they set their graves.

Jane Draycott

The Levitation of St. Christina

(from: Christina The Astonishing)

*(reputed by witnesses to have flown like a bird from her coffin
during her own requiem mass – Saint-Truiden, Flanders, 1182)*

I rise on a wing and a prayer. In the aisles Father Thomas
is singing his heart out O Lamb of God all shaven and shorn
and loud enough to waken the dead. Have mercy upon us.

Up here in the gods where anything goes I am Lucifer, born
like a swan from a box, striking the light and standing well clear
of the tears, of the tar and the feathers, and of the coffin's yawn

that takest away Father Thomas's face, that waning moon in
                                               the filthy air,
that gaping wound in the side of the world. And the O in his mouth
is the sins, is enough to make the angels weep. Receive our prayer.

Out of the hive of the yet to be born, I'm the queen bee, behemoth
in the candle's flame, shifting my shape in the smoke dance,
the dance of death, whose sting is the needle fixed on celestial north.

I leap, and my shadow's a shroud-span over the mountains, an icy stroke
down the cheek of the earth. I have only to touch the hills
                                    and they shall smoke.

Hilary Llewellyn-Williams

Making Man

Something of stone, the heft of it
in your palm, the way it moulds
to the curve around your thumb –
the Venus mount – yet resists it:

something of wood, the rasp
of bark on your arm, the damp moss
smell, webs of xylem
packed sinewy in your grasp:

something of earth, the dense
and crumbled soil, dirt in the whorls
of your skin, muddy boots in the hall,
that clod indifference

out of which things grow
haphazardly, and jostle into form:
and something brutish too, the tossed horns,
rank sweat, stamped hoof, a bellow

in the frost, the way they stand
to piss, the hairy pelt and jaw,
and the old thrust and tumble;
the way they squint at the wind.

Inside, we're all the same:
thinking, and passionate,
bloody and soft, and fearful;
we all lie down to sleep, we all dream.

But outside it's the other, stark and raw
that makes the sap rise; the them
and us, the border, brother earth
and mother sea colliding on a shore

salt-tongued and dangerous.
So we said *let us make man
from our own flesh* and let him be
stone, wood, and beast for us.

Carol Ann Duffy

Mrs Darwin

7 April 1852

Went to the Zoo.
I said to Him –
Something about that Chimpanzee over there reminds me of
    you.

Grace Schulman

Eve's Unnaming

Not horses, but roan
against the blue-green bay,

not crocuses, but wings
folded over suns,

not rhododendrons, but fire that wilts
to straw in the rain.

How to tag
stone, shell, gull,

hands enfolding lamb's-ear,
a bee sucking the delphinium,

when the sea writes and revises,
breaks, pours out, recoils,

when the elm's leaves
turn silver at dawn.

To see in the dark
the south window strew flowers

on the chapel floor,
or wind peel a sand rose,

is unnamable,
like joy,

like my love's grin
between a cap and a jacket.

Names are for things
we cannot own.

Linda Gregerson

Noah's Wife

is doing her usual for comic relief.
      She doesn't
    see why she should get on the boat, etc.,

etc., while life as we know it hangs by a thread.
      Even God's
    had one or two great deadpan lines:

Who told you (this was back at the start –
      the teeth
    of the tautology had just snapped shut) *Who*

told you you were naked? The world
      was so new
    that death hadn't been till this minute

required. *What makes you think* (the
      ground
    withers under their feet) *we were told?*

The woman's disobedience is good for
      plot,
    as also for restoring plot to human

scale: three hundred cubits by fifty
      by what?
    What's that in inches exactly? Whereas

an obstinate wife is common coin.
      In
    the beginning was nothing and then a flaw

in the nothing, a sort of mistake that amplified, the
      nothing
    mistranscribed (it takes such discipline

to keep the prospect clean) and now the lion
      whelps,
    the beetle rolls its ball of dung, and Noah

with no more than a primitive double-
      entry audit
    is supposed to make it right.

We find the Creator in an awkward bind.
        Washed back
    to oblivion? Think again. The housewife

at her laundry tub has got a better grip.
        Which may
    be why we've tried to find her laughable,

she's such an unhappy reminder of what
        understanding
    costs. Ask the boy who cannot, though

God knows he's tried, he swears
        each bar
    of melting soap will be his last, who cannot

turn the water off when once he's turned it on.
        His hands
    are raw. His body seems like filth to him.

Who told you (the pharmacopoeia has
        changed,
    the malady's still the same) *Who told you*

you were food for worms?
        What
    makes you think (the furrow, the fruit)

I had to be told?

Adelaide Crapsey

Susanna and the Elders

    "Why do
    You thus devise
    Evil against her?" For that
    She is beautiful, delicate:
    Therefore.

Kathryn Maris

Goddess

I love a bare world like the world I strode with my boy.
I held his hand. I said, 'This is a wall of wind.' I pitched

the words over the wall, but the wind-whirr deafened him.
His walk was a wrestle. The wan sky was his twin.

His father beckoned him to the swings
and the world grew barer. My son's love is a burden,

The oedipal beat, beat, beat of his fist on his
father's tee-shirted chest. I see

that his leaving will repeat itself; I will let him leave.
And I love a bare world.

Once my husband declared me a goddess
of destruction. I approved of that view. I view

myself that way, too: Queen of an uninhabited planet.
I tread on moon-rubble. Dust circles my knees.

My dress is Belgian deconstructionist. I am barefoot and regal
and unadorned but for the bracelet from the ward.

I am mother to all that is bare, all that is gone
for I have expected the bare world all along.

Jane Holland

The Knife

To be cured of the misery is to be cured of the poetry.
Germaine Greer: *Slip-Shod Sibyls*

I buy the knife
but keep it safely wrapped in leather;
    bone-handled,
something Hemingway might have owned.

    From time to time, I'll bring it out
like one of your letters;
    test the blade with my tongue
until blood comes,

    indulge in the dark dream of after.
I'll play it from hand to hand,
    watch myself for signs of readiness
in its sharp mirror.

It's a rich source of alternatives,
    my knife,
my merciful scythe,
    my one word thesaurus.

Tess Gallagher

Instructions to the Double

So now it's your turn,
little mother of silences, little
father of half-belief. Take up
this face, these daily rounds
with a cabbage under each arm
convincing the multitudes
that a well-made-anything
could save them. Take up
most of all, these hands
trained to an ornate piano
in a house on the other side
of the country.

I'm staying here
without music, without
applause. I'm not going
to wait up for you. Take
your time. Take mine
too. Get into some trouble
I'll have to account for. Walk
into some bars alone
with a slit in your skirt. Let
the men follow you on the street
with their clumsy propositions, their
loud hatreds of this and that. Keep
walking. Keep your head
up. They are calling to you – slut, mother,
virgin, whore, daughter, adulteress, lover,
mistress, bitch, wife, cunt, harlot,
betrothed, Jezebel, Messalina, Diana,
Bathsheba, Rebecca, Lucretia, Mary,
Magdelena, Ruth, you – Niobe,
woman of the tombs.

Don't stop for anything, not
a caress or a promise. Go
to the temple of the poets, not
the one like a run-down country club,
but the one on fire
with so much it wants
to be done with. Say all the last words
and the first: hello, goodbye, yes,
I, no, please, always, never.
If anyone from the country club
asks if you write poems, say
your name is Lizzie Borden.
Show him your axe, the one
they gave you with a silver
blade, your name engraved there
like a whisper of their own.

If anyone calls you a witch,
burn for him; if anyone calls you
less or more than you are
let him burn for you.

It's a dangerous mission. You
could die out there. You
could live for ever.

5. *How The Mind Works*

Memory, Existence, The Meaning of Life

Marilyn Hacker

Square Du Temple II

Moon on late daylight: green fruit plucked from a stalk.
Almost July; almost the end of cherry
season. I walked out on a literary
cocktail early, because I couldn't make more small talk
and because it's a pervasive joy to walk
across the square at not-yet-dusk. Its tutelary
geniuses, preadolescent, very
slender and supple African children, hawk-
swoop on skates around the resting lawn.
(The toddlers and their guardians have gone
home.) A breeze flies from their shoulder blades,
loquacious and invisible, in banners.
The duck pond is refreshed by small cascades,
as silence cures an overdose of manners.

Mary Baine Campbell

Novocaine

The music is coming from the engine, seven centuries old,
And the words of it say love has changed everything
For the singer and brought him to life, although he is dead,
And through the windshield a brown finch is visible
Muttering among the leaves. Dust over green, the green of summer's end.

Inside, the dentist explains to her helper that she always insists
On Novocaine for her patients if she sees the slightest facial twitch.
"I don't *feel* pain —" says one, "— but I do," she replies,
"I don't want to feel your pain or be the one
Who gave it" The helper says, "Why?"

I wish the dentist had answered, but the time had come
To concentrate on my tooth, which was finally numb.
So I lay in the eye of the lamp that brightened the face
of Dustin Hoffman in *Marathon Man*, in a Hollywood gym
Where the world entered the innocent patient through his teeth and gums.

The lamp hurt my eyes. I closed them, and thought of the real pain
Of Mengele's real Jews. But Dr. Bernstein
Was incredibly gentle, in their honor, I guess, in their memory.
She honored my nerves as though they were the nerves of the world,
Not wanting to feel the pain of the world or be the one who gave it.

So the stanza the pain should be in is missing in this poem,
Like a book about your disease in the library of what you need.
What good could it be to hear the tale of Novocaine
When 'anaesthetic' means artless or missing a sense of the beautiful?
But believe me, Dr. Bernstein was artful, and she was also beautiful.

The music came in on the P.A., seven centuries old,
And the troubador's words say love has changed everything
For him and brought him to life, though of course he's dead.
The sun is higher and summer's an hour older and Dr. Bernstein too
Is singing for no reason as she takes off her surgical mask.

Sandra McPherson

Eschatology

I accompany this life's events like a personal journalist:
"Little did she know when she got in the car that afternoon";
or "Despite inauspicious beginnings,
this was to be their happiest year."

Little did I expect that our horoscopes would prove true.
And how could we foresee an answer to
that frankly secular prayer, we with so little faith
as to be false prophets to our most fortunate gifts.

I am glad when doom fails. Inept apocalypse
is a specialty of the times: the suffering of the rich
at the hand of riches; the second and third comings of wars.

Shouldn't we refuse prediction
that the untried today is guilty, that immeasurable
as this child's hope is, it will break tomorrow?

Lorna Crozier

What Comes After

I am my own big dog.
Walk, and I'm at the door,
eat, and I take what I offer,
lie down, and I curl on the floor,
my heavy head between my paws.

I don't need anything but this,
I don't think of what comes after.

I sing the way a dog sings,
I weep the way a dog weeps.
Every night at my feet
I am a big sack of sleep
stinking of me.

Margaret Walker

Childhood

When I was a child I knew red miners
dressed raggedly and wearing carbide lamps.
I saw them come down red hills to their camps
dyed with red dust from old Ishkooda mines.
Night after night I met them on the roads,
or on the streets in town I caught their glance;
the swing of dinner buckets in their hands,
and grumbling undermining all their words.

I also lived in low cotton country
where moonlight hovered over ripe haystacks,
or stumps of trees, and croppers' rotting shacks
with famine, terror, flood, and plague near by,
where sentiment and hatred still held sway
and only bitter land was washed away.

Thylias Moss

The Warmth Of Hot Chocolate

Somebody told me I didn't exist even though he was
looking dead at me. He said since I defied logic,
I wasn't real for reality is one of logic's definitions.
He said I was a contradiction of terms, that one side
of me cancelled out the other side leaving nothing.
His shaking knees were like polite maracas in the small
clicking they made. His moustache seemed a misplaced
smile. My compliments did not deter him from insisting
he conversed with an empty space since there was no
such thing as an angel who doesn't believe in God.
I showed him where my wings had been recently trimmed.
Everybody thinks they grow out of the back, some people
even assume shoulder blades are all that man has left
of past glory, but my wings actually grow from my scalp,
a heavy hair that stiffens for flight by the release
of chemical secretions activated whenever I jump off a
bridge. Many angels are discovered when people trying
to commit suicide ride and tame the air. I was just
such an accident. We're simply a different species,
not intrinsically holy, just intrinsically airborne.
Demons have practical reasons for not flying; it's too
hot in their homebase to endure all the hair; besides,
when they jump they keep falling. Their homebase isn't
solid. Demons fall perpetually, deeper and deeper into
evil until they reach a level where even to ascend is
to fall.

I think God covets my wings. He forgot to create some
for himself when he was forging himself out of pure thoughts
rambling through the universe on the backs of neutrons.
Pure thoughts were the original cowboys. I suggested
to God that he jump off a bridge to activate the wings
he was sure to have, you never forget yourself when you
divvy up the booty, but he didn't have enough faith that
his fall wouldn't be endless. I suggested that he did
in fact create wings for himself but had forgotten; his
first godly act had been performed a long time ago, afterall.
I don't believe in him; he's just a comfortable
acquaintance, a close associate with whom I can

be myself. To believe in him would place him in
the center of the universe when I know he's more secure
in the fringes, the farthest corner so that he
doesn't have to look over his shoulder to nab the
backstabbers who want promotions but are tired of
waiting for him to die and set in motion the natural
evolution. God doesn't want to evolve. Has been
against evolution from its creation. He doesn't
figure many possibilities are open to him. I think
he's wise to bide his time although he pales in the
moonlight to just a glow, just the warmth of hot
chocolate spreading through the body like a subcutaneous
halo. But to trust him implicitly would
be a mistake for he then would not have to maintain
his worthiness to be God. Even the thinnest
flyweight modicum of doubt gives God the necessity
to prove he's worthy of the implicit trust I can
never give because I protect him from corruption,
from the complacence that rises within him sometimes,
a shadowy ever-descending brother.

Roz Cowman

Logic

Shameless she is,
her bare shoulders
rising like brown loaves,
fresh from the ovens,
and she is walking loose
with her sin upon her
and never a blush.

Now the other one's more
natural; small sign of joy
on that face, and look
at her wearing her disgrace
like a thieving bitch
with a stolen goose
hung round her neck.

Sylvia Plath
Sheep in Fog

The hills step off into whiteness.
People or stars
Regard me sadly, I disappoint them.

The train leaves a line of breath.
O slow
Horse the colour of rust,

Hooves, dolorous bells –
All morning the
Morning has been blackening,

A flower left out.
My bones hold a stillness, the far
Fields melt my heart.

They threaten
To let me through to a heaven
Starless and fatherless, a dark water.

Diane Wakoski
Meeting An Astronomer On The Buddha's Birthday

Vanity
guards us
from introspection.

What guards us
from vanity?

To think of ourselves
like the moon,
dead and beautiful,
and of an origin no one
can be sure of?

Diane Wakoski

The Conjurer

This woman in the russet dress holds a ball in her hand.
She will place it under a cup
and you,
bending over in your professional dress
will watch and say, "that one."

But, of course, the ball will appear in another cup
entirely.

I, in the background,
have performed this same trick,
know the secret of the balls. But you
would not gasp if I performed
would not think less of the lady dressed in red if I should
unmask
the trick.

The willing believer takes his lady's hand,
not because of her tricks,
but because of her.
He likes to say, "I take this lady for her tricks,"
but only because
the record looks better that way.

Josephine Dickinson

V. Mass
(from: This Night)

We have come into a hidden world

where silence hums
an invisible mass,
a shadow

of suns,
a music
philosophers don't know,
a rippling halo,

holy hope,
provisional dark
of burning star
and satellite.

What is it to see
in bent light?
to touch
the hand that locks

mass and gravity,
extent
that in our visible matter hide –
the moistness

in the golden ring
the bridegroom did for none provide
but for his bride,
the paradox

upon this hill
I need no glass
but that desire should fill
me more, not less?

Denise Riley

Shantung

It's true that anyone can fall
in love with anyone at all.
Later, they can't. Ouf, ouf.

How much mascara washes away each day
and internationally, making the blue one black.
Come on everybody. Especially you girls.

Each day I think of something about dying.
Does everybody? do they think too, I mean.
My friends! some answers. Gently
unstrap my wristwatch. Lay it face down.

Jane Hirshfield

Burlap Sack

A person is full of sorrow
the way a burlap sack is full of stones or sand.
We say, "Hand me the sack,"
but we get the weight.
Heavier if left out in the rain.
To think that the sand or stones are the self is an error.
To think that grief is the self is an error.
Self carries grief as a pack mule carries the side bags,
being careful between the trees to leave extra room.
The mule is not the load of ropes and nails and axes.
The self is not the miner nor builder nor driver.
What would it be to take the bride
and leave behind the heavy dowry?
To let the thin-ribbed mule browse in tall grasses,
its long ears waggling like the tails of two happy dogs?

Phillis Levin

Acorn

Under its hat
many secrets
asleep
keeping time

Soon it will tell
almost everything
if you wait
long enough
in the grass in the snow

if you look if you listen

and if you do nothing
it will be what it will be
nevertheless

With a hat like that

144

you could walk the windiest hall
of an endless wood

as the worst and the best rain down
out of nowhere

With a hat like that
you could hide the highest hope
the biggest fear

and appear once a year to disappear

O where is the loom
on which it is woven

How can a tomb
too small for a pebble
carry the body of autumn in its hull

Cradle of greenest memory

kernel dreaming
the weight of a starling

cupola cupping the fire of dawn

den of creation
shedding itself
again
for a song

O give me a room to keep a secret
until the leaf is ready
to be lit

and when it is time to go out
into the cold
give me a hat

like that

Phillis Levin

Box in Eden

Pink Pearl eraser
rubbing white paper,
diminishing into
a little hill, more

and more so the box
can fill: little container
a perfect promise,
ready to hold the feel

of skin, ready to nestle
a fingernail clipping,
a button, a marble,
a tooth or a pin.

Pink Pearl collecting,
sifted, sifting:
embers of kindness,
a bower of crumbs.

Here resides
whatever in itself
by itself
is enough

to touch, eyes closed,
not to covet or possess,
only to caress –
and where is it now,

my secret compartment,
humble casket,
barrow of being,
storehouse of

unsayable softness
unclaimed, asleep
at the bottom
of what drawer?

Colette Bryce

The Full Indian Rope Trick

There was no secret
murmured down through a long line
of elect; no dark fakir, no flutter
of notes from a pipe,
no proof, no footage of it –
but I did it,

Guildhall Square, noon,
in front of everyone.
There were walls, bells, passers-by;
then a rope, thrown, caught by the sky
and me, young, up and away,
goodbye.

Goodbye, goodbye.
Thin air. First try.
A crowd hushed, squinting eyes
at a full sun. There
on the stones
the slack weight of a rope

coiled in a crate, a braid
eighteen summers long,
and me –
I'm long gone,
my one-off trick
unique, unequalled since.

And what would I tell them
given the chance?
It was painful; it took years.
I'm my own witness,
guardian of the fact
that I'm still here.

Brenda Hillman

november moon

Length passed;
dimension fled;--

(ivy moon
a pale slug eating
a downed poppy)

i had knocked
on the door
   & wept –

& the moon didn't answer
but the door
   with three
corners did –

november moon

All souls, raise your hands –

(easier done than said)

i have a little headache,
you said to the word –

& the word described
as water came
in the style of a stem
by a stream
by a stone;

it is wild that you lived,
said the word –

Emily Dickinson

712

Because I could not stop for Death –
He kindly stopped for me –
The Carriage held but just Ourselves –
And Immortality.

We slowly drove – He knew no haste
And I had put away
My labor and my leisure too,
For His Civility –

We passed the School, where Children strove
At Recess – in the Ring –
We passed the Fields of Gazing Grain –
We passed the Setting Sun –

We paused before a House that seemed
A Swelling of the Ground –
The Roof was scarcely visible –
The Cornice – in the Ground –

Since then – 'tis Centuries – and yet
Feels shorter than the Day
I first surmised the Horses' Heads
Were toward Eternity –

6. A Word's Work

Language & Writing

Denise Levertov

To the Reader

As you read, a white bear leisurely
pees, dyeing the snow
saffron,

and as you read, many gods
lie among lianas: eyes of obsidian
are watching the generations of leaves,

and as you read
the sea is turning its dark pages,
turning
its dark pages.

Diane Glancy

Kemo Sabe

In my dream I take the white man
slap him til he loves me.
I tie him to the house,
take his land & buffalo.
I put other words into his mouth,
words he doesn't understand
like spoonfuls of smashed lima beans
until his cheeks bulge.
Chew now, dear, I say.
I flick his throat until he swallows.
He works all day,
never leaves the house.
The floors shine,
the sheets are starched.
He wipes grime from the windows
until clouds dance across the glass.
He feeds me when I'm hungry.
I can leave whenever I want.
Let him struggle for his dignity,
this time let him remember
my name.

Janet Frame

The Happy Prince

In the children's record of the Happy Prince,
before each gold flake is peeled from the Prince's body,
the voice orders, Turn the Page, Turn the Page,
supposing that children do not know when to turn,
and may live at one line for many years,
sliding and bouncing boisterously along the words,
breaking the closed letters for a warm place to sleep.
Turn the Page, Turn the Page.

By the time the Happy Prince has lost his eyes,
and his melted heart is given to the poor,
and his body taken from the market-place and burned,
there is no need to order, Turn the Page,
for the children have grown up, and know when to turn,
and knowing when, will never again know where.

Heather McHugh

Ghazal of the Better-Unbegun

A book is a suicide postponed. – Cioran

Too volatile, am I? too voluble? too much a word-person?
I blame the soup: I'm a primordially
stirred person.

Two pronouns and a vehicle was Icarus with wings.
The apparatus of his selves made an ab-
surd person.

The sound I make is sympathy's: sad dogs are tied afar.
But howling I become an ever more un-
heard person.

I need a hundred more of you to make a likelihood.
The mirror's not convincing – that at-best in-
ferred person.

As time's revealing gets revolting, I start looking out.
Look in and what you see is one unholy
blurred person.

The only cure for birth one doesn't love to contemplate.
Better to be an unsung song, an unoc-
curred person.

McHugh, you'll be the death of me – each self and second studied!
Addressing you like this, I'm halfway to the
third person.

Elizabeth Macklin

How To Wait

If there were a word that meant
thought, mind, spirit
and wish, desire,
appetite.

And memory,
and recall. And finally also
will, purpose, intention,

we might have it down:
The impatient child
filled without being filled,
filled despite

the longing, being just
sated enough. Pears poached long enough,
making their long, light syrup.

And if we did have the word?
Not just one thing alone,
and not just longing.

Christine Evans

Case History

There was a boy of twelve who'd never learned
To speak. Farm-bred, he had not understood
That he was more than livestock – turned
To dogs for company, came running for his food
With cats or chickens and woke with no surprise
At owl's homecoming or stars' breath on his face.
I saw him when they brought him in. His eyes
Were clear as sunlit water, held a space
We promptly crammed with language. Beyond reach
Soft wordless songs, the colours in wet stone
He loved: grass-smell, the old humanity of touch.
His brightness died, and we began to realise
Speech wakes in us so confident, so soon
What deeper dumbnesses might it disguise?

Merle Collins

"No Dialects Please..."

In this competition
dey was lookin for poetry of worth
for a writin that could wrap up a feelin
an fling it back hard
with a captive power to choke de stars
so dey say,
'Send them to us but NO DIALECTS PLEASE
We're British.'

Ay!
Well ah laugh till me boushet near drop
Is not only dat ah tink
of de dialect of de Normans and de Saxons
dat combine an reformulate
to create a language-elect
is not only dat ah tink
how dis British education mus really be narrow
if it leave dem wid no knowledge
of what dey own history is about
is not only dat ah tink
bout de part of my story

dat come from Liverpool in a big dirty white ship
mark
AFRICAN SLAVES PLEASE!
We're the British!

But as if dat not enough pain
for a body to bear
ah tink bout de part on de plantations down dere
Wey dey so frighten o de power
in the deep spaces
behind our watching faces
dat dey shout
NO AFRICAN LANGUAGES PLEASE!
It's against the law!
Make me ha to go
an start up a language o me own
dat ah could share wid me people
Den when we start to shout
bout a culture o we own
a language o we own
a identity o we own
dem an de others dey leave to control us say
STOP THAT NONSENSE NOW

We're all British!

Every time we lif we foot to do we own ting
to fight we own fight
dey tell us how British we British
an ah wonder if dey remember
dat in Trinidad in the thirties
dey jail Butler★★
who dey say is their British citizen
an accuse him of
Hampering the war effort!
Then it was
FIGHT FOR YOUR COUNTRY, FOLKS!
You're British!

Ày! Ay!
Ah wonder when it change to
NO DIALECTS PLEASE!
WE'RE British!

Huh!
To tink how still dey so dunce
an so frighten o we power
dat dey have to hide behind a language
that we could wrap round we little finger
in addition to we own!
Heavens o mercy!
Dat is dunceness oui!
Ah wonder where is de bright British?

* *Written in response to an advert requesting submissions for a poetry
competition. The organisers warned, "No Dialects Please, We're British"*
** *Grenadian trade union leader active in Trinidad strikes of the 1930s.*

Sue Hubbard

A Necklace of Tongues

All morning she sits
stitching a necklace of tongues
in her high window,
picking each inert slab

from the shallow porcelain dish
holding its brass-cold weight
muted as a muffled bell
heavy in the dip of her open palm.

Last night snow flakes
melted like kisses,
like salt
on their warm skin,

now her silver needle
pushes through the thick-muscled
root trussing each
glossal silence

with meticulous petit point.
If a worm has five hearts,
and an angel none,
how many tongues

does it take to tell lies
about love?

But for now she can only wait,
passing the leaden hours

with herringbone and cross stitch.
Later in front of her mirror of ice
she will lift the cold carrion
like a queen's fringed torque,

place it in the soft dip
at the base of her throat,
making visible the muted words,
that wounded song of herself.

Lyn Hejinian

Come October, It's the Lake, Not the border

Come October, it's the lake not the border
that has been redrawn. Thinking
about the event afterwards, I realize how remarkably well-prepared
the girls are. There don't seem to be any slouches
among them. Please tell them I say hello and that we'll need 14
for the green salad and 14 for the apple tarts between
with some rapid washing in clear water I remember as play
and planning in childhood, preparing until the very last moment
for a gripping narrative that was itself perpetually given over
to improvisations and asymmetrical collaborations that could run
for days. That makes another 14. It was 'the word' or 'the world' in 1981
when we undertook to talk about the phrase
'once in a while' once in a while
noting the vagueness then named 'a while' and how 'once' the phrase
recurs and therefore means more than once
the 'while' is defined. We too are in 'a while'
and when 'once' next occurs, if the basic design suits
you, we will need a bit of modestly biographical contextualization
for November. I'm going to put some thought to something
implausibly contemporary which perhaps isn't wise
since between then and now no new coincidences have been noted
just one large color photograph of bespangled cowgirls
herding heavy bulls up the avenue that opens this week carefully
wearing baby blue boots to take out the garbage
but it never rained. At the end of the month, Halloween
                                        should be clear.

Patience Agbabi

Transformatrix

I'm slim as a silver stiletto, lit
by a fat, waxing moon and a seance
of candles dipped in oil of frankincense.
Salt peppers my lips as the door clicks shut.
A pen poised over a blank page, I wait
for madam's orders, her strict consonants
and the spaces between words, the silence.
She's given me a safe word, a red light
but I'm breaking the law, on a death wish,
ink throbbing my temples, each vertebra
straining for her fingers. She trusses up
words, lines, as a corset disciplines flesh.
Without her, I'm nothing but without me
she's tense, uptight, rigid as a full stop.

Sarah Wardle

Author! Author!

Readers, know that writing is a private pleasure.
Each of you may interpret these words together,
yet the key to these usages, here, remains with me,
for it is your very absence that lets this poem be,
and though individually these words are public,
only the weaver understands their interrelationship,
so that these lines serve as blinds, or prison bars,
to keep an audience distant, guessing from afar,
while I remain inside my poem, mind and state,
for understand this print is not blood spilt on a page,
but, what is more uncanny, space beneath the stone,
a translation, chiselled in sand, hollowed on a tomb,
wherein lie the silent bones of this white sheet,
taking with them their true, unverified secret.

Gwendolyn MacEwen

Let Me Make This Perfectly Clear

Let me make this perfectly clear.
I have never written anything because it is a Poem.
This is a mistake you always make about me,
A dangerous mistake. I promise you
I am not writing this because it is a Poem.
You suspect this is a posture or an act.
I am sorry to tell you it is not an act.
You actually think I care if this
Poem gets off the ground or not. Well
I don't care if this poem gets off the ground or not
And neither should you.
All I have ever cared about
And all you should ever care about
Is what happens when you lift your eyes from this page.
Do not think for one minute it is the Poem that matters.
You can shove the Poem.
What matters is what is out there in the large dark
and in the long light,
Breathing.

Elaine Feinstein

Infidelities

Last night she ran out barefoot over
the wet gravel to call him back
from the street. This morning,
in the tranquillity of bath water,

she wonders when it was she first shivered
with the wish for more than ordinary happiness.
How did she fall in love with poetry
that clear eyed girl she was?

Late at night, by a one-bar heater,
her unpainted lips parted
on the words of dead poets.
She was safer in the dance hall.

'And if you can't love poetry,'
he muses. 'What was there of me
all those years ago, apart from
that life of which it is made?

Only an inhospitable hostess,
a young woman in an old dress.'

Martha Kapos

Accomplice

Begin by letting him be the word
you keep hidden under your tongue,
while you wait there innocent

as an envelope with a letter growing quietly
inside it. He'll tear open and unfold
the whole of it, come straight out

to meet you, leaping three steps at a time,
the screen-door banging behind him,
with a hundred demon arms and a smile.

Let him come out entirely himself, complete as a sperm,
bright as a moment in the mind.
He's the secret accomplice who sleeps with you.

All night, sharp as light, he'll be alive
inside the dark jack-in-the-box of your sleep,
prying an eyelid to spring the sky

open in the morning when you blink.
Blue will appear alert at the window, jump
to attention when he holds it up to the light.

The room, in a hurry to assemble
in perfect perspective, will throw its wall, floors,
corners together, so it stands straight up,

just like that, when you get out of bed. Now he's
beginning the words you hear in your mouth
coming in a sharp torrent of syllables.

Phillis Levin

Keep Reading

...and still, as he looked, he lived;/ and still, as he lived, he wondered.
Kenneth Grahame – The Wind in the Willows

'Keep reading,' you said, as we lay
In the boat of your bed, you
Almost asleep, I floating on words,

On a stream of lines flowing
To the river's edge, when I stopped,
For I wanted to be by your side,

There with you, your skin warm
Against mine. 'Keep reading,' you said:
Though I thought you were far away,

On the other side, on the brink of sleep,
You were listening, still, you were near,
Knowing how far from the end I was

As the sound of your voice (as a sound
Alive inside your voice) carried me on
To the weir, to a piper piping an alien

Song at the gates of dawn, on a shore
Changed by more than the touch
Of the sun. Then the words wavered,

The letters blurred, swelling
To dapples of darkness and light –
I looked away to see you there,

Your glistening lashes, a tear
That fell, running down your cheek
As you heard me start to weep

At a passage you knew so well,
The one you were longing to hear
As you floated far into night,

Waiting in the boat of your bed
To hear me reach what was so close by,
Where you led me to, having read my heart.

'Keep reading,' you said, without saying why.

Jo Shapcott

Muse

When I kiss you in all the folding places
of your body, you make that noise like a dog
dreaming, dreaming of the long runs he makes
in answer to some jolt to his hormones,
running across landfills, running, running
by tips and shorelines from the scent of too much,
but still going with head up and snout
in the air because he loves it all
and has to get away. I have to kiss deeper
and more slowly – your neck, your inner arm,
the neat creases under your toes, the shadow
behind your knee, the white angles of your groin –
until you fall quiet because only then
can I get the damned words to come into my mouth.

Penelope Shuttle

Poem

A poem stays awake long after midnight
talking you from room to room,

does not care that walls have ears,
las paredes oyen

A poem prefers tin to silver,
silver to gold,
gold to platinum

Every year
a poem tosses a young woman from the cliffs
to the rocky sea below

A poem accidentally sends the entire letter f
off to Florence

but keeps the letter t
in a matchbox, like a tiny contraband tortoise

Sometimes
a poem is your only daughter

busy and happy in the world,
China or Spain,
abundancia de riqueza

Like the partial Angel Gabriel
in Santa Sophia
a poem is half-gold, half-invisible

A poem will do things in England
she'll never do in France

It will take more than the ten thousand lakes
for which Minnesota is famous
to drown a poem

The poem pauses now and then
to look at nothing-much-in-particular

A poem likes scraping and burnishing
the prepared surface of the copper,

is frequently found note-taking copiously
from *The Fantastic Historia Animalium of the Rain*

A poem makes herself tiny as a waterbear
or a tardygrade,
a mite able to survive freezing, boiling

able to go into suspended animation
for one hundred years, if need be.

Anne Rouse

Virginia Arcady

My muse came up from the creek,
Taller than a man in the speckled shade,
Where crayfish imitate tiny stones,
And the brisk water plays.

Reckon it was my muse, being so
Ringletty and fair, with a child's eye.
In her head-dress bitter, living grapes
Nest on the wild vine.

Strolling the bogged paths
Of the bottom field, apart by arms length,
She talked low, reproachful, pretty:
Said I don't love her enough.

Marianne Moore

Poetry

I, too, dislike it: there are things that are important beyond all this fiddle.
  Reading it, however, with a perfect contempt for it, one discovers in
  it after all, a place for the genuine.
    Hands that can grasp, eyes
    that can dilate, hair that can rise
      if it must, these things are important not because a

high-sounding interpretation can be put upon them but because
                                                        they are
useful. When they become so derivative as to become unintelligible,
the same thing may be said for all of us, that we
    do not admire what
    we cannot understand: the bat
holding on upside down or in quest of something to

eat, elephants pushing, a wild horse taking a roll, a tireless wolf under
  a tree, the immovable critic twitching his skin like a horse that
                                      feels a flea, the base-
ball fan, the statistician –
    nor is it valid
to discriminate against 'business documents and

school-books'; all these phenomena are important. One must
                                     make a distinction
however: when dragged into prominence by half poets, the
                                     result is not poetry,

nor till the poets among us can be
  'literalists of
the imagination' – above
insolence and triviality and can present
for inspection, 'imaginary gardens with real toads in them,'
                                     shall we have
it. In the meantime, if you demand on the one hand,
the raw material of poetry in
    all its rawness and
    that which is on the other hand
      genuine, you are interested in poetry.

7. *Mother Nature*

Seasons, Animals, The Natural World

Mary Ruefle

Perfume River

She thinks fishing is an odd way
to make love: watching her husband rooted
in water, slick to the hips under the arch
of a bridge, his whole rod nodding
like hart's-tongue fern in its youth.
She has other thoughts hidden
inside of these, barely visible
like the stamens of crocus.

Ah spring! The cedar waxwing with a plume
in his ass, pumping seeds from his mouth
like a pinball machine.

Palaver of scents
and the boys standing naked under the waterfall.
Pachinko! The word enters her bloodstream:

Holy Mary mother of God-who's-gone-fishing-today,
she'll stay out bog-trotting until she's
blue in the face, like an orchid.

Josephine Jacobsen

from: Of Pairs

The mockingbirds, that pair, arrive,
one, and the other; glossily perch,
respond, respond, branch to branch.
One stops, and flies. The other flies.
Arrives, dips, in a blur of wings,
lights, is joined. Sings. Sings.

Actually, there are birds galore:
bowlegged blackbirds brassy as crows;
elegant ibises with inelegant cows;
hummingbirds' stutter on air;
tilted over the sea, a man-of-war
in a long arc without a feather's stir.

Brenda Hillman

Trois Morceaux En Forme De Poire

Titled after Satie

I.
Three pears ripen
On the ledge. Weeks pass.
They are a marriage.

The middle one's the conversation
The other two are having.
He is their condition.

Three wings without birds,
Three feelings.
How can they help themselves?

They can't.
How can they stay like that?
They can.

II.
The pears are consulting.
Business is bad this year,

D'Anjou, Bartlett.
They are psychiatrists,

Patient and slick.
Hunger reaches the hard stem.

It will get rid of them.

III.
The pears are old women;
They are the same.
Slight rouge,
Green braille dresses,
They blush in unison.
They will stay young.
They will not ripen.
In the new world,
Ripeness is nothing.

Maxine Kumin

In The Root Cellar

The parsnips, those rabbis
have braided their beards together
to examine the text. The word
that engrosses them is: February.

To be a green tomato
wrapped in the Sunday book section
is to know nothing. Meanwhile
the wet worm eats his way outward.

These cabbages, these clean keepers
in truth are
a row of impacted stillbirths.
One by one we deliver them.

The apples are easy abutters
a basket of pulltoys and smiles.
Still, they infect one another
like children exchanging the measles.

O potato, a wink of
daylight and you're up with
ten tentative erections.
How they deplete you!

Dusty blue warthogs, the squash
squat for a thump and a tuning.
If we could iron them out
they'd be patient blue mandolins.

The beets wait wearing their birthmarks.
They will be wheeled into the amphitheater.
Even before the scrub-up, the scalpel,
they bleed a little.

I am perfect, breathes the onion.
I am God's first circle
the tulip that slept in His navel.
Bite me and be born.

Margaret Atwood

February

Winter. Time to eat fat
and watch hockey. In the pewter mornings, the cat,
a black fur sausage with yellow
Houdini eyes, jumps up on the bed and tries
to get onto my head. It's his
way of telling whether or not I'm dead.
If I'm not, he wants to be scratched; if I am
he'll think of something. He settles
on my chest, breathing his breath
of burped-up meat and musty sofas,
purring like a washboard. Some other tomcat,
not yet a capon, has been spraying our front door,
declaring war. It's all about sex and territory,
which are what will finish us off
in the long run. Some cat owners around here
should snip a few testicles. If we wise
hominids were sensible, we'd do that too,
or eat our young, like sharks.
But it's love that does us in. Over and over
again, *He shoots, he scores!* and famine
crouches in the bedsheets, ambushing the pulsing
eiderdown, and the windchill factor hits
thirty below, and pollution pours
out of our chimneys to keep us warm.
February, month of despair,
with a skewered heart in the centre.
I think dire thoughts, and lust for French fries
with a splash of vinegar.
Cat, enough of your greedy whining
and your small pink bumhole.
Off my face! You're the life principle,
more or less, so get going
on a little optimism around here.
Get rid of death. Celebrate increase. Make it be spring.

Sarah Arvio

Starlings

All winter I watched the swarms of starlings
swooping in the northern sky like cast nets
or some foreign alphabets flying loose

and returning and rushing out again.
I wanted to live the life I desired,
as we all did, I think, our one desire,

wanting to do what we wanted to do,
sweeping and then spreading and turning back.
A flood of arrows, dare-arrows, daring to hope,

never horizontals or verticals,
not a straight arrow or as the crow flew,
though life, I think, looked daggers at me,

daring me write this letter now to you,
scratching the sky with a row of my words
(*those letters sent to him that lives away*).

Look me daggers, love, stare me in the eye,
dare me to love you and I'll dare you back.
Darling, I will say, my starling, my crow –

no, not a thrush as the century turned,
though I felt a rush looking at the sky
and all the devastations of desire,

as staggering as ever – startling, true,
or dulled, I think, by the drift of the years
or the drag of the years dragging me back

through the smudges of my alphabets,
cirrus clouds like rags cleaning up the sky
and the vast waste of my wasted desire.

Margaret Danner

The Painted Lady

The Painted Lady is a small African
butterfly, gayly toned orchid or peach
that seems as tremulous and delicately sheer
as the objects I treasure, yet, this cosmopolitan
can cross the sea at the icy time of the year
in the trail of the big boats, to France.
Mischance is as wide and somber grey as the lake here
in Chicago. Is there strength enough in my huge
peach paper rose, or lavender sea-laced fan?

Anne Cluysenaar

Yellow Meadow-Ants in Hallowed Ground

for Colin Titcombe, naturalist and teacher

I need to displace myself. I need to see,
when the tip of my finger disturbs the alignment of dust
over their open holes, how a human hand
might seem (as to them) nothing more than the foot of a vole.

I need to feel, more than I need to see,
as if I had helped to make it, that airy mass
hung in the solid dark of a marked-out grave.
An ancient pasture healing the shock of death.

I need to be glad, I must be, such intricate bronze,
such tiny aggressive life, can thrive as if cut
of spade, as if cry, were no more than the passing tricks
of storm or flood, or of geological heave.

Spare, like sea-shore stuff, dry grasses stand
deep in these ants' displacement of inner ground.
When the tips catch wind, my veins seem wrapped round the quiver
of those hidden columns, as if I had left myself.

A.E. Stallings

Listening to the Monkeys of the Nearby Yerkes Regional Primate Research Center

Humidity has made them homesick,
This thick, cicada'd Georgia June.
The heat is ancient and nostalgic,
Familiar is the doubling moon.

Upon my stoop I hear their calling,
Their long, lugubrious ululations,
In languages, rising, falling,
Of a thousand monkey nations.

The night is shallowed-out with lamp-gloss,
That streets may rise like tricky rivers
Raccoons think they can ford across
To join their families or lovers;

Or 'possums, with their human feet,
Who also cross, and see as stars
The kind lights swooping down to greet
Them from the swift, oncoming cars.

The night is hollowed-out with fear –
These voices, the bathometer,
This somewhere-past-the-second beer
Helps me but to hardly bear –

I want to call before they stop,
To bridge our two captivities,
But I would wake my neighbors up
Who frown on such proclivities

Of poets or of indigents
Abusing words or alcohol,
Confusing the experiments,
To ask the meaning of it all...

No answer comes, no answer comes –
But owls, air-conditioning, trains,
The silence of opposing thumbs,
Superior and sober brains.

Hilary Menos

Berg

After the Larson breakout of ninety-five,
when a mound the size of Rutland calved with a howl
into the Admunsen sea, and bergy bits and growlers
surrounded Cape Longing, we were on standby.

Glaciologists from Colorado to London
argued over fracture mechanics and bed forms.
Every satellite map looked like a storm
breaking. We put a watch on the ice tongue.

Now everything mattered; melt water ponding,
the crystallography of frazil ice, the hole in the ozone layer,
the thermodynamics of polar-bear hair.
We sandbagged East Anglia, Holland.

They came like brides, majestic over Barking Reach,
queued to check-in at the Barrier, their tabular tops
reflecting weak sun, waltzed towards Wapping
and Wandsworth, cold and hooded, each one

like an inmate from some asylum holding the flowered
hem of her ancient slip too high up her pale thighs,
a thousand mile stare in her eyes,
saving the last dance for the Post Office Tower.

Polly Clark

Elvis the Performing Octopus

hangs in the tank like a ruined balloon,
an eight-armed suit sucked empty,

ushering the briefest whisper
across the surface, keeping

his slurred drift steady with an effort
massive as the ocean resisting the moon.

When the last technician,
whistling his own colourless tune,

splashes through the disinfectant tray,
one might see, had anyone been left to look,

Elvis changing from spilt milk to tumbling blue,
pulsing with colour like a forest in sunlight.

Elvis does the full range, even the spinning top
that never quite worked out, as the striplight fizzes

and the flylamp cracks like a firework.
Elvis has the water applauding,

and the brooms, the draped cloths, the dripping tap,
might say that a story that ends in the wrong place

always ends like this –
fabulous in an empty room,

unravelled by the tender men in white,
laid out softly in the morning.

Joy Harjo

She Had Some Horses

She had some horses.

She had horses who were bodies of sand.

She had horses who were maps drawn of blood.

She had horses who were skins of ocean water.

She had horses who were the blue air of sky.

She had horses who were fur and teeth.

She had horses who were clay and would break.

She had horses who were splintered red cliff.

She had some horses.

She had horses with eyes of trains.

She had horses with full, brown thighs.

She had horses who laughed too much.

She had horses who threw rocks at glass houses.

She had horses who licked razor blades.

She had some horses.

She had horses who danced in their mothers' arms.

She had horses who thought they were the sun and their bodies

shone and burned like stars.

She had horses who waltzed nightly on the moon.

She had horses who were much too shy, and kept quiet in stalls

of their own making.

She had some horses.

She had horses who liked Creek Stomp Dance songs.

She had horses who cried in their beer.

She had horses who spit at male queens who made them afraid of
themselves.

She had horses who said they weren't afraid.

She had horses who lied.

She had horses who told the truth, who were stripped bare of their
tongues.

She had some horses.

She had horses who called themselves, "horse."

She had horses who called themselves, "spirit" and kept their

voices secret and to themselves.

She had horses who had no names.

She had horses who had books of names.

She had some horses.

She had horses who whispered in the dark, who were afraid to speak.

She had horses who screamed out of fear of the silence, who

carried knives to protect themselves from ghosts.

She had horses who waited for destruction.

She had horses who waited for resurrection.

She had some horses.

She had horses who got down on their knees for any savior.

She had horses who thought their high price had saved them.

She had horses who tried to save her, who climbed in her bed

at night and prayed as they raped her.

She had some horses.

She had some horses she loved.

She had some horses she hated.

These were the same horses.

Judith Kazantzis
The Dose

After a night dose of rain,
a steam noses up to the window,

the mangroves, ferns, sea grapes,
like a faint skunk whiff

— distinct from the damp earth after rain,
the rain I was born to, how it

sprang down to my greeting or I would run
with it on my eyelids, drop by drop

during each cloud's downpour;
then we would say, O rain, get to Spain

or those southern parts that really need it —
But here... is this smell

stealing along my path
like a sickbed stranger out of the stinking woods.

Amaryllis

It came above the water line, bottle-green
into the light, among the curtains and the lamps.
She told me how it started,
how she'd turned it to the clock of the sun

whose rays across the window
shifted through her day like a tide.
Heady as moon-rise unloading in a room of sickness.
A room whose surfaces keeled under bric-a-brac
– things she'd kept not knowing why –
the ghost of someone else's heirlooms.
Low tones of mothballs from the drawers,

silks she wouldn't touch again.
A coming magnified against the heavy furniture,
the flesh thick stem softly blowing out its flower.
She'd had the quick step of a dancer;
I thought of her lovers, her poise,

as the illness set her back again.
Bedroom days under dressings of lanolin,
a season breathed around the room.
Her wrists, her ankles – those fine bones –

and the way her breasts still cupped into a V,
defiant among bedsores.
Years later in a bar below the street, lonely
and single, there was that flower
lighting a corner above the seated crowd,

straightening its back to me.
And something I had to hear in her voice
to believe, when it came a second time,
she'd said the whiteness was like a liturgy,
like a wedding without regret.

Ruth Pitter

Morning Glory

With a pure colour there is little one can do:
Of a pure thing there is little one can say.
We are dumb in the face of that cold blush of blue,
Called glory, and enigmatic as the face of day.

A couple of optical tricks are there for the mind;
See how the azure darkens as we recede:
Like the delectable mountains left behind,
Region and colour too absolute for our need.

Or putting an eye too close, until it blurs,
You see a firmament, a ring of sky,
With a white radiance in it, a universe,
And something there that might seem to sing and fly.

Only the double sex, the usual thing;
But it calls to mind spirit, it seems like one
Who hovers in brightness suspended and shimmering,
Crying Holy and hanging in the eye of the sun.

And there is one thing more; as in despair
The eye dwells on that ribbed pentagonal round,
A cold sidereal whisper brushes the ear,
A prescient tingling, a prophecy of sound.

Heather Buck

The Poppy

The poppy cannot explain
The sun's turning away, cannot reproach
The sudden cold-shouldering,
After the warm fingering into the depths
Of its dark red centred self.

Amy Clampitt

Meadowlark Country

Speaking of the skylark in a New England classroom –
nonbird, upward-twirler, Old-World hyperbole –
I thought how the likewise ground-nesting
Western meadowlark, rather than soar unsupported
out over the cattle range at daybreak, takes up
its post on a fencepost. I heard them out there,
once, by the hundreds, one after another:
a liquid millennium arising from the still
eastward-looking venue of the dark –

like the still-evolving venue of the young, the faces
eastward-looking, bright with a mute,
estranged, ancestral puzzlement.

Ellen Bryant Voigt

The Lotus Flowers

The surface of the pond was mostly green –
bright green algae reaching out from the banks,
then the mass of waterlilies, their broad round leaves
rim to rim, each white flower spreading
from the center of a green saucer.
We teased and argued, choosing the largest,
the sweetest bloom, but when the rowboat
lumbered through and rearranged them,
we found the plants were anchored, the separate
muscular stems descending in the dense water –
only the most determined put her hand
into that frog-slimed pond
to wrestle with a flower. Back and forth
we pumped across the water, in twos and threes,
full of brave adventure. On the marshy shore,
the others hollered for their turns,
or at the hem of where we pitched the tents
gathered firewood –
                    this was wilderness,

although the pond was less than half an acre
and we could still see the grand magnolias
in the village cemetery, their waxy
white conical blossoms gleaming in the foliage.
A dozen girls, the oldest only twelve, two sisters
with their long braids, my shy neighbor,
someone squealing without interruption:
all we didn't know about the world buoyed us,
as the frightful water sustained and moved the flowers
tethered at a depth we couldn't see.

In the late afternoon, before they'd folded
into candles on the dark water,
I went to fill the bucket at the spring.
Deep in the pines, exposed tree roots
formed a natural arch, a cave of black loam.
I raked off the skin of leaves and needles,
leaving a pool so clear and shallow
I could count the pebbles
on the studded floor. The sudden cold
splashing up from the bucket to my hands
made me want to plunge my hand in –
and I held it under, feeling the shock that wakes
and deadens, watching first my fingers,
then the ledge beyond me,
the snake submerged and motionless,
the head propped on its coils the way a girl
crosses her arms before her on the sill
and rests her chin there.   Lugging the bucket
back to the noisy clearing, I found nothing changed,
the boat still rocked across the pond,
the fire straggled and cracked as we fed it
branches and debris into the night,
leaning back on our pallets –
spokes in a wheel – learning the names of the many
constellations, learning how each fixed
cluster took its name:
not from the strongest light, but from the pattern
made by stars of lesser magnitude,
so like the smaller stars we rowed among.

Gail Mazur

Bluebonnets

I lay down by the side of the road
in a meadow of bluebonnets, I broke
the unwritten law of Texas. My brother

was visiting, he'd been tired, afraid of
his tiredness as we'd driven toward Bremen,
so we stopped for the blue relatives

of lupine, we left the car on huge feet
we'd inherited from our lost father,
our Polish grandfather. Those flowers

were too beautiful to only look at;
we walked on them, stood in the middle
of them, threw ourselves down,

crushing them in their one opportunity
to thrive and bloom. We lay like angels
forgiven our misdeeds, transported

to azure fields, the only word for
the color eluded me – delft, indigo,
sapphire, some heavenly word you might

speak to a sky. I led my terrestrial brother
there to make him smile, and this
is my only record of the event.

We took no pictures, we knew no camera
could fathom that blue. I brushed
the soft spikes, I fingered lightly

the delicate earthly petals, I thought,
This is what my hands do well
isn't it, touch things about to vanish.

8. Mother Time

Mortality, Age & Ages

Marie Howe

Death, The Last Visit

Hearing a low growl in your throat, you'll know that it's started.
It has nothing to ask you. It has only something to say, and
it will speak in your own tongue.

Locking its arm around you, it will hold you as long as you ever wanted.
Only this time it will be long enough. It will not let go.
Burying your face in its dark shoulder, you'll smell mud and hair and water.

You'll taste your mother's sour nipple, your favorite salty cock
and swallow a word you thought you'd spit out once and were done with.
Through half closed eyes you'll see that its shadow looks like yours.

A perfect fit. You could weep with gratefulness. It will take you
as you like it best, hard and fast as a slap across your face,
or so sweet and slow you'll scream give it to me give it to me until it does.

Nothing will ever reach this deep. Nothing will ever clench this hard.
At last, (the little girls are clapping, shouting) someone has pulled
the drawstring of your gym bag closed enough and tight. At last

someone has knotted the lace of your shoes so it won't ever come undone.
Even as you turn into it, even as you begin to feel yourself stop,
you'll whistle with amazement between your residual teeth oh jesus

oh sweetheart, oh holy mother, nothing nothing ever felt this good.

Jane Kenyon

Otherwise

I got out of bed
on two strong legs.
It might have been
otherwise. I ate
cereal, sweet
milk, ripe, flawless
peach. It might
have been otherwise.
I took the dog uphill
to the birch wood.
All morning I did
the work I love.
At noon I lay down
with my mate. It might
have been otherwise.
We ate dinner together
at a table with silver
candlesticks. It might
have been otherwise.
I slept in a bed
in a room with paintings
on the walls, and
planned another day
just like this day.
But one day, I know,
it will be otherwise.

Eavan Boland

An Elegy For My Mother In Which She Scarcely Appears

I knew we had to grieve for the animals
a long time ago: weep for them, pity them.
I knew it was our strange human duty
to write their elegies after we arranged their demise.
I was young then and able for the paradox.
I am older now and ready with the question:
What happened to them all? I mean to those
old dumb implements which have
no eyes to plead with us like theirs,
no claim to make on us like theirs? I mean –

there's as a singing kettle. I want to know
why no one tagged its neck or ringed the tin
base of its next design or crouched to hear
its rising shriek in winter or wrote it down with
the birds in their blue sleeves of air
torn away with the trees that sheltered them.

And there were brass fire dogs which lay out
all evening on the grate and in the heat
thrown at them by the last of the peat fire
but no one noted down their history or put them
in the old packs under slate-blue moonlight.
There was a wooden clothes-horse, absolutely steady
without sinews, with no mane and no meadows
to canter in; carrying, instead of ladies
and lords or Irish monks, rinsed tea cloths
but still, I would have thought, worth adding to
the catalogue of what we need, what we always need

as is my mother, on this Dublin evening of
fog crystals and frost as she reaches out to test
one corner of a cloth for dryness as the pre-war
Irish twilight closes in and down on the room
and the curtains are drawn and here am I,
not even born and already a conservationist,
with nothing to assist me but the last
and most fabulous of beasts – language, language –
which knows, as I do, that it's too late
to record the loss of these things but does so anyway,
and anxiously, in case it shares their fate.

Denise Levertov

Despair

While we were visiting David's grave
I saw at a little distance

a woman hurrying towards another grave
hands outstretched, stumbling

in her haste; who then
fell at the stone she made for

and lay sprawled upon it, sobbing,
sobbing and crying out to it.

She was neatly dressed in a pale coat
and seemed neither old nor young.

I couldn't see her face, and my friends
seemed not to know she was there.

Not to distress them, I said nothing.
But she was not an apparition.

And when we walked back to the car in silence

I looked stealthily back and saw she rose
and quieted herself and began slowly

to back away from the grave.
Unlike David, who lives

in our lives, it seemed
whoever she mourned dwelt

there, in the field, under stone.
It seemed the woman

believed whom she loved heard her,
heard her wailing, observed

the nakedness of her anguish
and would not speak.

Alice Notley

The Person That You Were Will Be Replaced

In grief the person that you were is replaced by grief...
not the person you originally were but the one you'd become.

Grief is opportunistic and uncontrollable

     it doesn't exactly come
from you, you "allow it in"   It's godlike
     as in possession.

This was the night I was the craziest: near my birthday,
four months after Ted's death, walking
on Second Avenue I thought "It's possible
he didn't really die." I felt a maniacal joy
and then became sickened and distressed
I knew a depth of me had, up to then, believed he was alive.
That depth was now emptied of him and filled with grief.

I dreamed all that year; I divided into dreamer and interpreter
     A gigantic horse blocks
     the entrance to
my building; I wake up and think "The horse is a hearse"
     blocking my life. Or
a dream with a dawn in it, the sky purple-black,
but a hint of dawn, and when I awake I know it's the sky
in Lawrence's "Ship of Death" – thin white
thread – trying its way.

                  If a self can
contain the deaths of others, it's very large;
it's certainly larger than my body
     If the other who dies is partly me,
and that me dies and another grows, the medium it grows in
     is grief.

The wish to locate absence, that contemporary obsession to
     find the empty present –
grief will saturate the present.

Grief isn't glandular; though becomes somatic;
gets far into your body. Eats it changes it.

One is magically struck down at certain
moments, can't move, can't arise,
and inside is poison: grief gets caught
in intensifying pockets which when opened
cause sensations of illness. On Christmas morning
I can't stand up.

If you immerse your feet in icy water
you forget grief for a moment. I did this once, my
brother-in-law made us cross a cold stream barefoot,
that winter, walking in the woods – I was emptied, then elated,
blissful; but didn't try it again. Grief
returns vengeful after you've repulsed it.

Jean Earle

The Way It Goes

After you died, my love, in devastation
I said to you, "I'll come as soon as I can..."
Truly convinced I would follow you
Almost at once – perhaps in hours.

I soon learned the body won't let go
Until its time, no matter how the grief
Wills to an end. Before long
(To the grief's horror) the flesh shouts "Food!"
And, when denied, bothers for this and that
It fancies in particular,
Till, like an itch
That must be scratched, it eats

Even for two.
And next, one day it notices the warmth
On it's own side of the marital bed –
Or how the martins have returned
To the stricken house
Or how the light
Blazes those twigs when you glance, half-blind
From your would-be dying.

After a while,
However the spirit mourns
The face stops crying.

Catherine Fisher

Undertakers

The baker's doorway steams like Acheron.
They eat hot rolls and pasties, shiny grease
soaking the paper so their fingers tear it;
the thin one smokes, flicking off ash.
Their coats are raven, crypt-black, but they laugh,
swap jokes, wave at a passing van.
Later they crowd the car,
running its engines so the windows trickle;
one gazes at the bookie's wistfully.
They've done their part; performed
the silent secrets no-one asks about.
Now through fiery glass the final hymn
brings them out to stamp, rub hands,
uncrease coats and faces.
They line the porch, pull on gloves,
leave the singing to others;
their tribute no emotion and firm hands,
sharing unsteadily on shoulders
the box of dark that always weighs too much
and comes too soon.

Stevie Smith

Not Waving But Drowning

Nobody heard him, the dead man,
But still he lay moaning:
I was much further out than you thought
And not waving but drowning.

Poor chap, he always loved larking
And now he's dead
It must have been too cold for him his heart gave way,
They said.

Oh, no no no, it was too cold always
(Still the dead one lay moaning)
I was much too far out all my life
And not waving but drowning.

190

Fanny Howe

9-11-01

The first person is an existentialist

Like trash in the groin of the sand dunes
Like a brown cardboard home beside a dam

Like seeing things the same
Between Death Valley and the desert of Paran

An earthquake a turret with arms and legs
The second person is the beloved

Like winners taking the hit
Like looking down on Utah as if

It was Saudi Arabia or Pakistan
Like war-planes out of Miramar

Like a split cult a jolt of coke New York
Like Mexico in its deep beige couplets

Like this, like that... like call us all It,
Thou It. "Sky to Spirit Call us all It!"

The third person is a materialist.

Carole Satyamurti

My First Cup of Coffee

I'm sophisticated in my Cuban heels,
my mother's blue felt hat
with the smart feather like a fishing fly

as I sit with her in the Kardomah; and
coffee please, I say, not orange squash,
crossing my legs, elegant as an advert.

Beyond the ridges of my mother's perm
the High Street is a silent film
bustling with extras: hands grasping purses,

steering prams, eyes fixed on lists,
bolster hips in safe-choice-coloured skirts
– and then, centre screen, Nicolette Hawkins

(best in the class at hockey, worst at French)
and a boy – kissing,
blouse straining, hands

where they shouldn't be:
the grown-up thing. My hat's hot, silly;
coffee tastes like rust.

My mother, following my gaze, frowns: common.
I'm thinking, if I could do all that
I could be bad at French.

Kathryn Simmonds

The Men I Wish I'd Kissed

Adrian, two rows in front as we sang
yellow bird, way up in banana tree.
I sang for him,
his yellow hair.
His perfect pale ears.

Prematurely stubbled Mark
who never spoke to me, but ruled
the pack of fourth year girls –
his silver Zippo
seeking their Silk Cuts –
while I stared out at other boys
on other buses, school ties loose
as snapped lassos.

Dan, the eldest brother of my next-best friend,
all monosyllables and eyelashes,
exiting from his dark room
where Blondie offered up
her pop star breasts.

A man from Padua who asked if he might
kiss me at a party once, though
I declined. Prim fool:
I didn't know then kisses are just foreign fruits
that you should always try.

Alan Alda in his M★A★S★H years,
gangly and sweet and able
to tell jokes while saving lives.

Tan chested Dustin Hoffman in *The Graduate*
for whom I wouldn't mind the stoop.

And English men, not movie stars
but ordinary English men –
the one I trailed this hot spring afternoon,
who peeled off his t-shirt
clean as avocado from the skin
and walked half bare
before the gently frothing cherry trees.

Kimiko Hahn

In Childhood

Things don't die or remain damaged
but return: stumps grow back hands,
a head reconnects to a neck,
a whole corpse rises blushing and newly elastic.
Later this vision is not True:
the grandmother remains dead
not hibernating in a wolf's belly.
Or the blue parakeet does not return
from the little grave in the fern garden
though one may wake in the morning
thinking mother's call is the bird.

Or maybe the bird is with grandmother
inside light. Or grandmother was the bird
and is now the dog
gnawing on the chair leg.
Where do the gone things go
when the child is old enough
to walk herself to school,
her playmates already
pumping so high the swing hiccups?

Ros Barber

What Happens to Women

It's what happens to women, no matter who you are.
Divine inside? They'll only see the face.
It's coming, despite your warmth, your grit, your heart –
the sudden shift from beauty to disgrace.
A light snapped off, and you're gone. You're in the dark.
No-one can see you now. You are unglued,
for while you slept, the world took you softly apart.
Now man after man walks through the ghost of you.

On a morning like any other, she wakes to find
her lover moved out, and all her admirers gone
from her steps, as if with one breath, one mind,
they abandoned their roses there like skeletons.
A half-penned love note stutters towards the sea,
embarrassed, undoing its 'love', and 'dear', and 'we'.

Wendy Cope

II. Strugnell's Haiku

The leaves have fallen
And the snow has fallen and
Soon my hair also.

Patricia Beer

Middle Age

Middle age at last declares itself
As the time when could-have-been
Is not wishful thinking anymore,
Is not, say: I could have been at Oxford
If my parents had been richer
Or if the careers mistress had not thought
Exeter was good enough for me.

It is not misunderstanding either
As when at night in the first year of the war
Bombs could have been thunder
And later on in peace
Thunder could have been bombs.
Sights and sounds are more themselves now.

There have been real alternatives.
They have put on weight and yet faded.

Evening walks go past
Where we could have lived:
The coach-house that the mortgage company
Said had too much charm
And not enough rooms.

Everywhere I look it is the same,
The churchyard or the other side of the bed.
The one who is not lying there
Could have been.

Pamela Gillilan

Menopause

Moods' ebb and flow ruled
by bright or clouded days,
not by the forceful womb.

Belly will not grow round again
unless, like a man's, from excess;
but not unsexed, not done with love.

Invisibly new-seasoned.
Long vassaldom served through.
Self, while the light lasts.

Jenny Joseph

Warning

When I am an old woman I shall wear purple
With a red hat which doesn't go, and doesn't suit me.
And I shall spend my pension on brandy and summer gloves
And satin sandals, and say we've no money for butter.
I shall sit down on the pavement when I'm tired
And gobble up samples in shops and press alarm bells
And run my stick along the public railings
And make up for the sobriety of my youth.
I shall go out in my slippers in the rain
And pick the flowers in other people's gardens
And learn to spit.

You can wear terrible shirts and grow more fat
And eat three pounds of sausages at a go
Or only bread and pickle for a week
And hoard pens and pencils and beermats and things in boxes.

But now we must have clothes that keep us dry
And pay our rent and not swear in the street
And set a good example for the children.
We must have friends to dinner and read the papers.

But maybe I ought to practise a little now?
So people who know me are not too shocked and surprised
When suddenly I am old, and start to wear purple.

E.J. Scovell

Deaths of Flowers

I would if I could choose
Age and die outwards as a tulip does;
Not as this iris drawing in, in-coiling
Its complex strange taut inflorescence, willing
Itself a bud again though all achieved is
No more than a clenched sadness,

The tears of gum not flowing.
I would choose the tulip's reckless way of going;
Whose petals answer light, altering by fractions
From closed to wide, from one through many perfections,
Till wrecked, flamboyant, strayed beyond recall,
Like flakes of fire they piecemeal fall.

Sara Teasdale

Let It Be Forgotten

Let it be forgotten, as a flower is forgotten,
Forgotten as a fire that once was singing gold,
Let it be forgotten for ever and ever,
Time is a kind friend, he will make us old.

If anyone asks, say it was forgotten
Long and long ago
As a flower, as a fire, as a hushed footfall
In a long forgotten snow.

Sylvia Townsend Warner

Quiet Neighbours

Sitting alone at night
Careless of time,
From the house next door
I hear the clock chime

Ten, eleven, twelve;
One, two, three –
It is all the same to the clock,
And much the same to me.

But tonight more than sense heard it:
I opened my eyes wide
To look at the wall and wonder
To ask what lay on the other side.

They are quiet people
That live next door;
I never hear them scrape
Their chairs along the floor,

They do not laugh loud, or sing,
Or scratch at the grate,
I have never seen a taxi
Drawn up at their gate;

And though their back-garden
Is always neat and trim
It has a humbled look,
and no one walks therein.

So did not their chiming clock
Imply some hand to wind it,
I might doubt if the wall between us
Had any life behind it.

London neighbours are such
That I may never know more
Than this of the people
Who live next door.

While they for their part
Should they hazard a guess
At me on my side of the wall
Will know as little, or less;

For my life has grown quiet,
As quiet as theirs;
And the clock has been silent on my chimney-piece
For years and years.

Elinor Wylie

Wild Peaches

Down to the Puritan marrow of my bones
There's something in this richness that I hate.
I love the look, austere, immaculate,
Of landscapes drawn in pearly monotones.
There's something in my very blood that owns
Bare hills, cold silver on a sky of slate,
A thread of water, churned to a milky spate
Streaming through slanted pastures fenced with stones.

I love those skies, thin blue or snowy gray,
Those fields sparse-planted, rendering meager sheaves;
That spring, briefer than apple-blossom's breath,
Summer, so much too beautiful to stay,
Swift autumn, like a bonfire of leaves,
And sleepy winter, like the sleep of death.

Anne-Marie Fyfe

Novgorod Sidings

Virtual snow on the line, a starry
damask night, the train quits
the virtual station. Wellwishers
gather on the cinderpath, not knowing

how to say goodbye. Passengers
with tall hats in half windows alight
in the opening pages. A red-signal
power-cut lasts an entire chapter.

But the couple ring true; emerge from
lost strands. There is grey in her hair
now, cologne hangs in the lull
of stale compartments. Destination

their long-shut summer-house. He carries
her portmanteau in one hand, an octave
mandola in the other. No need
of words. Luggage racks cleared

supper-car mantles cooling. Unlit
factories, grain-stores, mosques dissolve
in the filters of darkness, past telegraph
poles, a lone traveller on a snow-stormed

bridge, isolated railroad hostels.
He notices she's lost an earring, one freshwater
pearl. A running motif. The rest is non-
linear and poorly focused. The engine

slows at the first tunnel, erases carriage
after relentless carriage from the frame.

Colette Inez

The Chairs

Our faces caught in the mirror
above the piano soften,
hands resting on each other's
shoulders after we clear the dishes.
With a flourish you call
my attention to the four chairs
upholstered in my absence,
deep burnt sienna, colour
of the wine we decant.
"This reminds me of..." you say,
lifting your glass.
Chairs, accept our humble bodies
heavy with memory and longing.
Once we sat on stones
on an island in the north,
seeking the key
to Spinoza's infinitely
infinite universe.
Love, the hour grows short.
What was the comparison

Rommi Smith

Tide

for Ken Saro-Wiwa

Look, look my friend, over there
how those white sand beaches are
turned by the lap of the tide
into wet Black gold by night.

See, my friend, nearer here,
how those flock of gulls,
grow fat off of Black gold;
gulp the lives out of smaller shells.

One day, we will not be here to witness this;
the lap of that tide will make
each one of us a tenant of its waves.
And only the rocks will testify
to the cackle, overhead, of those
same gulls. Each one, spreading
the long lies of its wings,
writing history out
across the thin blue sky.

Jane Yeh

Correspondence

I've gotten nothing for weeks. You might think of me

As dated in a blue housecoat, buttoning and unbuttoning,
Waiting you out: I have my ways

Of keeping time. When your letter comes, dogs will bark
Up and down the street. The tomatoes in the garden

Will explode like fireworks. Each day the mailman passes
In a reverie, illiterate, another cobweb

Grows across the door. Picture me
Going bald one hair at a time, combing and curling, burning

My hand on the iron once every hour: I like to
Keep myself busy. When I hear from you, *aurora*

Borealis will sweep across the sky. Every lottery ticket in my drawer
Will win. Even the mailman will know the letters

Of your name. If you bothered to notice, you would see me
Turning to gold rather slowly, bone

By bone, the way teeth come
Loose from the gums, the way animals go

Extinct, in geological time.

Mary Ursula Bethell

Response

When you wrote your letter it was April,
And you were glad that it was spring weather,
And that the sun shone out in turn with showers of rain.
I write in waning May and it is autumn,
And I am glad that my chrysanthemums
Are tied up fast to strong posts,
So that the south winds cannot beat them down.

I am glad that they are tawny coloured,
And fiery in the low west evening light.
And I am glad that one bush warbler
Still sings in the honey-scented wattle...

But oh, we have remembering hearts,
And we say "How green it was in such and such an April,"
And "Such and such an autumn was very golden"
And "Everything is for a very short time."

Emily Dickinson

465

I heard a Fly buzz – when I died –
The Stillness in the Room
Was like the Stillness in the Air –
Between the Heaves of Storm –

The Eyes around – had wrung them dry –
And Breaths were gathering firm
For that last Onset – when the King
Be witnessed – in the Room –

I willed my Keepsakes – Signed away
What portion of me be
Assignable – and then it was
There interposed a Fly –

With Blue – uncertain stumbling Buzz –
Between the light – and me –
And then the Windows failed – and then
I could not see to see –

Leland Bardwell

Dog-Ear

I am turning my death over
like a page in a book
I dog-ear it.
I need to remember the place.

Susan Wicks

Pistachios

A darkening January afternoon.
I stand at the kitchen window absently eating
pistachios left over from Christmas; outside, a blur
of hydrangea as I slide
the edge of my nail between the curved wings of a shell.
They say sex is a kind of dying.

At a certain time of life –
you never know exactly when
or where or how fast – sex leaves.
It's like a tide
slowly leaving a beach, imperceptibly exposing
rocks like bony fingers, hidden tongues of sand
and sometimes the rank on improbable rank
of mussels close as bristles –
millions of them, blue-black,
crowding the surface – like the teeth of combs
or petrified fur
that teases the soles of your bare feet
raw – a whole glittering expanse
of blue-black points, and, hidden inside,
that throb of flesh. As the tide recedes
a million brittle mouths lean shut.

A skeleton hydrangea bowls across the dusk,
shivers. I crack another shell open,
feeling saliva spurt
at the green thought
of pistachios, salt on my lips, shells light as paper.

Nina Bogin

Going Up The Hudson River, After Twenty Years

The river continues its hard work,
shunting the heavy waters
through the ailing land,
southbound, out of Albany.

In the stunned light the world is mud –
the dank riverbank, the eddies of debris.
And the train too is a dark sleek brown,
rustling with headlines and ennui.

Has some unspoken disaster occurred?
I feel almost at home here,
wedged against the window,

but nothing's the same. The present throws itself
under the wheels. The future
waves from the bridge.

It's too late for nostalgia.
I'll take the stale sandwich,
yesterday's news, the one long hoot of adieu.

9. The Art of Work
Homework, All Kinds of Work

Gwendolyn Brooks

The Pool Players Seven at the Golden Shovel

We real cool. We
Left school. We

Lurk late. We
Strike straight. We

Sing sin. We
Think gin. We

Jazz June. We
Die soon.

Sarah Hannah

Cassetta Frame (Italy, circa 1600)
Robert Lehmann Collection, Metropolitan Museum of Art

I wonder what his hands were like – skin,
Thumbprint's orbits, half moon of the nail –
The artisan who plied bough and alloy, chisel,
Stone, for the sake of circumscription:
Poplar, walnut, ebony, pear, niello,
Crystal, lapis. The words abscond from wood
And bloom in trees: Pioppo tremulo;
Forma di pera. I confess to find
Myself astonished by outskirts of things:
Hem and shirr, ice storm, sea coast, shadow, fringe,
To find myself forsworn to the mixture,
Poplar, walnut, ebony, pear,
Niello, crystal, lapis. Lapse! No life
But in the rim; no word but on the lips.

Note: The materials used were typed out on a small card beneath the
frame display and are considered by this author to be a found poem.

Deborah Garrison

"Please Fire Me"

Here comes another alpha male,
and all the other alphas
are snorting and pawing,
kicking up puffs of acrid dust

while the silly little hens
clatter back and forth
on quivering claws and raise
a titter about the fuss.

Here comes another alpha male –
a man's man, a dealmaker,
holds tanks of liquor,
charms them pantsless at lunch:

I've never been sicker.
Do I have to stare into his eyes
and sympathize? If I want my job
I do. Well I think I'm through

with the working world,
through with warming eggs
and being Zenlike in my detachment
from all things Ego.

I'd like to go
somewhere else entirely,
and I don't mean
Europe.

Mary Stewart Hammond

Making Breakfast

There's this ritual, like a charm,
Southern women do after their men
make love to them in the morning.
We rush to the kitchen. As if possessed.
Make one of those big breakfasts
from the old days. To say thank you.
When we know we shouldn't. Understanding
the act smacks of Massah, looks shuffly as
all getout, adds to his belly, which is bad
for his back, and will probably give him
cancer, cardiac arrest, and a stroke. So,
you do have to wonder these days as you
get out the fat-back, knead the dough,
adjust the flame for a slow boil,
flick water on the cast-iron skillet
to check if it's ready and the kitchen
gets steamy and close and smelling
to high heaven, if this isn't an act
of aggressive hostility and/or a symptom
of regressed tractability. Although
on the days we don't I am careful
about broiling his meats instead of
deep-fat frying them for a couple of hours,
dipped in flour, serving them smothered
in cream gravy made from the drippings,
and, in fact, I won't even do
that anymore period, no matter what
he does to deserve it, and besides, we are
going on eighteen years so it's not as if we
eat breakfast as often as we used to,
and when we do I now should serve him –
forget the politics of who serves whom –
oatmeal after? But if this drive answers
to days when death, like woolly mammoths
and Visigoth hordes and rebellious kinsmen,
waited outside us, then it's healthy, if
primitive, to cook Southern. Consider it
an extra precaution. I look at his face,
that weak-kneed, that buffalo-eyed,
Samson-after-his-haircut face, all of him

burnished with grits and sausage
and fried apples and biscuits and my
power, and adrift outside himself,
and the sight makes me feel all over
again like what I thank him for
except bigger, slower, lasting, as if,
hog-tied, the hunk of him were risen
with the splotchy butterfly on my chest,
which, contrary to medical opinion, does not
fade but lifts off into the atmosphere,
coupling, going on ahead.

Carol Rumens

Two Women

Daily to a profession – paid thinking
and clean hands – she rises,
unquestioning. It's second nature now.
The hours, though they're all of daylight, suit her.
The desk, typewriter, carpets, pleasantries
are a kind of civilisation, built on money,
of course, but money, now she sees, is human.
She has learned giving from her first chequebook,
intimacy from absence. Coming home
long after dark to the jugular torrent
of family life, her smile
cool as the skin of supermarket apples,
she's half the story. There's another woman
who wears her name, a silent, background face
that's flushed with effort.
The true wife, she picks up scattered laundry
and sets the table with warmed plates to feed
the clean-handed woman. They've not met.
If they were made to touch, they'd scald each other.

Gillian Clarke

Overheard in County Sligo

I married a man from County Roscommon
and I live at the back of beyond
with a field of cows and a yard of hens
and six white geese on the pond.

At my door's a square of yellow corn
caught up by its corners and shaken,
and the road runs down through the open gate
and freedom's there for the taking.

I had thought to work on the Abbey stage
or have my name in a book,
to see my thought on the printed page,
or still the crowd with a look.

But I turn to fold the breakfast cloth
and to polish the lustre and brass,
to order and dust the tumbled rooms
and find my face in the glass.

I ought to feel I'm a happy woman
for I lie in the lap of the land,
and I married a man from County Roscommon
and I live in the back of beyond.

Charlotte Mew

The Farmer's Bride

Three Summers since I chose a maid,
Too young maybe — but more's to do
At harvest-time than bide and woo.
When us was wed she turned afraid
Of love and me and all things human;
Like the shut of a winter's day.
Her smile went out, and 'twasn't a woman —
More like a little, frightened fay.

One night, in the Fall, she runned away.
"Out 'mong the sheep, her be," they said,
Should properly have been abed;
But sure enough she wasn't there
Lying awake with her wide brown stare.
So over seven-acre field and up-along across the down
We chased her, flying like a hare
Before our lanterns. To Church-Town
All in a shiver and a scare
We caught her, fetched her home at last
And turned the key upon her, fast.

She does the work about the house
As well as most, but like a mouse:
Happy enough to chat and play
With birds and rabbits and such as they,
So long as men-folk stay away.
"Not near, not near!" her eyes beseech
When one of us comes within reach.
The women say that beasts in stall
Look round like children at her call.
I've hardly heard her speak at all.

Shy as a leveret, swift as he,
Straight and slight as a young larch tree,
Sweet as the first wild violets, she,
To her wild self. But what to me?

The short days shorten and the oaks are brown,
The blue smoke rises to the low gray sky,
One leaf in the still air falls slowly down,
A magpie's spotted feathers lie
On the black earth spread white with rime,
The berries redden up to Christmas-time.
What's Christmas-time without there be
Some other in the house than we!

She sleeps up in the attic there
Alone, poor maid. 'Tis but a stair
Betwixt us. Oh, my God! – the down,
The soft young down of her; the brown,
The brown of her – her eyes, her hair, her hair!

Elma Mitchell

Thoughts After Ruskin

Women reminded him of lilies and roses.
Me they remind rather of blood and soap,
Armed with a warm rag, assaulting noses,
Ears, neck, mouth and all the secret places:

Armed with a sharp knife, cutting up liver,
Holding hearts to bleed under a running tap,
Gutting and stuffing, pickling and preserving,
Scalding, blanching, broiling and pulverising,

– All the terrible chemistry of their kitchens.
Their distant husbands lean across mahogany
And delicately manipulate the market,
While safe at home, the tender and the gentle
Are killing tiny mice, dead snap by the neck,
Asphyxiating flies, evicting spiders,
Scrubbing, scouring aloud, disturbing cupboards,
Committing things to dustbins, twisting, wringing,

Wrists red and knuckles white and fingers puckered,
Pulpy, tepid. Steering screaming cleaners
Around the snags of furniture, they straighten
And haul out sheets from under the incontinent
And heavy old, stoop to importunate young,
Tugging, folding, tucking, zipping, buttoning,
Spooning in food, encouraging excretion,
Mopping up vomit, stabbing cloth with needles,

Contorting wool around their knitting needles,
Creating snug and comfy on their needles...
And when all's over, off with overalls,
Quickly consulting clocks, they go upstairs,
Sit and sigh a little, brushing hair,
And somehow find, in mirrors, colours, odors,
Their essence of lilies and roses.

Clare Pollard

The Chain

I am pale as tequila
in black, and my skirt's made of smoke,
I smile at your joke

give you change to feed to machines
that flicker like adverts in puddles,
like terrible dreams.

Ice?
Do you think that I'm nice?
Perhaps I'm just cheap,

minimum wage, yet you all get this show,
get to patronise, blow me a kiss.
Crisp?

I'm your optic illusion
Let's face it, I'm better than real –
walk into a place like this,

any time, it's the same place:
same girl with a different face,
framed posters of postery things,

and the carpets,
the carpets –
inspired by the crash

of a tray full of office girl drinks:
shooters and bitch fizz,
liquid kids' TV,

and the music,
the music,
that's sweeter and safer than shandy.

The menu you know:
wraps, bangers, comb.
Mayo?

It's been a long day, yes?
Sit down and talk –
I've plenty of empties to stack.

Don't worry, you've no need to listen back.
Wife selfish? Job poo?
Poor darling, poor You.

I cut up raggedy lemons,
like combs jammed full with blonde hair,
whilst you outline the things you deserve...

What does it take around here to get served?
Slice? Ice?
The other staff live in a squat,

what with not being paid the price
of a whisky and Coke in an hour.
What did you call me then? Flower?

How kind, when I hum of the booze,
a fug I can't lose
even with all that chill walk home

past the taxis and dark spots and darlings,
trailing a veil of men's breath,
my hands tacky with froth

my hair like that splash of Sauvignon Blanc
I tip down the sink at the end.
You think I'm your friend?

In this nowhere you come with your cash,
I clean up the ash.
You think this is real?

Nothing I show you I feel.
That's a small? Extra-Cold? And with glass?
Special Meal Deal?

Julie O'Callaghan

Schmooze-Fest

They bought my life
so I'm off to Lake Geneva, Wisconsin
for a corporate bonding weekend.
I'll get through this schmooze-fest
if it's the last thing I do.
Marv says avoid the loser
in the snappy tie.
He says pack a jumbo bottle
of Bug-Off: those little varmints
can be murder.
There goes my watch alarm.
Time for a whacky round
of executive whirlyball.

Kate Bingham

Things I Learned at University

How to bike on cobblestones and where to signal right.
How to walk through doors held open by Old Etonians
and not scowl. How to make myself invisible in seminars
by staring at the table. How to tell Victorian Gothic from Medieval.
How to eat a Mars Bar in the Bodleian. When to agree
with everything in theory. How to cultivate a taste for sherry.

Where to bike on the pavement after dark. How to sabotage a hunt.
When to sunbathe topless in the Deer Park. When to punt.
How to hitch a lift and when to walk and where to run.
When not to address my tutors formally. How to laugh at Latin puns
and when to keep quiet and preserve my integrity.
How to celebrate an essay crisis. When to sleep through fire alarms.

How to bike no-handed, how to slip a condom on with one.
When to smoke a joint and when to swig champagne.
When to pool a tip and how to pull a pint. A bit of history.
When to listen to friends and whether to take them seriously.
At the same time how to scorn tradition and enjoy it.
How to live like a king, quite happily, in debt.

Ruth Fainlight

Moving

Sit down among the boxes and write a poem,
he told me; obedient, I'm writing.
Moving house, he said, is such an ordinary
thing to do – a regular activity,
especially for you – no obligation
to unpack at once or be too dutiful.

Find a vacant corner and there among
half-empty cartons spilling crumpled paper,
piles of sofa cushions and rolled-up carpets,
dining chairs like acrobatic couples
or swimmers, chest to chest, one pair of legs
trailing through water, the other flailing air,

and think about important things – not builders,
plumbers, electricians. I try to remember
how it began, this restlessness: a lifetime
trying to feel at home. A need and hope, he
hints, which might be programmed in my genes,
bred in the bone – nothing to do with him –

and makes me realise again those complex
ties that hold us together: everywhere,
both of us are strangers. Then: "Let's open
a bottle of wine and drink a toast to life,"
he smiles and holds me close, "then go upstairs."
Why not? I ponder, putting the poem aside.

Ruth Fainlight

Thunder

I am very good at chimpanzee's work:
shelling almonds, picking stones out of lentils,
scratching a smear of food off a sleeve or collar.
I find a satisfaction in repetition,
superstition, and know the myopic's refusal
to look above or beyond the horizon. Half
of my nature is simple as a medieval
peasant. The other isn't, and that's the problem.

It's harder to date the complex of discontents
shared by any metaphysical primate,
who soon learns that pain is surer than pleasure.
A stubbed toe hurts, and the soul asserts itself
by the same token. Such thoughts are as timeless
as wondering how the planets started spinning
and why one cannot live forever.
Elegies must be the oldest art form.

Thunder rolls from the northern hills, and the lamp
on my desk flickers. Once, it would have been
an omen, a god's voice or seven-league tread.
Now it's only a nuisance, or a warning
reminder of how easily the world could end.
There are days in the present when I imagine, far
in the future, someone brooding on first and last things,
keening the dead, and tending her garden.

Elizabeth Macklin

Despite the Temptation

I wasn't allowed to write the poem
about the asparagus, fattest white asparagus,
trying to open the can of asparagus
without a can-opener, where he was finally

down on the floor on his knees with hammer & chisel,
at which point he said I was not allowed
to write a poem about any of this.
And yet ever after I was tempted

to say how I'd loved the experience (*you
in the experience*). At least he'll know now
we all know about the asparagus, & will
guess that, despite explicit orders,

I did 'love' him. Or maybe the can of asparagus,
fattest white asparagus, & opening the can
of asparagus without a can-opener. And yet
look how well we did with the tools at hand.

Molly Peacock

Cutting Tall Grass

I love the sound of lawnmowers each year.
There's a woman in her workpants smelling of
gasoline and cut grass, wiping a smear
of grease on her head while blotting a swelling of
sweat from her head under her plastic visor.
I'm not sure whether she loves that machine.
Short grass is none the wiser for the razor,
so the love of mowing it is love of sheen.
But one must love the vehicle, the sun,
the bugs thrown up behind and the swallows
snatching bugs at the wheels to love a lawn,
the old grass spewn in the bleak shadows,
the new grass smelling of wet and slight rot,
to love to live between what is and is not.

Leontia Flynn

For Stuart, Who Accidentally Obtained a Job in the Civil Service

I have it in my diary as May the 6th
and a beautiful evening. We walk in silence
back to my house. There are condolences;
sitting round as though we are at a wake,
somebody mentions Kafka.

You explain about your mother.
For now I tell you, just for now...
the evening light and a spark, fallen
from your cigarette butt onto the woolly jumper
over your truculent heart, quietly dying.

Saskia Hamilton

Elegy

The work of burial is never done. First the interruption,
then the interruption, so it's carried on in sleep,
over to argument, floating in the water with the flowers
the shit the shells the debris from the city after the rains
have washed it to the beaches and the sea
has taken it up into itself. The figure with the shovel:
the figure with the shovel: the figure with
the book, the shoulders rising, the dog reading news
on the pavement washed then by rain running off the asphalt
down into the gulley where it goes under the city with the tunnelling
animals, the cunning animals, the readers under
the city.

Mimi Khalvati

Ghazal: The Servant

Ma'mad, hurry, water the rose.
Blessed is the English one that grows
    out in the rain.

Water is scarce, blood not so.
Blood is the open drain that flows
    out in the rain.

Bring in the lamp, the olive's flame.
Pity the crippled flame that blows
    out in the rain.

Where are the children? What is the time?
Time is the terror curfew throws
    out in the rain.

Hurry, Ma'mad, home to your child.
Wherever my namesake, Maryam, goes
    out in the rain.

Fleur Adcock

Things

There are worse things than having behaved foolishly in public.
There are worse things than these miniature betrayals,
committed or endured or suspected; there are worse things
than not being able to sleep for thinking about them.
It is 5 a.m. All the worse things come stalking in
and stand icily about the bed looking worse and worse and
                                          worse.

Fleur Adcock

The Ex-Queen Among the Astronomers

They serve revolving saucer eyes,
dishes of stars; they wait upon
huge lenses hung aloft to frame
the slow procession of the skies.

They calculate, adjust, record,
watch transits, measure distances.
They carry pocket telescopes
to spy through when they walk abroad.

Spectra possessed their eyes; they face
upwards, alert for meteorites,
cherishing little glassy worlds:
receptacles for outer space.

But she, exile, expelled, ex-queen,
swishes among the men of science
waiting for cloudy skies, for nights
when constellations can't be seen.

She wears the rings he let her keep;
she walks as she was taught to walk
for his approval, years ago.
His bitter features taunt her sleep.

And so when these have laid aside
their telescopes, when lids are closed
between machine and sky, she seeks
terrestrial bodies to bestride.

She plucks this one or that among
the astronomers, and is become
his canopy, his occultation;
she sucks at earlobe, penis, tongue

mouthing the tubes of flesh; her hair
crackles, her eyes are comet-sparks.
She brings the distant briefly close
above his dreamy abstract stare.

Joan Murray
You Talk Of Art

You talk of art, of work, of books.
Have you ever sat down, thought all that's to do?
That book to read, that book to write,
Sat down, stood up, walked back and forth,
Because not an action you could do would
Fill the gap that's wanting action to the chin?

Look. Look into the past one damned moment,
And on that you ask me to work, to dream, to do?
Try it yourself on nothing. I can't.
Every confounded one has had so much of life
That left them gasping in a stinking or a lighter air,
Left out of breath and glad to think at last,
Higher or lower, their there and there and there.

And where am I? Where I began, and where I'll end:
Sitting, sitting, with the last grain of will
Rotting in time, and there's no time or tide in me.

You talk of art, of work, of books.
I'll talk of nothing in its lowest state,
Talk till my jaw hangs limply at the joint,
And the talk that's one big yawn in the face of all of you,
Empty as head, empty as mood, and weak.
And I can hear all the watery wells of desolation
Lapping a numbing sleep within the head.

U.A. Fanthorpe

The Poet's Companion

Must be in mint condition, not disposed
To hayfever, headaches, hangovers, hysteria, these being
The Poet's prerogative.
Typing and shorthand desirable. Ability
To function on long walks and in fast trains an advantage.
Must be visible/invisible
At the drop of a dactyl. Should be either
A mobile dictionary, thesaurus and encyclopedia,
Or have instant access to same.
Cordon bleu and accountancy skills essential,
Also cooking of figures and instant recall of names
Of once-met strangers.
Should keep a good address book. In public will lead
The laughter, applause, the unbearably moving silence.
Must sustain with grace
The role of Muse, with even more grace the existence
Of another eight or so, also camera's curious peeping
When the Poet is reading a particularly
Randy poem about her, or (worse) about someone else.
Ability to endure reproaches for forgetfulness, lack of interest,
Heart, is looked for,
Also instant invention of convincing excuses for what the Poet
Does not want to do, and long-term ability to remember
Precise detail of each.
Must be personable, not beautiful. The Poet
Is not expected to waste time supervising
The Companion. She will bear
Charming, enchanted children, all of them
Variations on the Poet theme; and
Impossibly gifted.
Must travel well, be fluent in the more aesthetic
European languages; must be a Finder
Of nasty scraps of paper
And the miscellany of junk the Poet loses
And needs *this minute, now.* Must be well-read,
Well-earthed, well able
To forget her childhood's grand trajectory,
And sustain with undiminished poise
That saddest dedication: lastly *my wife,*
Who did the typing.

10. The Work of Art

The Arts, Fine and Otherwise

Naomi Shihab Nye

The Small Vases from Hebron

Tip their mouths open to the sky
The turquoise, amber,
the deep green with fluted handle,
pitcher the size of two thumbs,
tiny lip and graceful waist.

Here we place the smallest flower
which could have lived invisibly
in loose soil beside the road,
sprig of succulent rosemary,
bowing mint.

They grow deeper in the center of the table.

Here we entrust the small life,
thread, fragment, breath.
And it bends. It waits all day.
As the bread cools and the children
open their gray copybooks
to shape the letter that looks like
a chimney rising out of a house.

And what do the headlines say?

Nothing of the smaller petal
perfectly arranged inside the larger petal
or the way tinted glass filters light.
Men and boys, praying when they died,
fall out of their skins.
The whole alphabet of living,
heads and tails of words,
sentences, the way they said,
"Ya' Allah!" when astonished,
or "ya'ani" for "I mean" –
a crushed glass under the feet
still shines.
But the child of Hebron sleeps
with the thud of her brothers falling
and the long sorrow of the colour red.

Kay Ryan

A Bad Time for the Sublime

The sublime is now
a less popular topic
than if El Greco was myopic.
Yes El Greco may very well
have been, which may very
well have made his men
so thin and his women so
distressed. If pressed,
the oculists confess that
the shape taken by the
aqueous humor makes
or breaks us, and have
devised anti-vision devices
that restore noses to their
right lengths and places.
Witness how a speckled plain
condenses to a field
or farmyard, the ecstasy
or pain of space
erased by moving the lens
back or forward.
We now discover there were
many thin kings and
many chubby martyrs,
many ordinary trees
and water always very
similar to our water.

Patricia Goedicke

The Reading Club

Is dead serious about this one, having rehearsed it for two weeks
They bring it right into the Old Fellows Meeting Hall.
Riding the backs of the Trojan Women,
In Euripides' great wake they are swept up,

But the women of the chorus, in black stockings and kerchiefs,
Stand up bravely to it, shawled arms thrash
In a foam of hysterical voices shrieking,
Seaweed on the wet flanks of a whale,

For each town has its Cassandra who is a little crazy,
Wed to some mystery or other and therefore painfully sensitive,
Wiser than anyone but no one listens to her, these days the terror
Reaches its red claws into back yard and living room alike,

For each town has its Andromache who is too young,
With snub nose and children just out of school
Even she cannot escape it, from the bombed city she is led out
Weeping among the ambulances,

And each community has its tart, its magical false Helen
Or at least someone who looks like her, in all the makeup she can muster
The gorgeous mask of whatever quick-witted lie will keep her alive
At least a little longer, on the crest of the bloody wave,

That dolorous mountain of wooden ships and water
In whose memory the women bring us this huge gift horse,
This raging animal of a play no one dares to look in the eye
For fear of what's hidden there:

Small ragdoll figures toppling over and over
From every skyscraper and battlement hurtling
Men and women both, mere gristle in the teeth of fate.
Out over the sea of the audience our numb faces

Are stunned as Andromache's, locked up there on the platform
Inside Euripides' machine the women sway and struggle
One foot at a time, up the surging ladder
Of grief piled on grief, strophe on antistrophe,

In every century the same, the master tightens the screws,
Heightens the gloss of each bitter scene
And strikes every key, each word rings out
Over our terrified heads like a brass trumpet,

For this gift is an accordion, the biggest and mightiest of all,
As the glittering lacquered box heaves in and out,
Sigh upon sigh, at the topmost pitch a child
Falls through midnight in his frantically pink skin.

As the anguished queen protests, the citizens in the chorus wail
Louder and louder, the warriors depart
Without a glance backwards, these captains of the world's death
Enslaved as they are enslavers, in a rain of willess atoms

Anonymity takes over utterly: as the flaming city falls
On this bare beach, in the drab pinewood hall
The Reading Club packs up to go; scripts, coffee cups, black stockings
Husbands and wives pile into the waiting cars

Just as we expect, life picks up and goes on
But not art: crouched back there like a stalled stallion
Stuffed in its gorgeous music box is the one gift
That will not disappear but waits, but bides its time and waits

For the next time we open it, that magical false structure
Inside whose artifice is the lesson, buried alive,
Of the grim machinations of the beautiful that always lead us
To these eternally real lamentations, real sufferings, real cries.

Anne Waldman

The Lie

Art begins with a lie
    The separation is you plus me plus what we make
        Look into lightbulb, blink, sun's in your eye

I want a rare sky
    vantage point free from misconception
        Art begins with a lie

Nothing to lose, spontaneous rise
    of reflection, paint the picture
        of a lightbulb, or eye the sun

How to fuel the world, then die
    Distance yourself from artfulness
        How? Art begins with a lie

The audience wants to cry
    when the actors are real & passionate
        Look into footlight, then feed back to eye

You fluctuate in an artful body
    You try to imitate the world's glory
        Art begins with a lie

        That's the story, sharp speck in the eye.

Frances Williams

The Actress
(from Persona)

Here is the oval face of Bibi Andersson.
Her head is wide as a planet. But instead

Of craters and volcanoes, she carries
The softness of being infinitely human.

Dark moods migrate across her skin
Like lost tribes forcing a way to memory.

She's held, for a daringly long duration,
By the four-corners of Ingmar Bergman.

He smothers her with Bach, a solemn hood
Of notes, aching through light. It's 1966

And over the pores of her powdered skin
A day is ending. But something else lets

itself in. Watching and feeling watched –
The two compete in the interrogation

Her eyes witness and rival. The sun still
Abandons Scandinavia as it stole away from

Bergman and the crew who might surround
Her like the Magi intent, perhaps, and listening.

The score was later stripped, over the action,
To create the exact moment, journeying still,
That now passes through itself, like an eclipse.

Lauris Edmond

Trapeze

She is a flare of crimson light in the dark
a nerve of motion
arms open she flies alone
a crucifixion of longing.

Our hands are wet with fear.

In her lyric expectation
she soars to the narrow bar:
released one second after its time
it comes down twisting,
not straight,
held as though by the hesitations
of an uncertain lover.

And so she falls,

no cramp of the wings
no clotting of that fluid body
no sound but the gasp we do not know we give.

The sun and moon have fallen into the earth
gravity has swallowed the air. My eyes
are dry and fiercely hot, staring
into that burning streak.

There's the net. There's a moving tangle,
a roll, a rolling, something that begins to rise
and stand and stretch
and valiantly at last to wave.

But we stay slumped in the high ringed seats
some spirit in us
that never left earth before
has gone too far. We are weak with loss.
We can do nothing. We watch and wait.

And now it happens; she dazzles again
but it is our hands that reach and touch
and find the place. Our breath.
We hold the strong bar.

So she has taken us; she has drawn us
into herself for ever.

Carrie Etter

The Daughters of Prospero

When gales make a house a boat to toss on water,
and Gonzalo scrutinizes me, says I'm ripe

for hanging, and loquaciously heads below deck,
I know this isn't the oceanic feeling

Freud wrote of, this lingering image of a child
placing paper boat after boat onto a brook,

though each one drowns in a short drop ten feet downstream.
Placing white boat after boat onto a brook,

because she has learned beginner's origami,
because her fingers have amassed a score of cuts,

because some of the boats never looked seaworthy,
because a surprising number can glide like swans,

the girl sets her boats on a fatal course, and though
her head is bent, I can just see her eyes' fierce gleam.

Ruth Padel

Blown Ruby

As if they were itinerant stained-glass-makers
setting up camp outside a mediaeval town
at the edge of forest – or here, by Plinteria ti Merimna –
and lighting their transformation fires to conjure glass
from wood and sand. Bellows. Three furnaces
for heating, cooling, melting. Cristallo, azurite,

blown ruby. They come, villagers would say,
they speak in foreign languages
and when they go, our windows are alive
with coloured light. By the fire, at night,
you'd hear their stories of the other worlds
they brought to life in glass. Slow

campfire melting. Sun scatters unevenly
through imperfections in everything they made
at the corner of Ayias Annas and Spiridonos.
You transform us we'd say, in welcome.
They will not come again. Close your eyes. A branch
is being broken and the soot-bruised earth is warm.

Isabella Gardner

In The Museum

Small and emptied woman, you lie here a thousand years dead your hands
on our diminished loins, flat in this final bed, teeth jutting from your
unwound head, your spiced bones black and dried. Who knew you and
kissed you and kept you and wept when you died? Died you young? Had
you grace? Risus sardonicsu replied. Then quick I siezed my husband's hand
while he stared, at his bride.

Lyn Moir

Velázquez on Picasso's Pigeons

That man, that manic clown, he's painting pigeons!
He excuses himself, to be sure, with the claim
it's the view from my windows. Ojalá fuera!
If only it were – it's a view calls to mind
my native Sevilla, or the coastline at Cádiz,
expanses of water and waving pine trees,
birds on the balcony, a fresh summer breeze
instead of this arid Castilian plain,
pine-cloaked Guadarrama range sawing the sky,
league after league of boulders and rock
weighing us down, we arse-lickers at court.

If there were a pigeon-loft around my windows,
one of two things: her highness would be cooing,
handling their feathers, laughing, smiling, playing
like a child in any village watching living creatures grow;
or, more sinister, more likely, the courtiers
would pluck them from their nesting boxes, eat them,
that is, if his good majesty had not had them first.
I fear a game bird's life at Philip's court is short.
Eat or be eaten, crawl and curry favour. Simple rules
to keep oneself alive in a world of fools.

Judith Wright

Request to a Year

If the year is meditating a suitable gift,
I should like it to be the attitude
of my great- great- grandmother,
legendary devotee of the arts,

who having eight children
and little opportunity for painting pictures,
sat one day on a high rock
beside a river in Switzerland

and from a difficult distance viewed
her second son, balanced on a small ice flow,
drift down the current toward a waterfall
that struck rock bottom eighty feet below,

while her second daughter, impeded,
no doubt, by the petticoats of the day,
stretched out a last-hope alpenstock
(which luckily later caught him on his way).

Nothing, it was evident, could be done;
And with the artist's isolating eye
My great-great-grandmother hastily sketched the scene.
The sketch survives to prove the story by.

Year, if you have no Mother's Day present planned,
Reach back and bring me the firmness of her hand.

Leah Fritz

Rembrandt

Dear God, they want me to write about nothing,
to paint with paint, of paint, by paint, for paint –
and he in his chair with sublimely human face
half-turned to a light no light on earth has seen.

Words have an awkward way of meaning something.
A mindless soul, a soulless mind is what
they want, art to reflect their heartlessness
but give it dignity, and he in Holland,

dead, by all accounts, turning slowly,
pig-on-a-spit, they wonder why nothing's holy.

Mary Ruefle

The Last Supper

It made a dazzling display:
the table set with the meat
from half of a walnut, a fly
on a purple grape, the grape
lit from within and the fly
bearing small black eggs.
We gathered round the oval table
with our knives, starved
for some inner feast.
We were not allowed to eat,
as we had been hired as models
by the man at our head.
Days passed
in which we grew faint with hunger.
Later we were told
that although we did not appear
on the canvas
our eyes devouring these things
provided the infinite light.

Vicki Feaver

Oi Yoi Yoi
(to Roger Hilton)

The lady has no shame.
Wearing not a stitch
she is lolloping across
an abstract beach
towards a notional sea.

I like the whisker of hair
under her armpit. It suggests
that she's not one of those women
who are always trying to get rid
of their smell.

You were more interested
in her swinging baroque tits
and the space between her thighs
than the expression on her face.
That you've left blank.

But her mons veneris
you've etched in black ink
with the exuberance of a young lad
caught short on a bellyful of beer
scrawling on a wall in the Gents.

As a woman I ought to object.
But she looks happy enough.
And which of us doesn't occasionally
want one of the old gods to come down
and chase us over the sands.

Medbh McGuckian

Hand Reliquary, Ave Maria Lane

God knows that there is no proof
That part returns to wholeness
Simply because miracles happen
At a single church-going.

Her verdant branches labelled
With the names of the five senses,
The garden not ours, she prayed
For her illness to last beyond the grave,

And be the unsealer of that tree.
She might have been dead for a week,
Though she went on with her deep
Dying, her womb a transparent crystal

Turning into a brown relic
Even before her death. The blinding
Beauty of her hood opening
Acted upon me as my own ghost

Would do, sounding silk,
As with a lifting gesture
She tore off flesh from her hand,
Driving wide her middle finger

Into the palm of the other.
Till being a vessel, Christ appeared to her
As a dish filled with carved-up bread
So unnaturally sweet, so lightly crushed,

She could quench the tall language
Of his image in her mouth,
Which was the breast-wound, always on the point
Of being taken, in his female side.

11. On The Seventh Day, No Work

Spirit & Soul, Religion

Brigit Pegeen Kelly

Imagining Their Own Hymns

What fools they are to believe the angels
in this window are in ecstasy. They
do not smile. Their eyes are rolled back in annoyance
not in bliss, as my mother's eyes roll back
when she finds us in the dirt with the ciderflies
and juice blackening our faces and hands.
When the sun comes up behind the angels
then even in their dun robes they are beautiful,
with their girlish hair and their mean lit faces,
but they do not love the light. As I
do not love it when I am made clean
for the ladies who bring my family money.
They stroke my face and smooth my hair. So sweet,
they say, so good, but I am not sweet or good.
I would take one of the 'possums we kill
in the dump by the woods where the rats slide
like dark boats into the dark stream and leave it
on the heavy woman's porch just to think
of her on her knees scrubbing and scrubbing
at a stain that will never come out.
And these angels that the women turn to
are not good either. They are sick of Jesus,
who never stops dying, hanging there white
and large, his shadow blue as pitch, and blue
the bruise on his chest, with spread petals,
like the hydrangea blooms I tear from
Mrs. Macht's bush and smash on the sidewalk.
One night they will get out of here. One night
when the weather is turning cold and a few
candles burn, they will leave St. Blase standing
under his canopy of glass lettuce
and together, as in a wedding march,
their pockets full of money from the boxes
for the sick poor, they will walk down the aisle,
imagining their own hymns, past the pews
and the water fonts in which small things float,
down the streets of our narrow town, while
the bells ring and the birds fly up in the fields
beyond – and they will never come back.

Jane Hirshfield

The Bell Zygmunt

For fertility, a new bride is lifted to touch it with her left hand,
or possibly kiss it.
The sound close in, my friend told me later, is almost silent.

At ten kilometers, even those who have never heard it know what it is.

If you stand near during thunder, she said,
you will hear a reply.

Six weeks and six days from the phone's small ringing,
replying was over.

She who cooked lamb and loved wine and wild-mushroom pastas.
She who when I saw her last was silent as the great Zygmunt mostly is,
a ventilator's clapper between her dry lips.

Because I could, I spoke. She laid her palm on my cheek to answer.
And soon again, to say it was time to leave.

I put my lips near the place a tube went into
the back of one hand.
The kiss — as if it knew what I did not yet — both full and formal.

As one would kiss the ring of a cardinal, or the rim
of that cold iron bell, whose speech can mean "Great joy",
or — equally — "The city is burning. Come."

Jane Hirshfield

In Praise of Coldness

"If you wish to move your reader,"
Chekhov wrote, "you must write more coldly."

Herakleitos recommended, "A dry soul is best."

And so at the center of many great works
is found a preserving dispassion,
like the vanishing point of quattrocento perspective,
or the tiny packets of desiccant enclosed
in a box of new shoes or seeds.

But still the vanishing point
is not the painting,
the silica is not the blossoming plant.

Chekhov, dying, read the timetables of trains.
To what more earthly thing could he have been faithful?–
Scent of rocking distances,
smoke of blue trees out the window,
hampers of bread, pickled cabbage, boiled meat.

Scent of the knowable journey.

Neither a person entirely broken
nor one entirely whole can speak.

In sorrow, pretend to be fearless. In happiness, tremble.

Gwyneth Lewis

Pentecost

The Lord wants me to go to Florida.
I shall cross the border with the mercury thieves,
as foretold in the faxes and prophecies,
and the checkpoint angel of Estonia
will have alerted the uniformed birds
to act unnatural and distract the guards

so I pass unhindered. My glossolalia
shall be my passport; I shall taste the tang
of travel on the atlas of my tongue
salt Poland, sour Denmark and sweet Vienna
and all men in the Spirit shall understand
that, in His wisdom, the Lord has sent

a slip of a girl to save great Florida.
I shall tear through Europe like a standing flame,
not pausing for long, except to rename
the occasional city; in Sofia
thousands converted and hundreds slain
in the Holy Spirit along the Seine.

My life is your chronicle; O Florida
revived, look forward to your past,
and prepare your perpetual Pentecost
of golf course and freeway, shopping mall and car
so the fires that are burning in the orange groves
turn light into sweetness and the huddled graves

are hives of the future – an America
spelt plainly, translated in the Everglades
where palm fruit hang like hand grenades
ready to rip whole treatises of air.
Then the S in the tail of the crocodile
will make perfect sense to the bibliophile

who will study this land, his second Torah.
All this was revealed. Now I wait for the Lord
to move heaven and earth to send me abroad
and fulfil His bold promise to Florida.
As I stay put, He shifts His continent:
Atlantic closes, the sheet of time is rent.

The Saints

You see them praying, sometimes headless,
or wearing their hearts, flaming.
Often in groups, cluttering the landscape
with attributes, framed in the glow

of haloed light. They offer gaping wounds
as they float with the angels, silent,
apocryphal. Their benign patrons pose
beside them, tourists in the divine.

They suffer beautifully – Lawrence,
roasted, Ignatius, devoured whole,
Ursula, massacred with her virgins,
Peter Martyr, writing *Credo*

in his last drop of blood. Vermilion,
cardinal, crimson, it sputters on the canvas,
the holy ghost fluttering above –
but their eyes are fixed on you,

the future; you can barely hold their gaze.
A shop girl has the face of Catherine,
she pales as she hands you change,
and the man beside you on the bus,

wise behind his beard, is the Matthew
from your tattered children's Bible,
his lips moving soundlessly – as a siren
parts the traffic, then grows faint.

Christina Rossetti

In The Bleak Mid-Winter

1. In the bleak mid-winter
   Frosty wind made moan,
Earth stood hard as iron,
   Water like a stone;
Snow had fallen, snow on snow,
   Snow on snow,
In the bleak mid-winter
   Long ago.

2. Our God, Heaven cannot hold Him
   Nor earth sustain;
Heaven and earth shall flee away
   When He comes to reign:
In the bleak mid-winter
   A stable-place sufficed
The Lord God Almighty,
   Jesus Christ.

3. Enough for Him, whom cherubim
   Worship night and day,
A breastful of milk
   And a mangerful of hay;
Enough for Him, whom angels
   Fall down before,
The ox and ass and camel
   Which adore.

4. Angels and archangels
   May have gathered there,
Cherubim and seraphim
   Thronged the air,
But only His mother
   In her maiden bliss,
Worshipped the Beloved
   With a kiss.

5. What can I give Him,
   Poor as I am?
   If I were a shepherd
   I would bring a lamb,
   If I were a wise man
   I would do my part,
   Yet what I can I give Him,
   Give my heart.

Amy Gerstler

A Non-Christian On Sunday

Now we heathens have the town to ourselves
we lie around, munching award-winning pickles
and hunks of coarse, seeded bread smeared
with soft, sweet cheese. The streets seem
deserted, as if Godzilla had been sighted
on the horizon, kicking down skyscrapers
and flattening cabs. Only two people
are lined up to see a popular movie
in which the good and bad guy trade
faces. Churches burst into song. Trees wish
for a big wind. Burnt bacon and domestic tension
scent the air. So do whiffs of lawn mower exhaust
mixed with the colorless blood of clipped hedges.
For whatever's about to come crashing down
on our heads, be it bliss-filled or heinous,
make us grateful. OK? Hints of the saviour's
flavour buzz on our tongues, like crumbs
of a sleeping pill shaped like a snowflake.

Susan Wheeler

The Stable Earth, The Deep Salt Sea

After the dark and in the quaking
the candles on the lawn go out.
You make a path across the slate like a snail.
Everybody spooks.

Duo Seraphim clamabant, alter ad alterum.
What whistling comes from within the trees,
from the bushes there that bend beneath
the breezes?

There were children on the lawn barely walking.

Plena est omnis terra. And you were divided
like wells and like windows, as access to a thing
you represent. Take what regret allows and go
toward light.

Many years ago the woman watched the child
from the stoop. The doorknob broke, and then –

Whom shall I send? And who will go for us?
Then I said, *Here am I! Send me.*

Sylvia Kantaris

Annunciation

It seems I must have been more fertile than most
to have taken that wind-blown
thistledown softly-spoken word
into my body and grown big-bellied with it.
Nor was I the first: there had been
rumours of such goings-on before my turn
came – tales of swansdown. Mine
had no wings or feathers actually
but it was hopeless trying to convince them.
They like to think it was a mystical
encounter, although they must know
I am not of that fibre and to say I was
'troubled' is laughable.
What I do remember is a great rejoicing,
my body's arch and flow, the awe,
and the ringing and singing in my ears –
and then the world stopped for a little while.
But still they will keep on about the Word,
which is their name for it, even though I've
told them that is definitely
not how I would put it.
I should have known they'd try to take
possession of my ecstasy and
swaddle it in their portentous terminology.
I should have kept it hidden in the dark
web of my veins.
Though this child grows in me –
not unwanted certainly, but
not intended on my part; the risk
did not concern me at the time, naturally.
I must be simple to have told them anything.
Just because I stressed the miracle of it
they've rumoured it about the place that I'm
immaculate – but then they always were afraid
of female sexuality.
I've pondered these things lately in my mind.
If they should canonise me
(setting me up as chaste and meek and mild)
God only knows what nonsense
they'll visit on the child.

Jean Valentine

Annunciation

I saw my soul become flesh   breaking open
the linseed oil breaking over the paper
running down   pouring
no one to catch it my life   breaking open
no one to contain it   my
pelvis thinning out into God

Sinéad Morrissey

& Forgive Us Our Trespasses

Of which the first is love. The sad, unrepeatable fact
That the loves we shouldn't foster burrow faster and linger longer
Than sanctioned kinds can. Loves that thrive on absence, on lack
Of return, or worse, on harm, are unkillable, Father.
They do not die in us. And you know how we've tried.
Loves nursed, inexplicably, on thoughts of sex,
A return to touched places, a backwards glance, a sigh –
They come back like the tide. They are with us at the terminus
When cancer catches us. They have never been away.
Forgive us the people we love – their dragnet influence.
Those disallowed to us, those who frighten us, those who stay
On uninvited in our lives and every night revisit us.
Accept from us the inappropriate
By which our dreams and daily scenes stay separate.

Louise Erdrich

Fooling God

I must become small and hide where he cannot reach.
I must become dull and heavy as an iron pot.
I must be tireless as rust and bold as roots
growing through the locks on doors
and crumbling the cinderblocks
of the foundations of his everlasting throne.
I must be strange as pity so he'll believe me.
I must be terrible and brush my hair
so that he finds me attractive.
Perhaps if I invoke GCare, the patron saint of television.
Perhaps if I become the images
passing through the cells of a woman's brain.
I must become very large and block his sight.
I must be sharp and impetuous as knives.
I must insert myself into the bark of his apple trees,
and cleave the bones of his cows. I must be the marrow
that he drinks into his cloud-wet body.
I must be careful and laugh when he laughs.
I must turn down the covers and guide him in.
I must fashion his children out of Playdough, blue, pink, green.
I must pull them from between my legs and set them before the
                                                    television.
I must hide my memory in a mustard grain
so that he'll search for it over time until time is gone.
I must lose myself in the world's regard and disparagement.
I must remain this person and be no trouble.
None at all. So he'll forget.
I'll collect dust out of reach,
a single dish from a set, a flower made of felt,
a tablet the wrong shape to choke on.

I must become essential and file everything
under my own system,
so we can lose him and his proofs and adherents.
I must be a doubter in a city of belief
that hails his signs (the great footprints
long as limousines, the rough print on the wall).
On the pavement where his house begins
fainting women kneel. I'm not among them
although they polish the brass tongues of his lions
with their own tongues
and taste the everlasting life.

Jane Kenyon

Things

The hen flings a single pebble aside
with her yellow, reptilian foot.
Never in eternity the same sound –
a small stone falling on a red leaf.

The juncture of twig and branch,
scarred with lichen, is a gate
we might enter, singing.

The mouse pulls batting
from a hundred-year-old quilt.
She chewed a hole in a blue star
to get it, and now she thrives....
Now is her time to thrive.

Things: simply lasting, then
failing to last: water, a blue heron's
eye, and the light passing
between them: into light all things
must fall, glad at last to have fallen.

Kay Ryan

Blandeur

If it please God,
let less happen.
Even out Earth's
rondure, flatten
Eiger, blanden
the Grand Canyon.
Make valleys
slightly higher,
widen fissures
to arable land,
remand your
terrible glaciers
and silence
their calving,
halving or doubling
all geographical features
toward the mean.
Unlean against our hearts.
Withdraw your grandeur
From these parts.

Lucie Brock-Broido

Domestic Mysticism

In thrice 10,000 seasons, I will come back to this world
In a white cotton dress. Kingdom of After My Own Heart.
Kingdom of Fragile. Kingdom of Dwarves. When I come home,
Teacups will quiver in their Dresden saucers, pentatonic chimes
Will move in wind. A covey of alley cats will swarm on the side
Porch & perch there, portents with quickened heartbeats
You will feel against your ankles as you pass through.

After the first millennium, we were supposed to die out.
You had your face pressed up against the coarse dyed velvet
Of the curtain, always looking out for your own transmigration:
What colors you would wear, what cut of jewel,
What kind of pageantry, if your legs would be tied
Down, if there would be wandering tribes of minstrels
Following with woodwinds in your wake.

This work of mine, the kind of work which takes no arms to do,
Is least noble of all. It's peopled by Wizards, the Forlorn,
The Awkward, the Blinkers, the Spoon-Fingered, Agnostic Lispers,
Stutterers of Prayer, the Flatulent, the Closet Weepers,
The Charlatans. I am one of those. In January, the month the owls
Nest in, I am a witness & a small thing altogether. The Kingdom
Of Ingratitude. Kingdom of Lies. Kingdom of How Dare I.

I go on dropping words like little pink fish eggs, unawares, slightly
Illiterate, often on the mark. Waiting for the clear whoosh
Of fluid to descend & cover them. A train like a silver
Russian love pill for the sick at heart passes by
My bedroom window in the night at the speed of mirage.
In the next millennium, I will be middle aged. I do not do well
In the marrow of things. Kingdom of Trick. Kingdom of Drug.

In a lung-shaped suburb of Virginia, my sister will be childless
Inside the ice storm, forcing the narcissus. We will send
Each other valentines. The radio blowing out
Vaughan Williams on the highway's purple moor.
At nine o'clock, we will put away our sewing to speak
Of lofty things while, in the pantry, little plants will nudge
Their frail tips toward the light we made last century.

When I come home, the dwarves will be long
In their shadows & promiscuous. The alley cats will sneak
Inside, curl about the legs of furniture, close the skins
Inside their eyelids, sleep. Orchids will be intercrossed & sturdy.
The sun will go down as I sit, thin armed, small breasted
In my cotton dress, poked with eyelet stitches, a little lace,
In the queer light left when a room snuffs out.

I draw a bath, enter the water as a god enters water:
Fertile, knowing, kind, surrounded by glass objects
Which could break easily if mishandled or ill-touched.
Everyone knows an unworshipped woman will betray you.
There is always that promise, I like that. Kingdom of Kinesis.
Kingdom of Benevolent. I will betray as a god betrays,
With tenderheartedness. I've got this mystic streak in me.

12. The Mechanics of a Body

The Body, Science

Carol Ann Duffy

Small Female Skull

With some surprise, I balance my small female skull in my hands.
What is it like? An ocarina? Blow in its eye.
It cannot cry, holds my breath only as long as I exhale,
mildly alarmed now, into the hole where the nose was,
press my ear to its grin. A vanishing sigh.

For some time, I sit on the lavatory seat with my head
in my hands, appalled. It feels much lighter than I'd thought;
the weight of a deck of cards, a slim volume of verse,
but with something else, as though it could levitate. Disturbing.
So why do I kiss it on the brow, my warm lips to its papery bone,

and take it to the mirror to ask for a gottle of geer?
I rinse it under the tap, watch dust run away, like sand
from a swimming-cap, then dry it-firstborn-gently
with a towel. I see the scar where I fell for sheer love
down treacherous stairs, and read that shattering day like braille.

Love, I murmur to my skull, then, louder, other grand words,
shouting the hollow nouns in a white-tiled room.
Downstairs they will think I have lost my mind. No. I only weep
into these two holes here, or I'm grinning back at the joke, this is
a friend of mine. See, I hold her face in trembling, passionate hands.

Anne Stevenson

The Spirit Is Too Blunt An Instrument

The spirit is too blunt an instrument
to have made this baby.
Nothing so unskilful as human passions
could have managed the intricate
exacting particulars: the tiny
blind bones with their manipulating tendons,
the knee and the knucklebones, the resilient
fine meshings of ganglia and vertebrae,
the chain of the difficult spine.

Observe the distinct eyelashes and sharp crescent
fingernails, the shell-like complexity
of the ear, with its firm involutions
concentric in miniature to minute
ossicles. Imagine the
infinitesimal capillaries, the flawless connections
of the lungs, the invisible neural filaments
through which the completed body
already answers to the brain.

Then name any passion or sentiment
possessed of the simplest accuracy.
No, no desire or affection could have done
with practice what habit
has done perfectly, indifferently,
through the body's ignorant precision.
It is left to the vagaries of the mind to invent
love and despair and anxiety
and their pain.

The Fury of Cocks

There they are
drooping over the breakfast plates,
angel-like,
folding in their sad wing,
animal sad,
and only the night before
there they were
playing the banjo.
Once more the day's light comes
with its immense sun,
its mother trucks,
its engines of amputation.
Whereas last night
the cock knew its way home,
as stiff as a hammer,
battering in with all
its awful power.
That theater.
Today it is tender,
a small bird,
as soft as a baby's hand.
She is the house.
He is the steeple.
When they fuck they are God.
When they break away they are God.
When they snore they are God.
In the morning they butter the toast.
They don't say much.
They are still God.
All the cocks of the world are God,
blooming, blooming, blooming
into the sweet blood of woman.

Carolyn Jess-Cooke

Inroads

My vein stands up to the mic and sings out a long red note.
I'm at the clinic giving blood, giving what I half-forgot
was brushed under my carpet
of skin at birth, the life-force quietly
moving through cracks under my surface
and now under the spotlight of a nurse's badge
in a sunset, on-stage, belting out a full vial
of velvety Joni blues.
It is shocking that it pours so willingly, that so much births
from the pore-hole needle, but then it seems
that the blood is a kind of blade
parting the air around it
rivering through so much whiteness
and is almost umbilical: the perfect original expressway
that flew from my mother and her mother to me,
the rich blue-red road
that echoes now on the inside of my elbow,
knocking at my skin.
I wish I could become this knife, or at least find a way to mimic
the tuning fork of the needle
that summons the silence of my body to sing.
I wish I could follow the end of the road of blood
that leads not to death
but to all things, to the unseen atom-cloth
from which they cut me and sewed me inside to be cut out again,
to the moment of the wish of me,
over the hip-sweeped dunes to the nebulae nurseries where bone
and tissue and blood weave the soul's coat.

*

You were born of a dying star
so all the melodies of time could storm through your veins,
so the silence of inertia would be drowned
in the aria of your dreams.
Now sing.

Tiffany Atkinson

Sonnet to Hand-Rolled Golden Virginia

You are right. It does come first. White
touchpaper thin as a host, then gunpowder,
fuse, and the rest will follow, sure as breath.
Little promethean acts that set the world
alight. Ritual origami for the spiritually lost.
Forgive the quick intimacy at bars and parties,
for we know each other in the lung, the heart;
smoke-screen wizards all. And I a good enough
person otherwise. I take the stairs. Buy vegetables.
Am a paid-up member of Amnesty International.
I hold down a job, between fag-breaks. Angel I am
not. Everyone needs forgiving. So forgive me, but
I won't quit. And if this helps you to overlook my
other, many, far more grave shortcomings, so be it.

Pattiann Rogers

When You Watch Us Sleeping

When you see us lying scented
in our nightclothes, the patchwork
quilt wadded at our feet, coverlet
kicked aside, when you see us still
at midnight, our bare arms covered
with the moon-shadows of the hemlock
by the window, our hands latent
and half-open on the pillows by our heads;

When you come upon any of us buried
but breathing, close to the earth,
motionless as oak leaves beneath drifts
of oak leaves or curled inside silk
body-vases hanging from greasewood
and vetch or sprawled, languid
under the broad branches
of the baobab in summer heat,
when you hear us humming hoarsely
sometimes, scarcely wheezing, murmuring
like white hens at their roost;

When you watch the green anole
on the banyan, cool and slender
as a pod, the onyx grain of his eye
closed deep in green sunlight,
when you can see how he obviously
possesses in his body, even in the slack
scaly skin of rose beneath his jaw,
even in the posing net of his ribs,
even in the corpuscle of blood
at the tip of his tail,
how he possesses in his body alone
all the power he needs to rise
and declare, not merely truth,
but rapture;

The living body asleep, so great
a sum of beauty that a billion
zeroes follow it, the eyes
sealing the head so tightly
during those moments
that the infinity of possible
heavens inside can be clearly
perceived by anyone;
when you watch us sleeping,
when you see the purest
architecture of the ear,
the explicit faith of the knee,
the old guiltless unforgiving adoring
sweet momentary tremble of claim
in the breast...

Aren't you sorry?
Don't you love us?

Gwendolyn Brooks

The Mother

Abortions will not let you forget.
You remember the children you got that you did not get,
The damp small pulps with a little or with no hair,
The singers and workers that never handled the air.
You will never neglect or beat
Them, or silence or buy with a sweet.
You will never wind up the sucking-thumb
Or scuttle off ghosts that come.
You will never leave them, controlling your luscious sigh,
Return for a snack of them, with gobbling mother-eye.
I have heard in the voices of the wind the voices of my dim
killed children.
I have contracted. I have eased
My dim dears at the breasts they could never suck.
I have said, Sweets, if I sinned, if I seized
Your luck
And your lives from your unfinished reach,
If I stole your births and your names,
Your straight baby tears and your games,
Your stilted or lovely loves, your tumults, your marriages, your aches,
and your deaths,
If I poisoned the beginnings of your breaths,
Believe that even in my deliberateness I was not deliberate.
Though why should I whine,
Whine that the crime was other than mine? –
Since anyhow you are dead.
Or rather, or instead,
You were never made.
But that too, I am afraid,
Is faulty: oh, what shall I say, how is the truth to be said?
You were born, you had body, you died.
It is just that you never giggled or planned or cried.

Believe me, I loved you all.
Believe me, I knew you, though faintly, and I loved, I loved you
All.

Sarah Corbett

Kisses

They are a kiss just in the way they stand.
He leans softly in to her; they have that look.
He holds his first decade in his hands
like his awareness of her, her small heat.

In the next frame they have turned to kiss,
the boy's black hair a scruff in her fist
as she holds him to her. There is intimation
of tongues, of give, and something fiercer.

There is innocence in this, an untaught wisdom,
a curdled-down riff in the pit of it,
a beetle brilliance that catches us once in its heat
as children taking our first kiss.

In the alley by your grandmother's house
he held you to the wall, his mouth open-lipped
on yours, tongued the gaps. You recall
the pressing heat of his breast, a faint tinge

of urine on his breath, the kissing
of legs as he lifted your yellow dress.

Jane Duran

Stillborn

This hurt has beat so long,
turns up with the tide
each month – memorial.

The midwife waits by the bed.
A hand rests on my belly,
trails its design
with sympathy.
Who weeps with me?
I do not recognise
the long white hair.

Bygone – the fire escape,
a point of entry,
a wedge.
The fire hand is austere
all night long
all labour long
undoing.

I touch your foot
before you go
stepping blindly off
no toehold, no notches
to catch at
nothing binding, nothing soft

our child
dropped down through time
through the slats
like a dime.

Here in my bed
I exchange coinage with the night.
The curtain whisks up – seagull edge,
its white barely flaring.
The roof is smitten with rain
and the ends of stories.

Grace Nichols

Because She Has Come

Because she has come
with geometrical designs
upon her breasts

Because she has borne five children
and her belly is criss-crossed
with little tongues of fire

Because she has braided her hair
in the cornrow, twisting it upwards
to show her high inner status

Because she has tucked
a bright wrap
about her Nubian brownness

Because she has stained her toes
with the juice of the henna
to attract any number of arrant males

Because she has the good sense
to wear a scarab
to protect her heart

Because she has a pearl
in the middle
of her lower delta

Give her honour
Give her honour, you fools,
Give her honour.

Sandy Solomon

My Friend Seems Near Tears

My friend seems near tears over a man
she's just visited in another city.
Probably he didn't want to see her
no bear hugs in the kitchen anymore,
no walks with locked arms, no casual kisses.
She says she feels fat and ugly, assuming
the fault is hers and that it's in her body;
something she swallowed, like responsibility;
something she must remember, like, first thing
each day, to shower, curl reluctant hair,
shade the angles of the face again, and dress
so as not to draw attention or cause offense.
I want to shake her to free her of such lessons
as she sits hunched and strangely quieted
across the booth, stirring her coffee too much.
Look at her, so tall and beautiful
when she forgets herself, her whole body
lit with a sloppy, ungovernable brightness,
enthusiasm that doesn't know its place.
Even in despair, it gives itself away,
throwing the mannered order of her face:
one eye tinted perfectly, the other smudged
because she got to talking and forgot and rubbed.

Carol Rumens

Women, Veiled

Because the mouth has been known to tell lies
Because beauty isn't better than compassion
Because we live with two terrors: being looked at, not being looked at
Because we shine without photosynthesis.

Because our eyes are lost birds, beating from dark to dark
Because our foreheads were scorched by the explosion
Because you need room for your house, when you must leave it
And because we mourn for the children, butchered in Crazy Park.

And because you should give death time, though your body blooms with plenty
Because you are mostly liquid. Because you need somewhere to laugh
Because you're the sleeve of Allah. Because of the man you have chosen
Because he is simple. Because you have chosen yourself.

Vuyelwa Carlin

Lydia
(Born, 1910)
from Plaques and Tangles

Tiny Lydia, each little bone outlined;
transulcent Lydia – the vein-map of you:

your fragile fierce arm clings –
"Help me – I've been wrong all my life."

Miniature ivory, flake of alabaster,
airy puff of hair; you mark at a touch –

fairyish thing bruised by the pea
twenty mattresses down. "I'm wrong –

he said so – you know it" – over and over;
Thumbelina's seed of heart, pinched with cold.

Brittle, pressed blanchflower, you hold on –
the lodged hook drags, and drags.

Samantha Wynne-Rhydderch

The X-Ray Room

I am dismantled in monochrome
on the screen opposite the student doctors,
their gaze moving from me here to

me translated into porcelain
there. I am Exhibit A, my symmetry
unmasked by this cut and paste version

of my guts hermeneutically sealed
in negative. I stand by my parallel
text as if to elucidate

evisceration. My bones
in triplicate have nowhere to hide.
Their fragility becomes heraldic

when these exegetes invoke them
in Latin. You see, my other
has been deceiving me all along.

Vassar Miller

On Approaching My Birthday

My mother bore me in the heat of summer
when the grass blanched under sun's hammer stroke
and the birds sang off key, panting between notes,
and the pear trees once all winged with whiteness
sagged, breaking with fruit, and only the zinnias,
like harlots, bloomed out vulgar and audacious,
and when the cicadas played all day long
their hidden harpsichords accompanying
her grief, my mother bore me, as I say,
then died shortly thereafter, no doubt
of her disgust and left me her disease
when I grew up to wither into truth.

Amy Lowell

Penumbra

As I sit here in the quiet Summer night,
Suddenly, from the distant road, there comes
The grind and rush of an electric car.
And, from still farther off,
An engine puffs sharply,
Followed by the drawn-out shunting scrape of a freight train.
These are the sounds that men make
In the long business of living.
They will always make such sounds,
Years after I am dead and cannot hear them.
Sitting here in the Summer night,
I think of my death.
What will it be like for you then?
You will see my chair
With its bright chintz covering
Standing in the afternoon sunshine,
As now.
You will see my narrow table
At which I have written so many hours.
My dogs will push their noses into your hand,
And ask-ask-
Clinging to you with puzzled eyes.
The old house will still be here,
The old house which has known me since the beginning.
The walls which have watched me while I played:
Soldiers, marbles, paper-dolls,
Which have protected me and my books.
The front-door will gaze down among the old trees
Where, as a child, I hunted ghosts and Indians;
It will look out on the wide gravel sweep
Where I rolled my hoop,
And at the rhododendron bushes
Where I caught black-spotted butterflies.
The old house will guard you,
As I have done.
Its walls and rooms will hold you,
And I shall whisper my thoughts and fancies
As always,

From the pages of my books.
You will sit here, some quiet Summer night,
Listening to the puffing trains,
But you will not be lonely,
For these things are a part of me.
And my love will go on speaking to you
Through the chairs, and the tables, and the pictures,
As it does now through my voice,
And the quick, necessary touch of my hand.

Marie Ponsot

Living Room

The window's old & paint-stuck in its frame.
If we force it open the glass may break.
Broken windows cut, and let in the cold

to sharpen house-warm air with outside cold
that aches to buckle every saving frame
& let the wind drive ice in through the break

till chair cupboard walls stormhit all goods break.
The family picture, wrecked, soaked in cold,
would slip wet & dangling out of its frame.
Framed, it's a wind-break. It averts the worst cold.

Eva Salzman

Brooklyn Bridge
designed by Roebling and finished by his daughter-in-law Emily

This one's mine: not a nail-less Bridge of Sighs
nor a stage, where enemies or film crews shoot
but trembling on a net of "wheres" and "whys",
part Asses' Bridge, part Al-Sirat, less Iron Brute,

more hunkering church, grown from Gothic grey
with its cables spun from spiders bred in books.
That dark harp was made for me to play.
And however dark, I couldn't help but look

at ever darker slights, their height and girth
stringing me high above the traffic's hum.
I was harnessed by a yoke of fear, from birth,
less myself while adding to that sum –

the way the architect's now ailing daughter
laid her father's body, right across the water.

Carolyn Beard Whitlow

Rockin' A Man, Stone Blind

Cake in the oven, clothes out on the line,
Night wind blowin' against sweet, yellow thighs,
Two-eyed woman rockin' a man stone blind.

Man smell of honey, dark like coffee grind;
Countin' on his fingers since last July.
Cake in the oven, clothes out on the line.

Mister Jacobs say he be colorblind,
But got to tighten belts and loosen ties.
Two-eyed woman rockin' a man stone blind.

Winter becoming angry, rent behind.
Strapping spring sun needed to make mud pies.
Cake in the oven, clothes out on the line.

Looked in the mirror, Bessie's face I find.
I be so down low, my man be so high.
Two-eyed woman rockin' a man stone blind.

Policeman's found him; damn near lost my mind.
Can't afford no flowers; can't even cry.
Cake in the oven, clothes out on the line.
Two-eyed woman rockin' a man stone blind.

Roo Borson

Water Memory

Water does not remember, it moves
among reeds, nudges the little boat
(a little), effloresces a shadowy fog
which forgets for us the way home
though the warm dry rooms are
in us. (Stretched on the examining table we
feel it when the unfamiliar hand
presses just there.) Water,
on its own, would not remember,
but herd follows herd, and memory is a shepherd
of the gentlest wants. Not even blood
can recall, though the live
kidney shipped in its special box
wakes up one day in someone new.
No one made this world, there's no need
to feel ashamed. Be water,
find a lower place, go there.

Linda Hogan

Skin

The men wore human skins
but removed them at night
and fell to the bottom of darkness
like crows without wings.

War was the perfect disguise.
Their mothers would not have known them,
and the swarming flies could not find them.

When they met a spirit in the forest
it thought they were bags of misfortune
and walked away
without taking their lives.

In this way, they tricked the deer.
It had wandered into the forest at night,
thinking antlers of trees
were other deer.

If I told you the deer was a hide of light
you wouldn't believe it, or that it was a hunting song
that walked out of a diviner's bag
sewn from human skin.

It knew it could pass
through the bodies of men and could return.
It knew the arrow belonged to the bow,
and that men only think they are following
the deaths of animals
or other men
when they are walking into the fire.

That's why fire is restless
and smoke has become
the escaped wings of crows,
why war is only another skin,
and hunting,
and why men are just the pulled-back curve of the bow.

Sandra Alcosser

Mare Frigoris

Coming home late spring night, stars a foreign
Language above me, I thought I would know

The moons like family, their dark plains – sea of
Crises, sea of nectar, serpent sea.

How quickly a century passes,
Minerals crystallize at different speeds,

Limestone dissolves, rivers sneak through its absence.
This morning I learned painted turtles

Sleeping inches below the streamback
Freeze and do not die. Fifteen degrees

Mare Frigoris, sea of cold, second
Quadrant of the moon's face. I slide toward

The cabin, arms full of brown bags, one light
Syrups over drifts of snow. Night rubs

Icy skin against me and I warm
Small delicates – cilantro, primrose –

Close to my body. A hundred million
Impulses race three hundred miles an hour

Through seventeen square feet of skin and
Gravity that collapses stars, lifts earth's

Watery dress from her body, touches me
With such tenderness I hardly breathe.

13. Insiders, Outsiders

Culture, Heritage, Identity, Displacement & Exile

Nuala Ní Dhomhnaill

The Language Issue

I place my hope on the water
in this little boat
of the language, the way a body might put
an infant

in a basket of intertwined
iris leaves
its underside proofed
with bitumen and pitch,

then set the whole thing down amidst
the sedge
and bulrushes by the edge
of a river

only to have it borne hither and thither,
not knowing where it might end up;
in the lap, perhaps,
of some Pharaoh's daughter.

(translated from Irish by Paul Muldoon)

Diane Glancy

Christopher

Here come Christopher Columbus comming ober t'wabes.
PUFF, PUFF.
He think he come to the segund part of urth.
His shups bump inter land at night
y haze la senal dla cruz.
Hey Yndias. He say. HEY ERMERICA.
He brang glaz beads & bells.
Luego se ayunto alli mucha gente dla Isla.
We think he god from skie. Yup. Yup. Wedu.
The blue oshen sprad like a table napkin by his shups.
Como el por ante todos toma
va como de hecho tomo possession dla dha.
Yaz. He say. I take. Now whar find GOLD?
Our har like harsehair. He say.
He look our fish tooth on spears. HAR HAR. He laf.
Los reyes wand gold. Gloria religion xpiana.
Gloria Yndias. He say. Y load his shups. Wedu.
Thar go Christopher. Huf. Huf.
Wid gold he own t'segund urth.
Wid gold he buy our souls inter heaben.

Donna Kate Rushin

The Bridge Poem

I've had enough
I'm sick of seeing and touching
Both sides of things
Sick of being the damn bridge for everybody

Nobody
Can talk to anybody
Without me
Right?

I explain my mother to my father
My father to my little sister
My little sister to my brother
My brother to the white feminists
The white feminists to the Black church folks
The Black church folks to the ex-hippies
The ex-hippies to the Black separatists
The Black separatists to the artists
The artists to my friends' parents...

Then
I've got to explain myself
To everybody

I do more translating
Than the Gawdamn U.N.

Forget it
I'm sick of it.

I'm sick of filling in your gaps

Sick of being your insurance against
The isolation of your self-imposed limitations
Sick of being the crazy at your holiday dinners
Sick of being the odd one at your Sunday Brunches
Sick of being the sole Black friend to 34 individual white people

Find another connection to the rest of the world
Find something else to make you legitimate
Find some other way to be political and hip

I will not be the bridge to your womanhood
Your manhood
Your humanness

I'm sick of reminding you not to
Close off too tight for too long

I'm sick of mediating with your worst self
On behalf of your better selves

I am sick
Of having to remind you
To breathe
Before you suffocate
Your own fool self
Forget it
Stretch or drown
Evolve or die
The bridge I must be
Is the bridge to my own power
I must translate
My own fears
Mediate
My own weaknesses
I must be the bridge to nowhere
But my true self
And then
I will be useful

Angelina Weld Grimke

Fragment

I am the woman with the black black skin
I am the laughing woman with the black black face
I am living in the cellars and in every crowded place
    I am toiling just to eat
      In the cold and in the heat
        And I laugh
I am the laughing woman who's forgotten how to weep
I am the laughing woman who's afraid to go to sleep

Nikki-Rosa

childhood remembrances are always a drag
if you're Black
you always remember things like living in Woodlawn
with no inside toilet
and if you become famous or something
they never talk about how happy you were to have
your mother
all to yourself and
how good the water felt when you got your bath
from one of those
big tubs that folk in Chicago barbecue in
and somehow when you talk about home
it never gets across how much you
understood their feelings
as the whole family attended meetings about Hollydale
and even though you remember
your biographers never understand
your father's pain as he sells his stock
and another dream goes.
And though you're poor it isn't poverty that
concerns you
and though they fought a lot
it isn't your father's drinking that makes any difference
but only that everybody is together and you
and your sister have happy birthdays and very good
Christmases
and I really hope no white person ever has cause
to write about me
because they never understand
Black love is Black wealth and they'll
probably talk about my hard childhood
and never understand that
all the while I was quite happy

Marilyn Nelson

Chopin

It's Sunday evening. Pomp holds the receipts
of all the colored families on the Hill
in his wide lap, and shows which white store cheats
these patrons, who can't read a weekly bill.
His parlor's full of men holding their hats
and women who admire his girls' good hair.
Pomp warns them not to trust the Democrats,
controlling half of Hickman from his chair.
The varying degrees of cheating seen,
he nods toward the piano. Slender, tall,
a Fisk girl passing-white, almost nineteen,
his Blanche folds the piano's paisley shawl
and plays Chopin. And blessed are the meek
who have to buy in white men's stores next week.

P.K. Page

Brazilian Fazenda

That day all the slaves were freed
their manacles, anklets
left on the window ledge to rust in the moist air

and all the coffee ripened
like beads on a bush or balls of fire
as merry as Christmas

and the cows all calved and the calves all lived
such a moo.

On the wide verandah where birds in cages
sang among the bell flowers
I in a bridal hammock
white and tasselled
whistled

and bits fell out of the sky near Nossa Senhora
who had walked all the way in bare feet from Bahia

and the chapel was lit by a child's
fistful of marigolds on the red velvet altar
thrown like a golden ball.

Oh, let me come back on a day
when nothing extraordinary happens
so I can stare
at the sugar white pillars
and black lace grills
of this pink house.

Eva Salzman

The Refinery

You cannot look at narrow-brush moustaches.
You cannot think about gas-cookers, their ovens
flame-rimmed, the diadem of fire, or hear the bell
when it's done. Or think of teeth, lamp-shades, soap,
the refinery chimney-stacks, puffing cheerfully.

You cannot raise your hand in history class
to ask a simple question; your arm freezes
in a parody of salute. You cannot write "horror"
because horror is a good film for anyone
with a strong stomach and a taste for gore.

Anyway, the antique photographs are grainy,
have blurred into art – that Vaseline trick with the lens.

At dinner you sip the rot-gut wine
and listen to the table-talk – an operation botched
or an ache in the joints the doctor couldn't diagnose.
You choke with rage at the meal, gibbering,
while the devil samples your soul like buttered croissant.

Gertrude Stein
America

Once in English they said America. Was it English to them.
Once they said Belgian.
We like a fog.
Do you for weather.
Are we brave.
Are we true.
Have we the national colour.
Can we stand ditches.
Can we mean well.
Do we talk together.
Have we red cross.
A great many people speak of feet.
And socks.

Emma Lazarus
The New Colossus

Not like the brazen giant of Greek fame,
With conquering limbs astride from land to land;
Here at our sea-washed, sunset gates shall stand
A mighty woman with a torch, whose flame
Is the imprisoned lightning, and her name
Mother of Exiles. From her beacon-hand
Glows world-wide welcome; her mild eyes command
The air-bridged harbor that twin cities frame.
"Keep, ancient lands, your storied pomp!" cries she
With silent lips. "Give me your tired, your poor,
Your huddled masses yearning to breathe free,
The wretched refuse of your teeming shore.
Send these, the homeless, tempest-tost to me,
I lift my lamp beside the golden door!"

Judith Rodriguez

How Come The Truck-Loads?

Somehow the tutorial takes an unplanned direction:
anti-semitism.
A scholastic devil advances the suggestion
that two sides can be found to every question.
Right.
Now, who's an anti-Semite?
One hand.
Late thirties, in the 1960s. Bland.
Let's see now; tell us, on what texts or Jews
do you base your views?
There was a landlord, from Poland, that I had.
Bad?
A shrug. Well, what did he do?
Pretty mean chasing up rent. Ah. Tough.
And who
else? No one else. One's enough.

Sandra M. Gilbert

Going To Connecticut
for J.R.

More than a third of a century later,
meeting for the first time in almost all those years,

we face each other's still somewhat familiar faces
across a table in a California restaurant,

and wonder why we did it, why we suddenly said
that night in July in Greenwich Village

"Let's go to Connecticut," and got on a train
and ended up at midnight in Old Greenwich, Connecticut,

holding hands on an empty road that wound past
serious grown-up sleeping houses ....

Well, I was fifteen, you were nearly twenty-one, we were
                                                      experimentally
"in love," and I guess it must have seemed

like "something to do" – better than Remo anyway,
or the coffee houses, or the Eighth Street Bookstore,

even, in that scratchy heat,
better than Jones Beach: the long low

sober train boring into a wall of black, the alien
townships spurting past on either side

(nothing very built up then),
each with its deserted, brilliant platform

waiting for the next day's passengers, the real
people who really needed to ride that train.

How cindery the windows were,
and spooky with moths outside the glamorous

club car where we sat with sodas
on itchy plush reclining seats!

And how the crickets simmered
where we got out, dizzy on 7UP!

Remember the hedges – lilac, honeysuckle –
along the way, as we walked toward

we didn't know where?
We kissed a little

under one, tasting salt and 7UP
on each other, not sure what next

or where, then peered at
the shadows on lawn after lawn, the dim

bulk of chimneys, shapes of shutters,
here a trike, there a plastic pool,

and couples snoring, mysterious,
behind those tall white walls,

until we got embarrassed, still not sure what next,
retraced our steps, boarded another train,

and were hurried back to where we came from,
feeling like voyeurs, like trespassers.

Stephanie Bolster

Train Windows

The first train came to me
like this: unstoppable force.
I stood aside at Fredericton Junction
and let the speed and flare approach.
Wind flailed my hair, the gathered dark

dispersed. I found my room
of pull-out bed and pull-up blind.
A solitude so rare, uncracked, I
couldn't sleep. Morning: I tugged

the shade and empty ponds appeared.
We were that close to something;
the surface still rippled.
We were late for Montréal, New York,

for the years that would come, were gone,
were here. Years of blurred views through
windows. The engine approached,
I was alone, I held my breath

and didn't let it out, and haven't.

Chase Twichell

Horse

I've never seen a soul detached from its gender,
but I'd like to. I'd like to see my own that way,
free of its female tethers. Maybe it would be like
riding a horse. The rider's the human one,
but everyone looks at the horse.

Fiona Sampson

Hay-on-Wye

Slim as a nun, I lie along
the margin of a borrowed bed
whose springs are texting, through my bones,
Abandon hope. Abandonment –

ecstasy of fall. I gaze
up into a godless dark
as if it might disclose some way
of getting right back, to the start

of that unselfconscious wish
for (old-fashioned diction…) *joy.*
And dark stares back. True, I'm pissed
again. But must the old alloy

always split along these seams –
is this, then, what incarnation means?

Lucille Clifton

The Lost Women

i need to know their names
those women i would have walked with
jauntily the way men go in groups
swinging their arms, and the ones
those sweating women whom i would have joined
after a hard game to chew the fat
what would we have called each other laughing
joking into our beer? where are my gangs,
my teams, my mislaid sisters?
all the women who could have known me,
where in the world are their names?

Amanda Dalton

How To Disappear

First rehearse the easy things.
Lose your words in a high wind,
walk in the dark on an unlit road,
observe how other people mislay keys,
their diaries, new umbrellas.
See what it takes to go unnoticed
in a crowded room. Tell lies:
I love you. I'll be back in half an hour.
I'm fine.

Then childish things.
Stand very still behind a tree,
become a cowboy, say you've died,
climb into wardrobes, breathe on a mirror

until there's no one there, and practise magic,
tricks with smoke and fire –
a flick of the wrist and the victim's lost
his watch, his wife, his ten pound note. Perfect it.
Hold your breath a little longer every time.

The hardest things.
Eat less, much less, and take a vow of silence.
Learn the point of vanishing, the moment
embers turn to ash, the sun falls down,
the sudden white-out comes.
And when it comes again – it will –
just walk at it, walk into it, and walk,
until you know that you're no longer
anywhere.

Sujata Bhatt

Muliebrity

I have thought so much about the girl
who gathered cow-dung in a wide, round basket
along the main road passing by our house
and the Radhavallabh temple in Maninagar.
I have thought so much about the way she
moved her hands and her waist
and the smell of cow-dung and road-dust and wet canna lilies,
the smell of monkey breath and freshly washed clothes
and the dust from crows' wings which smells different –
and again the smell of cow-dung as the girl scoops
it up, all these smells surrounding me separately
and simultaneously – I have thought so much
but have been unwilling to use her for a metaphor,
for a nice image – but most of all unwilling
to forget her or to explain to anyone the greatness
and the power glistening through her cheekbones
each time she found a particularly promising
mound of dung –

Moniza Alvi

Map of India

If I stare at the country long enough
I can prise it off the paper,
lift it like a flap of skin.

Sometimes it's an advent calendar –
each city has a window
which I leave open
a little wider each time.

India is manageable – smaller than
my hand, the Mahanadi River
thinner than my lifeline.

Choman Hardi

My Children

I can hear them talking, my children
fluent English and broken Kurdish.

And whenever I disagree with them
they will comfort each other by saying:
Don't worry about mum, she Kurdish.

Will I be the foreigner in my own home?

Rosemary Tonks

Done For!

Take care whom you mix with in life, irresponsible one,
For if you mix with the wrong people
– And you yourself may be one of the wrong people –
if you make love to the wrong person,

In some old building with its fabric of dirt,
As clouds of witchcraft, nitro-glycerine and cake,
Brush by (one autumn night) still green
From our green sunsets... and then let hundreds pass, unlit,

They will do you ferocious, indelible harm!
Far beyond anything you can imagine, jazzy sneering one,
And afterwards you'll live in no man's land,
You'll lose your identity, and never get yourself back.

It may have happened already, and as you read this
Ah, it *has* happened already. I remember, in an old building;
Clouds which had cut themselves on a sharp winter sunset
(With its smoking stove of frosts to keep it cold) went by,
bleeding.

Josephine Miles
Ride

It's not my world, I grant, but I made it.
It's not my ranch, lean oak, buzzard crow,
Not my fryers, mixmaster, well-garden.
And now it's down the road, and I made it.

It's not your rackety car but you drive it.
It's not your four-door, top-speed, white-wall tires,
Not even our state, not even, I guess, our nation,
But now it's down the road, and we're in it.

Carol Ann Duffy
Selling Manhattan

All yours, Injun, twenty-four bucks worth of glass beads,
gaudy cloth. I got myself a bargain. I brandish
fire-arms and fire-water. Praise the Lord.
Now get your red ass out of here.

I wonder if the ground has anything to say.
You have made me drunk, drowned out
the world's slow truth with rapid lies.
But today I hear again and plainly see. Wherever
you have touched the earth, the earth is sore.

I wonder if the spirit of the water has anything
to say. That you will poison it. That you
can no more own the rivers and the grass than own
the air. I sing with true love for the land;
dawn chant, the song of sunset, starlight psalm.

Trust your dreams. No good will come of this.
My heart is on the ground, as when my loved one
fell back in my arms and died. I have learned
the solemn laws of joy and sorrow, in the distance
between morning's frost and firefly's flash at night.

Man who fears death, how many acres do you need
to lengthen your shadow under the endless sky?
Last time, this moment, a boy feels his freedom
vanish, like a salmon going mysteriously
out to sea. Loss holds the silence of great stones.

I will live in the ghost of grasshopper and buffalo.
The evening trembles and is sad.
A little shadow runs across the grass
and disappears into the darkening pines.

Emily Dickinson

67

Success is counted sweetest
By those who ne'er succeed.
To comprehend a nectar
Requires sorest need.

Not one of all the purple Host
Who took the Flag today
Can tell the definition
So clear of Victory

As he defeated – dying –
On whose forbidden ear
The distant strains of triumph
Burst agonized and clear!

14. How The World Works

History, Politics, War, Society

Carolyn Forché

The Colonel

What you have heard is true. I was in his house. His wife carried
a tray of coffee and sugar. His daughter filed her nails, his son went
out for the night. There were daily papers, pet dogs, a pistol on the
cushion beside him. The moon swung bare on its black cord over
the house. On the television was a cop show. It was in English.
Broken bottles were embedded in the walls around the house to
scoop the kneecaps from a man's legs or cut his hands to lace. On
the windows there were gratings like those in liquor stores. We had
dinner, rack of lamb, good wine, a gold bell was on the table for
calling the maid. The maid brought green mangoes, salt, a type of
bread. I was asked how I enjoyed the country. There was a brief
commercial in Spanish. His wife took everything away. There was
some talk of how difficult it had become to govern. The parrot
said hello on the terrace. The colonel told it to shut up, and pushed
himself from the table. My friend said to me with his eyes: say
nothing. The colonel returned with a sack used to bring groceries
home. He spilled many human ears on the table. They were like
dried peach halves. There is no other way to say this. He took one
of them in his hands, shook it in our faces, dropped it into a water
glass. It came alive there. I am tired of fooling around he said. As
for the rights of anyone, tell your people they can go fuck them-
selves. He swept the ears to the floor with his arm and held the last
of his wine in the air. Something for your poetry, no? he said. Some
of the ears on the floor caught this scrap of his voice. Some of the
ears on the floor were pressed to the ground.

Louise Bogan

Question in a Field

Pasture, stone wall, and steeple
what most perturbs the mind:
the heart-rending homely people,
or the horrible beautiful kind?

Kate Clanchy

War Poetry

The class has dropped its books. The janitor's
disturbed some wasps, broomed the nest
straight off the roof. It lies outside, exotic
as a fallen planet, a burst city of the poor;
its newsprint halls, its ashen, tiny rooms ,
all open to the air. The insects' buzz
is low-key as a smart machine. They group,
regroup, in stacks and coils, advance
and cross like pulsing points on radar screens.

And though the boys have shaven heads
and football strips, and would, they swear,
enlist at once, given half a chance, yes,
march down Owen's darkening lanes
to join the lads and stuff the Boche –
they don't rush out to pike the nest,
or lap the yard with grapeshot faces.
They watch the wasps through glass,
silently, abashed, the way we all watch war.

Emily Dickinson

341

After great pain, a formal feeling comes –
The Nerves sit ceremonious, like Tombs –
The stiff heart questions was it He, that bore,
And Yesterday, or Centuries before?

The Feet, mechanical, go round –
Of Ground, or Air, or Ought –
A Wooden way
Regardless grown,
A Quartz contentment, like a stone –

This is the Hour of Lead –
Remembered, if outlived,
As Freezing persons, recollect the Snow –
First – Chill – then Stupor – then the letting go –

Katha Pollitt

Trying to Write a Poem Against the War

My daughter, who's as beautiful as the day,
hates politics: Face it, Ma,
they don't care what you think! All
passion, like Achilles,
she stalks off to her room,
to confide in her purple guitar and await
life's embassies. She's right,
of course: bombs will be hurled
at ordinary streets
and leaders look grave for the cameras,
and what good are more poems against war
the real subject of which
so often seems to be the poet's superior
moral sensitivities? I could
be mailing myself to the moon
or marrying a palm tree,
and yet what can we do
but offer what we have?
and so I spend
this cold gray glittering morning
trying to write a poem against war
that perhaps may please my daughter
who hates politics
and does not care much for poetry, either.

Olive Senior

Join-the-Dots

*In the sample of 282 plantation maps drawn from the
National Library of Jamaica's collection, some 25 per cent
show the "village" area as a blank.*
    – Barry Higman, *Jamaica Surveyed*

We played at Join-the-Dots, Grandma and me,
but never could we win the prize.
For I saw pictures she could not see.
They said I had clear-seeing eyes.

Our house was built on land where once
a village stood. Where fragments
floating in the air sometimes cried out
for personhood.

They pounded on the rooftop, tore at
the gutter. "Hush, it is the wind",
Grandma said, but I knew better
though I would never

utter a word. For I was sworn to secrets.
"This is where we once lived too,"
the children said. "We'd like
to play with you."

When I could not sleep for black dots
floating, Grandma said, "Hush,
I'll bring you cocoa-tea sweetened
with cane sugar and

a hint of nutmeg. That will calm you
down." I'd try to share it with my
ghostly friends who said they
lived in land-snail shells

and sailed all night the village round.
Their Old One said: "No. You drink up,
child. For this our bodies
turned to dust. Ground

into fields of sugar cane, of cocoa-walks,
of nutmeg groves. Drink.
In remembrance of us".
I'd drain the cup.

The cocoa, cane sugar, the nutmeg, touched me
so sweetly, I'd sleep long. Sleep deeply.

Maya Angelou

These Yet-To-Be-United States

Tremors of your network
cause kings to disappear.
Your open mouth in anger
makes nations bow in fear.

Your bombs can change the seasons,
obliterate the spring.
What more do you long for?
Why are you suffering?

You control the human lives
in Rome and Timbuktu.
Lonely nomads wandering
owe Telstar to you.

Seas shift at your bidding,
your mushrooms fill the sky.
Why are you unhappy?
Why do your children cry?

They kneel alone in terror
with dread in every glance.
Their rights
are threatened daily
by a grim inheritance.

You dwell in whitened castles
with deep and poisoned moats
and cannot hear the curses
which fill your children's throats.

Marilyn Hacker

Ghazal: min al-hobbi ma khatal

for Deema Shehabi

You, old friend, leave, but who releases me from the love that kills?
Can you tell the love that sets you free from the love that kills?

No mail again this morning. The retired diplomat
stifles in the day's complacency from the love that kills.

What once was home is across what once was a border
which exiles gaze at longingly from the love that kills.

The all-night dancer, the mother of four, the tired young doctor
all contracted HIV from the love that kills.

There is pleasure, too, in writing easy, dishonest verses.
Nothing protects your poetry from the love that kills.

The coloratura keens a triumphant swan-song
as if she sipped an elixir of glee from the love that kills.

We learn the maxim: "So fine the thread,
so sharp the necessity" from the love that kills.

The calligrapher went blind from his precision
and yet he claims he learned to see from the love that kills.

Spare me, she prays, from dreams of the town I grew up in,
from involuntary memory, from the love that kills.

Homesick soldier, do you sweat in the glare of this check-point
to guard the homesick refugee from the love that kills?

Elizabeth Daryush

Children of Wealth

Children of wealth in your warm nursery,
Set in the cushioned window-seat to watch
The volleying snow, guarded invisibly
By the clear double pane through which no touch
Untimely penetrates, you cannot tell
What winter means; its cruel truths to you
Are only sound and sight; your citadel
Is safe from feeling, and from knowledge too.
Go down, go out to elemental wrong,
Waste your too round limbs, tan your skin too white;
The glass of comfort, ignorance, seems strong
Today, and yet perhaps this very night
You'll wake to horror's wrecking fire – your home
Is wired within for this, in every room.

Valerie Bloom

Yuh Hear 'bout...?

Yuh hear 'bout de people dem arres
fi bun dung de Asian people dem house?
Yuh hear 'bout de policeman dem lock up
fi beat up de black bwoy widout a cause?
Yuh hear 'bout de M.P. dem sack
because im refuse fi help im black constituents
eena dem fight 'gainst deportation?
Yuh noh hear 'bout dem?
Me neida.

Diane Ackerman

Afterthought

Toadies thick as an Egyptian plague
line your office each afternoon.
Wit-lame and mincing, they backpat or effuse.
People stop in the hallways to discuss your mood,
the deft, the spoonfed, those with brains of rattan.
Stricken, I wince as you rally each
with well-tried, if tonic, deceits.
Sweet years, I rode your faith's catamaran,
thought I'd a special affection specially won.
When my metal fretted, lest it fly apart,
I coiled you round the mainspring of my heart.
But you were lukewarm to me as to any other,
nesting your indifference in charm.
All the while I flourished in your countenance,
you gulled me, you led me a dance,
wooed me as protégé, lady-love, confrere,
when you never cared, you never cared.

Lynette Roberts

Englyn

Where poverty stikes the pavement – there is found
No cripple like contentment
Which stultifies all statement
Of bright thought from the brain's tent.

Some Bores Are Just Born

Why are you wearing those trousers?
My mother is famous in America.
I'm going to get three new pairs of jeans and a jumper
    and four tops at the weekend. My granddad gave me
    three hundred pounds.
And he bought me a huge encyclopaedia. All the boys
    hate your new clothes, I went round and asked them
    all and they all said it and I said she's my best friend.
    All the boys like me best, they said it at break time.
    You look so weird in that coat and your small head
    in that hat. Lyra said so.
Please, I'm speaking and anyway there I was and I broke
    my leg and I couldn't walk and the teachers were
    horrible to me.
That book looks really boring and that German teacher,
    she's horrible, she doesn't know her job. I don't mind
    telling her either.
But I couldn't believe how horrible he was to you.
Why is your mother slapping those playing cards so hard
    on the table?
Why is she always playing Patience when I come
    around?
Oh, yes, well I've been to France seventeen times.
She is horrible, she is.
And rude, too. You are mental, but please you are, please
    I'm speaking, it's very rude to interrupt, my very best
    friend.

Daisy Fried

A Story Having To Do With Walt Whitman

A friend of mine used to be, and still is, but only
legally, married to a dancer. The girl, this dancer,
his wife, had a teacher, one of those beautiful menschy
dancer men, who was dying of AIDS. He, the teacher,
as I imagine it, though it's not always true for dancers
in his company, had done nothing in his life but dance.
Well, that's perfectly good enough. But the girl, this dancer, this
wife, who read as well as danced, thought she would bring him
Leaves of Grass, with the not inconsiderable presumption
that it would comfort him to the great end. (Presumptions need
not be false. It would have.) But this girl, the dancer, the wife,
once she realized that she had presumed, ascribing to her
gift and thus to herself a certain importance, worried
about it so much that she put off bringing it to him.

He lay at home and sometimes in the hospital, with
many friends in bright-colored clothes around him (they all used
to wear black and white, but thinking of death, they put on
rainbows). The girl, the wife, the dancer, worried and worried,
about walking into the room of many colors. It
was not her wardrobe, she was not worried about that, though
she wore mostly grays, maroons, browns. She worried about
stepping forward in that crowd, having them look at her,
who did not even know if the dying man cared about her.
She worried she would be seen for what she was, not a friend,
but a pupil, and adorer. So he died and she
never brought the book. When she realized her foolishness,
as she always did, immediately after the moment
when it was too late, she just went down to the East River

and sat on a pier and looked at Manhattan and felt shame.
The book, a pretty hardback, in her lap. She sat and read
it, the whole thing. She thought several things as she read. One,
how can you die, not having read everything. Another,
how all actions should be as if for others, even if
none truly are. Three, how awful to die in the summer.
Four. She missed her husband, my friend. Five. She must work harder
at dancing. Six, what did it really matter if he
never read *Leaves of Grass*. Did it matter to the soul?
Seven, oh for goodness sake, what soul? The next day, she
agreed at his funeral to help clean out his
apartment. On his coffee table there was a Monet
with bad reproductions, Richardson's *Life of Picasso,*
Vol. 2 (the cubist years), autobiographies of

choreographers, and a battered paperback: *Leaves of Grass,*
what do you think? She opened it and found it all marked
up inside, with comments and all. Comments about how one could
make a dance with all this in mind. And she all of a
sudden remembered seeing the title "Afraid of the
Merge" on his list of choreography credits. Inside
the front cover it said "To my darling, from Gary." Instead
of this making this girl, the dancer, the wife laugh, or see the
humor in the whole thing, or at least see that she had read
him right, and picked the right gift, she just felt miserable.
This is why my friend and she had trouble getting along, for
he is not so complex and constipated as this girl, this
dancer, his wife. What happened? Oh, I expect she'll get over it.
Oh, one more thing. I am the girl, this dancer, this wife.

Ruth Stone

Resonance

The universe is sad.
I heard it when Artur Rubenstein played the piano.
He was a little man with small hands.
We were bombing Germany by then.
I went to see him in a dark warehouse
where a piano had been placed for his practice –
or whatever he did before a recital.
He signed the book I had with me –
it was called *Warsaw Ghetto.*
I later heard about about him –
his affairs with young women
– if only I had known – but I was
in love with you.
Artur is dead;
and you, my darling,
the imprint of your face, alert like a deer –
oh god, it is eaten away –
the earth has taken it back
but I listen to Artur –
he springs out of the grave –
his genius wired to this tape –
a sad trick of the neural pathways, resonating flesh
and my old body remembers the way you touched me.

June Jordan

The Reception

Doretha wore the short blue lace last night
and William watched her drinking so she fight
with him in flying collar slim-jim orange
tie and alligator belt below the navel pants uptight

"I flirt. You hear me? Yes I flirt.
Been on my pretty knees all week
to clean the rich white downtown dirt
the greedy garbage money reek.

I flirt. Damned right. You look at me."
But William watched her carefully
his mustache shaky she could see
him jealous, "which is how he always be

at parties." Clementine and Wilhelmina
looked at trouble in the light blue lace
and held to George while Roosevelt Senior
circled by the yella high and bitterly light blue face

he liked because she worked
the crowded room like clay like molding men
from dust to muscle jerked
and arms and shoulders moving when

she moved. The Lord Almighty Seagrams bless
Doretha in her short blue dress
and Roosevelt waiting for his chance:
a true gut-funky blues to make her really dance.

Peggy Shumaker

Oatmeal

Dry slide of Bob's Red Mill
Extra Thick Rolled Oats
off the scoop tiny
dustcloud
settling like ash
from stirred coals.
Waking together,
happy, not
our first try.

Zoë Skoulding

The Mirror Trade

Air shines. We snare it in our glass
with furnaces and transubstantiations,
quicksilver and tin amalgams.
We steal water from fire

then craft pure depth to capture space, annex
the country of illusions which looks in on us,
envying our every move,
always identical and opposite.

It's death to leave the island with this knowledge.
As we load mirrors, ships
bleed pictures of more ships
which lap the warehouse steps; we send out
pieces of ourselves which bear no trace of us.

Elizabeth Spires

Waving Goodbye

The world bends us to its purpose.
In the public gardens, we found
a "gazing globe" balanced
on a waist-high pedestal,
a silver ball a foot in circumference,
reflecting sky and ground,
ourselves as we stood above it.
We stared into its depths,
as in a crystal ball,
our faces large and wild,
arms and legs unnaturally small,
as if a spell were on the world,
or, finally, we clearly saw the world
for what it was: too brightly
shining, circular, unadorned.

Trees bent toward us, mere shadows
of themselves, their shadows
more substantial than the trees themselves.
The sky at one o'clock
a milky white, light-filled,
yet without sun or cloud. And beds
of tulips rising from the groundswell,
each one a little mouth.
I knelt beside you on one knee,
caught up in walls of air
I couldn't touch or see, the outer world
around me wavering, as on a hot summer day.

We looked out to the future. Our future
selves. You stood dead center
in the globe and raised your hand to stop
the scene, your palm enlarging
until it dwarfed the tallest trees.
Then waving goodbye, we walked,
as a joke, backward and away,
farther and farther away –
the globe still gazing on us –
leaving ourselves behind
to live forever in that silver room,
to watch and spy on lovers like ourselves.

Kathleen Raine

The Moment

To write down all I contain at this moment
I would pour the desert through an hour-glass,
The sea through a water-clock,
Grain by grain and drop by drop
Let in the trackless, measureless, mutable seas and sands.

For earth's days and nights are breaking over me,
The tides and sands are running through me,
And I have only two hands and a heart to hold the desert and the sea.

What can I contain of it? It escapes and eludes me,
The tides wash me away,
The desert shifts under my feet.

Siobhán Campbell

Recall

Pitiless, disease and hunger spread.
Our people fled. We live now
knowing we are those
who bullied, stole and beat.
O'Hare, Kelly, Campbell, Helly –
take heed for we survived.
Our curse is that we've understood
what hurts: we know the will
that curls a feeding smile;
we have been merciless and thrived.

Katrina Porteous

Seven Silences

(excerpt from 'An Ill Wind')

These are the seven silences of a black season:
First, all movement frozen. Shut down
The invisible machinery of the countryside – the hunt, the patter,
The auctioneer's song.

Next comes the silence you wait for the telephone to shatter.
You can't sleep. Can't eat. The silence of fear
Crackles like electricity down the wires; and the silence of paper
Drifts like snow through the door.

Such a queer thing to tell in sheep: a lamb a bit "hangy"
Or a ewe that will not come to the trough.
Ice-sharp, the silence after the vet has given his verdict.
This is the silence of disbelief.

The next silence is the worst silence. This is the silence
Of the steaming kitchen at three a.m.
When half the cattle lie stiff in the yard and half are still waiting.
This is a silence with no name.

The sixth silence is the silence of grass growing,
Oceans of grass that hush, hush in the wind.
It is hard to get used to this silence: grass growing, and questions
Swelling like streams underground.

And what will you do with all the questions? When a whisper,
    a rush, a torrent
Bursts from the farmyard into Whitehall, what will you get?
Nothing but frozen faces, and the last silence:
A barred gate.

Jane Routh

Tell Me What Else

Now tell me why. Tell me about greed.
Show me how to think about infinity.
How far does war go down with you?
Make me a list of what counts. Explain
why you think the moon's the same size
as the sun: your answer's who you are.
Say how three brothers trouble sleep,
turn, and draw their brown cloaks close
as they approach the arch – whether
they visit from another life, or whether
they're already dreamed and something
in your brain has named them wrongly.
No more about roses or snowdrops
but tell me about your sly animal self
among the dry ochre grasses of winter.
Or tell me about the moment when you sit
on a boulder in the river and you are the river,
you are the alders and the early morning air
and the deer who doesn't see you, high-stepping
among cobbles at the crossing place
on such thin legs.

Kate Lilley

Cento/Around Vienna

A girl may harden herself
in the conviction that she does possess a penis
I had the usual feeling of anxiety that one has
in the somewhat haphazard order in which it recurs
I saw myself particularly distinctly
"Why did I say nothing about the scene by the lake
for some days after it had happened?
Why did I then suddenly tell my parents about it?"
A normal girl, I am inclined to think,
will deal with a situation of this kind by herself
I will begin by mentioning the subject-matter
he intended to come forward as a suitor one day
what was the source of the words "if you like?"
there was a question mark after this word, thus "like?"

She might calmly read whatever she chose
"vorhof" ["vestibulum"; literally "fore-court"] –
an anatomical term for a particular
region of the female genitals
She had left home and gone among strangers
to this came the addendum not the least sadly
her father's heart had broken with grief and longing
he could not get to sleep without a drink of brandy
sexual satisfaction is the best soporific
She then recognized these words as a quotation
her knowing all about such things and at the same time
pretending not to know was really too remarkable
the feelings of pity for him which she remembered
from the day before would be quite in keeping with this

In repeating the dream she said "two hours"
so here we were back again at the scene by the lake
no sooner had she grasped the purport of his words
than she had slapped him in the face and hurried away
"you know I get nothing out of my wife"
Her father was dead and she had left home by her own choice
this fact determines the psychical coating
In the background of the picture there were *nymphs*
the neurosis had seized upon this chance event
and made use of it for an utterance of its own
They are therefore questions referring to – the genitals

wandering about in a strange town was overdetermined
my expectations were by no means disappointed
You give me a fortnight's warning just like a governess

Denise Levertov

Hypocrite Women

Hypocrite women, how seldom we speak
of our own doubts, while dubiously
we mother man in his doubt!

And if at Mill Valley perched in the trees
the sweet rain drifting through western air
a white sweating bull of a poet told us

our cunts are ugly – why didn't we
admit we have thought so too? (And
what shame? They are not for the eye!)

No, they are dark and wrinkled and hairy,
caves of the Moon...   And when a
dark humming fills us, a

coldness towards life,
we are too much women to
own to such unwomanliness.

Whorishly with the psychopomp
we play and plead-and say
nothing of this later.   And our dreams,

with what frivolity we have pared them
like toenails, clipped them like ends of
split hair.

Elizabeth Garrett

Russian Dolly

Down decades, centripetal, like a Russian dolly,
I unpack these bright impenetrable women.
Beside a pond, when the gift first came to me

Of knowing ignorance, where frogs grappled
In desperate scrum, I pared my curiosity
To taste beyond the hard gloss of an apple.

Dream fruit, the ever smaller seed within
The seed, down to this last generation's
Flowering of bright impenetrable women.

I took my wooden matron. And where the spikeless
Roses wreathed her apron-strings, I split
Her open. Inside, her smaller smiling likeness,

And inside her, and inside her again –
I understood the game, but could not see
The joke, nor how the game should end.

In broken calm, between the glaucous bloom
Of frogspawn, wooden faces wobble up
At me. Their upturned skirts, like currachs blown

From girdled shores, turn silently, and turn.
Around my waist the spikeless roses twine.

Ann Lauterbach

Hum

The days are beautiful.
The days are beautiful.

I know what days are.
The other is weather.

I know what weather is.
The days are beautiful.

Things are incidental.
Someone is weeping.

I weep for the incidental.
The days are beautiful.

Where is tomorrow?
Everyone will weep.

Tomorrow was yesterday.
The days are beautiful.

Tomorrow was yesterday.
Today is weather.

The sound of the weather
Is everyone weeping.

Everyone is incidental.
Everyone weeps.

The tears of today
Will put out tomorrow.

The rain is ashes.
The days are beautiful.

The rain falls down.
The sound is falling.

The sky is a cloud.
The towers are raining.

The towers are rain.
The days are beautiful.

The sky is dust.
The weather is yesterday.

The weather is yesterday.
The sound is weeping.

What is this dust?
The weather is nothing.

The days are beautiful.
The towers are yesterday.

The towers are incidental.
What are these ashes?

Here is the hat
That does not travel

Here is the robe
That smells of the night

Here are the words
Retired to their books

Here are the stones
Loosed from their settings

Here is the bridge
Over the water

Here is the place
Where the sun came up

Here is a season
Dry in the fireplace.

Here are the ashes.
The days are beautiful.

Sarah Hannah

The Linen Closet

Oh, the linen closet, imperial
Ladder of shelves, gold towels glowing
With repose, night creams pearled, in pots,
Their risen oils yellowed at the rims,
Tubed salves, perfumed proteins.

Tall and narrow, narrow and deep,
The linen closet of worry and care!
On the highest shelves, the recondite liquids
In brown, bottled sternly: Peroxide,
Witch Hazel, and the dread purgative,

Ipecac. You might have died or been renewed,
Clavicles dewed by that arched-back soap,
Inimitably scented, cuts bridged by red
Tinctures, muscles slackened in the heating pad's
Green mosses. But no matter the potion

You could not ignore the space
At the back, the absolute black
In the bowels of the shelves, beyond the patch
And blanch of gauze, the catch of clots –
That unflagging question (past cure)

No tonic or robe could appease,
No meter or prodding inspection
Could probe – you could not quite make it out,
And you would not forget it.

Lorine Niedecker

What Horror To Awake At Night

What horror to awake at night
and in the dimness see the light
    Time is white
    mosquitoes bite
I've spent my life on nothing.

The thought that stings. How are you, Nothing.
sitting around with Something's wife.
    Buzz and burn
    is all I learn
I've spent my life on nothing.

I'm pillowed and padded, pale and puffing
lifting household stuffing –
    carpets, dishes,
    benches, fishes,
I've spent my life on nothing.

Adrienne Rich

Diving Into The Wreck

First having read the book of myths,
and loaded the camera,
and checked the edge of the knife-blade,
I put on
the body-armor of black rubber
the absurd flippers
the grave and awkward mask.
I am having to do this
not like Cousteau with his
assiduous team
aboard the sun-flooded schooner
but here alone.

There is a ladder.
The ladder is always there
hanging innocently
close to the side of the schooner.
We know what it is for,
we who have used it.

Otherwise
it is a piece of maritime floss
some sundry equipment.

I go down.
Rung after rung and still
the oxygen immerses me
the blue light
the clear atoms
of our human air.
I go down.
My flippers cripple me,
I crawl like an insect down the ladder
and there is no one
to tell me when the ocean
will begin.

First the air is blue and then
it is bluer and then green and then
black I am blacking out and yet
my mask is powerful
it pumps my blood with power
the sea is another story
the sea is not a question of power
I have to learn alone
to turn my body without force
in the deep element.

And now: it is easy to forget
what I came for
among so many who have always
lived here
swaying their crenellated fans
between the reefs
and besides
you breathe differently down here.

I came to explore the wreck.
The words are purposes.
The words are maps.
I came to see the damage that was done
and the treasures that prevail.

I stroke the beam of my lamp
slowly along the flank
of something more permanent
than fish or weed
the thing I came for:
the wreck and not the story of the wreck
the thing itself and not the myth
the drowned face always staring
toward the sun
the evidence of damage
worn by salt and away into this threadbare beauty
the ribs of the disaster
curving their assertion
among the tentative haunters.

This is the place.
And I am here, the mermaid whose dark hair
streams black, the merman in his armored body.
We circle silently
about the wreck
we dive into the hold.
I am she: I am he

whose drowned face sleeps with open eyes
whose breasts still bear the stress
whose silver, copper, vermeil cargo lies
obscurely inside barrels
half-wedged and left to rot
we are the half-destroyed instruments
that once held to a course
the water-eaten log
the fouled compass

We are, I am, you are
by cowardice or courage
the one who find our way
back to this scene
carrying a knife, a camera
a book of myths
in which
our names do not appear.

Author biographical information and credits

Diane Ackerman was born in 1948 in Waukegan, Illinois, and received her MA, MFA and Ph.D from Cornell University. The author of six poetry collections she is also a noted non-fiction and popular science writer. She has taught at several universities and has hosted a five hour PBS tv series inspired by her book, *A Natural History of the Senses*. 'Afterthought' is from *Jaguar of Sweet Laughter*, ©1991 Diane Ackerman and reprinted with permission from Random House, USA.

Fleur Adcock was born in New Zealand in 1934, and is now a London resident. She has published a dozen collections of poems and has edited several anthologies, including *The Faber Book of Twentieth Century Women's Poetry*. She has translated collections by two Romanian poets and a book of medieval Latin poems and has received numerous prizes including a Cholmondeley Award in 1976, and a New Zealand National Book Award in 1984. She was made an OBE in 1996 and was awarded the Queen's Gold Medal for Poetry in 2006. 'The Ex-Queen Among the Astronomers' and 'Things' both appear in *Poems:1960-2000*, ©Fleur Adcock and reprinted with permission of Bloodaxe Books.

Kim Addonizio was born in 1954 in Washington, D.C. and has a BA and MA from San Francisco State University. She is the author of four poetry collections. A fifth, *Lucifer at the Starlite*, is forthcoming from W.W. Norton in 2009, as is a prose book, *Ordinary Genius: A Guide for the Poet Within*. Addonizio is also the author of a collection of stories, *In the Box Called Pleasure*, and co-author of *The Poet's Companion: A Guide to the Pleasures of Writing Poetry* (1997). She co-edited Dorothy Parker's *Elbow: Tattoos on Writers, Writers on Tattoos* (2002). Among her awards are Fellowships from the National Endowment for the Arts and the Guggenheim Foundation, a Pushcart Prize, and a Commonwealth Club Poetry Medal. Addonizio lives in Oakland, CA and is online at www.kimaddonizio.com. 'What Do Women Want?' is from *Tell Me*, ©2000 by Kim Addonizio. Reprinted with the permission of BOA Editions, Ltd.

Patience Agbabi was born in London in 1965. She has performed her poetry all over the world and lectured in Creative Writing at several UK universities including Cardiff, Greenwich and Kent. In 2004 she was nominated one of the UK's Next Generation Poets. Her most recent collection is *Bloodshot Monochrome* (Canongate, 2008). We feature the title poem from *Transformatrix*, ©2000 Patience Agbabi, first published in Great Britain by Canongate Books Ltd.

Sandra Alcosser was born in Washington D.C. in 1944, and has published poems in *The New Yorker, The New York Times* and *The Paris Review*. Her seven books have been selected for numerous honours including the National Poetry Series, the Associated Writing Programs Award Series in Poetry, and the Academy of American Poets James Laughlin Award. 'Mare Frigoris' first appeared in *Sleeping Inside the Glacier*, published by Brighton Press in 1997. She is the National Endowment for the Arts first conservation poet and Montana's first poet laureate. Alcosser directs the Master of Fine Arts Program in Creative Writing at San Diego State University.

Elizabeth Alexander was born in 1962 in Harlem, New York and grew up in Washington D.C. A poet, essayist, playwright, and teacher, she is the author of four books of poems, *The Venus Hottentot, Body of Life, Antebellum Dream Book*, and *American Sublime*, which was a finalist for the 2005 Pulitzer Prize. She is also a scholar of African-American literature and culture and recently published a collection of essays, *The Black Interior*. She is a professor at Yale University, and for the academic year 2007-2008 she was a fellow at the Radcliffe Institute for Advanced Study at Harvard University. 'My Grandmother's New York Apartment' is from *American Blue: Selected Poems* and is reprinted with permission from Bloodaxe Books.

Gillian Allnutt was born in January, 1949, in London, but spent much of her childhood in Newcastle upon Tyne. Since 1973 she has taught English and creative writing in London and Newcastle, and has also worked as a performer, publisher, journalist and editor. She was a collective member of Sheba Feminist Publishers (1981-83), and from 1983 to 1988 was poetry editor at *City Limits* magazine. She has published seven collections of poetry and has twice been nominated for the T.S. Eliot Prize. She is also the co-editor of *The New British Poetry, 1968-1988* (1988) and the author of *Berthing: A Poetry Workbook* (1991). She lives in Esh Winning, County Durham. 'Sarah's Laughter' is from *How the Bicycle Shone: New and Selected Poems*, ©2007 Gillian Allnutt and is reprinted with permission from Bloodaxe Books.

Moniza Alvi was born in Lahore, Pakistan in 1954 and raised in Hertfordshire, she now lives in London where she works as a writer and tutor. The first of her five poetry collections, *The Country at My Shoulder*, was shortlisted for the T.S. Eliot Prize and the Whitbread Poetry Award, and led to her being named as one of the 1994 Next Generation Poets. In 2002 she was presented with a Cholmondeley Award for her poetry. Her latest books are *Europa* (2008) and *Split World: Poems 1990-2005* (2008) 'Map of India' is from *Split World*, ©2008 Moniza Alvi and is reprinted with permission from Bloodaxe Books.

Maya Angelou was born in St. Louis, Missouri in 1928, and has had a remarkably varied career as author, poet, historian, performer, director, songwriter, dancer, singer and civil rights activist. A memoir, *I Know Why the Caged Bird Sings*, was nominated for the National Book Award and a collection of poetry, *Just Give Me a Cool Drink of Water 'fore I Die* (1971) was nominated for the Pulitzer Prize. 'These Yet-To-Be United States' is from *I Shall Not Be Moved*, ©1990 Maya Angelou and reprinted with permission from Little, Brown Book Group (UK) and Random House, New York (USA).

Sarah Arvio's books of poems are *Visits from the Seventh and Sono: cantos* (Knopf 2002 and 2006). A combined edition of those two books will be published next year in England by Bloodaxe Books. For *Visits* she was awarded a Guggenheim Fellowship and the Rome Prize of the American Academy of Arts and Letters; Sono was written during a year-long stay at the American Academy in Rome. 'Mirrors', a poem from *Visits* was recently reprinted in *The Best American Erotic Poems: From 1800 to the Present* (Scribner 2008). Arvio (born 1954, Pennsylvania) has been a translator for the United Nations in New York and Switzerland for many years; she now teaches poetry at Princeton. 'Starlings' was first published in *The Kenyon Review*, and later featured on *Verse Daily*. 'Starlings' was also published in *Sono: cantos*, ©2006 by Sarah Arvio. Reprinted by permission of Alfred A. Knopf, a division of Random House, Inc., N.Y.

Tiffany Atkinson was born in Berlin in 1972 to an army family and has lived in Germany, Cyprus and various parts of Britain. She now lectures in English at the University of Wales, Aberystwyth. She has won the Cardiff International Poetry Competition and her work has appeared widely in journals and anthologies. Her first collection, *Kink and Particle*, appeared in 2006 and won the Jerwood First Collection Prize. 'Sonnet to Hand-Rolled Golden Virginia' is from *Kink and Particle*, ©2006 Tiffany Atkinson and is reprinted with the permission of Seren.

Margaret Atwood was born in 1939 in Ottawa, Ontario, Canada. She is the author of more than forty books of fiction, poetry, and critical essays. Her new book of poetry is *The Door*. Another recent book, *Moral Disorder*, is a collection of interconnected short stories and was published by Nan A. Talese/Doubleday. Her novel, *Oryx and Crake*, was short-listed for the Man Booker Prize and the Giller Prize in Canada. Her other books include the 2000 Booker Prize winning, *The Blind Assassin*, and *Alias Grace*, which won the Giller Prize in Canada and the Premio Mondello in Italy, *The Robber Bride*, *Cat's Eye*, *The Handmaid's Tale*, *The Penelopiad*, and *The Tent*. Margaret Atwood lives in Toronto with writer Graeme Gibson. 'February' is from *Morning in the Burned House* and is reprinted with permission from: Houghton Mifflin in the USA, Curtis Brown in the UK, and McClelland & Stewart in Canada.

Ros Barber is a prize-winning poet and fiction writer, whose work has been published or anthologised by Anvil, Bloomsbury, Faber, the *Daily Telegraph*, and a variety of newspapers and magazines; broadcast on Radio 4's 'Poetry Please' and Radio 3's 'The Verb'. Her books include, *Not The Usual Grasses Singing* (Four Shores 2005), and *Material* (Anvil 2008). In addition to a number of residencies and public art commissions in the UK, she has received awards from Arts Council England, the Authors Foundation, and the Arts and Humanities Research Council. 'What Happens to Women' is taken from a series called 'Embassy Court' in, *How Things Are on Thursday*, ©2004 Ros Barber and reprinted with permission from Anvil Press Poetry.

Leland Bardwell was born in India in 1922, educated in Dublin and is the author of five novels and five collections of poetry, the most recent being *The Noise of Masonry Settling*, (Dedalus 2006). 'How My True Love and I Lay Without Touching' is from *Dostoevsky's Grave* (Dedalus). 'Dogear' is from *The White Beach: New & Selected Poems 1960-1998* (Salmon) ©1998 Leland Bardwell. Reprinted with permission from Salmon Poetry and the author.

Elizabeth Bartlett was born in 1924 and grew up in Kent and lives in Burgess Hill, West Sussex. She published her major retrospective book: *Two Women Dancing: New and Selected Poems* in 1995. Edited by Carol Rumens, this selected drew on more than fifty years of writing and was a Poetry Book Society Recommendation. She has since published a further collection, *Appetites of Love* (2001). 'Birth' is from *Two Women Dancing*, ©1995 Elizabeth Bartlett and reprinted with permission from Bloodaxe Books.

Patricia Beer (1924-1999) was born in Exmouth, Devon, into a Plymouth Brethren family she vividly described in her autobiography *Mrs Beer's House*. She taught English literature in Italy and at Goldsmith's College, London, then left teaching in 1968 to become a full-time writer in Devon. For twenty-five years she worked for *The London Review of Books* and the *Times Literary Supplement*. She was once described by an editor as "an iron fist in an elbow-length velvet glove". 'Middle Age' is from *Collected Poems*, ©1990 Patricia Beer and reprinted with permission from Carcanet Press Limited.

Connie Bensley was born in south-west London in 1929, and has always lived there, apart from wartime evacuation. Until her retirement she worked as a secretary to doctors and to an M.P., and as a medical copywriter. She has published: *Central Reservations: New & Selected Poems* which draws on two earlier collections, as well as *Choosing To Be a Swan* in which 'Politeness' appears. ©1994 Connie Bensley and reprinted here with permission from Bloodaxe Books. Her recent title is *Private Pleasures* (2007).

Barbara Bentley was born in Bolton, Lancashire in 1950. She currently works as a manager in a sixth form college in Orrell, Wigan, and is hoping that this might be her final post before she hangs up her clogs and divides her time between gardening, writing, and the travelling she always meant to do. A late convert to the joys of writing, as opposed to 'literary criticism', Bentley was one of the first cohort of students to take an MA in Creative Writing from the University of Glamorgan. She has won prizes in several competitions. 'Fax' is part of a sequence, 'Telephone Sonnets' from *Living Next to Leda*, ©1996 Barbara Bentley and reprinted with the permission of Seren.

Sara Berkeley was born in Dublin in 1967 and graduated from Trinity College in 1989, after which she wandered somewhat aimlessly round the globe for a while pretending she had a plan. She finally settled in a rural valley just northwest of San Francisco, where she lives with her husband and young daughter. She has published four collections of poems, a volume of short stories, *The Swimmer in the Deep Blue Dream*, and a novel, *Shadowing Hannah*. 'The Call' is from *Strawberry Thief*, ©2005 Sara Berkeley and reprinted with permission from Gallery Press, Ireland.

Mary Ursula Bethell (1874-1945) was born in England but spent her life travelling back and forth from New Zealand and Europe. She finally settled for a decade in Rise Cottage near Christchurch in New Zealand where she wrote most of her published poetry. She was inspired by nature, religion, social and educational work and a close relationship with a companion, Effie Pollen. 'Response' is from *A Garden in the Antipodes* (Sidgewick & Jackson).

Sujata Bhatt was born in Ahmedabad, India in 1956. She grew up in Pune (India) and in the USA. She received her MFA from the University of Iowa. To date, she has published seven collections of poetry, received the Commonwealth Poetry Prize (Asia) and the Alice Hunt Bartlett Prize, a Cholmondeley Award and the Italian Tratti Poetry Prize. She has translated Gujarati poetry into English and has also translated poems by Günter Grass and Günter Kunert. She has been a visiting writer and fellow at a number of universities and was poet-in-residence at the Poetry Archive in London. Her work has been widely anthologised and broadcast and has been translated into more than twenty languages. She currently lives in Germany with her husband and daughter. 'Muliebrity' is from *Brunizem*, ©2008 Sujata Bhatt and is reprinted with permission from Carcanet Press Limited.

Jill Bialosky was born in Cleveland, Ohio. She is the author of two books of poetry, *The End of Desire* and *Subterranean*. A third collection, *Intruder*, is forthcoming in 2008. Her poems have appeared in leading periodicals including *The New Yorker*, *Poetry* and *Kenyon Review*. She studied poetry at Johns Hopkins University and the University of Iowa Writers' Workshop. She has published two novels, *House Under Snow* and *The Life Room* and co-edited with Helen Schulman an anthology, Wanting a Child. She is an editor at W.W. Norton and lives in New York City with her family. 'Fathers in the Snow' is from *The End of Desire* and is reprinted here with permission from the author and Random House, New York, 1997.

Kate Bingham was born in London in 1971, a novelist (*Mummy's Legs* and *Slipstream*) (Virago) and filmmaker as well as a poet, Kate Bingham's recently published second collection, *Quicksand Beach*, was nominated for the Forward Prize for Best Collection. Her first collection, *Cohabitation*, received an Eric Gregory Award in 1996. She has two children and lives with her family in London. 'Things I Learned at University' is from *Cohabitation*, ©1998 Kate Bingham and reprinted with the permission of Seren.

Sophie Cabot Black was born in New York City in 1958 and raised in New England. Her first poetry collection, *The Misunderstanding of Nature*, received the Poetry Society of America's Norma Farber First Book Award. Her poetry has appeared in numerous magazines, including *The Atlantic Monthly*, *The New Republic*, *The New Yorker*, *The Paris Review*, and *Poetry*. *The Descent*, a second collection, received the 2005 Connecticut Book Award, and was also nominated for the 2005 Colorado Book Award and subsequently chosen as a "hot pick" on MSNBC's program, 'Topic A With Tina Brown'. She has been awarded several fellowships, including at Macdowell Colony and the Radcliffe Institute. She teaches at Columbia University. 'Interrogation' is from *The Misunderstanding of Nature*, ©1993 Sophie Cabot Black and is reprinted with the permission of Graywolf Press.

Valerie Bloom was born in Clarendon, Jamaica in 1956 and came to England in 1974. She gained a First in English with African and Caribbean Studies at the University of Kent. She has published a number of poetry collections and two novels, run writing courses for the Arvon foundation, led workshops for students, teachers and librarians in schools and colleges and has had residencies worldwide. She has performed her work at festivals, on television and radio in Britain, Europe, Africa and the Caribbean. She writes poetry in both English and in Jamaican patois for readers of all ages. She currently lives in Kent with her husband and three children. 'Yuh Hear 'bout?', ©1983 Valerie Bloom is from *Touch Mi Tell Mi* published by Bogle L'Ouverture Publications Ltd.

Louise Bogan (1897-1970) was born in Maine and raised in mill towns in the northeastern USA. She went to Boston University but only completed her freshman year. She turned down a fellowship to Radcliffe, was married briefly, had a daughter, moved to New York and spent several years in Vienna. Her volatile personal life was punctuated by mental illness, she nevertheless worked as poetry reviewer for *The New Yorker* from 1931 until her retirement in 1969. Her *Collected Poems: 1923-53* won the Bollingen Prize in 1955. 'Cassandra' and 'Questions in a Field' are from *The Blue Estuaries*, ©1968 The Estate of Louise Bogan. Copyright renewed 1996 by Ruth Limmer. Reprinted by permission of Farrar, Straus and Giroux.

Nina Bogin was born in New York City in 1952 and has been a resident of France since 1976 where she works as a translator and as a teacher of English. Her poems have appeared in literary magazines in the United States, England and France. She received a National Endowment for the Arts grant in 1989 and published her first volume of poems, In the North, in the same year. 'Going Up The Hudson River, After Twenty Years' is taken from *The Winter Orchards*, ©2001 Nina Bogin and reprinted with permission from Anvil Press Poetry.

Eavan Boland was born in Dublin in 1944 and studied in Ireland, London and New York. Her first book was published in 1967. She has taught at Trinity College, University College and Bowdoin College, Dublin, and at the University of Iowa. She is currently Mabury Knapp Professor in the Humanities at Stanford University, California. A pioneering figure in Irish poetry, her poems and essays have appeared in magazines such as *The New Yorker, The Atlantic, Kenyon Review* and *American Poetry Review*. She divides her time between California and Dublin where she lives with her husband. 'The Black Lace Fan My Mother Gave Me' is from *Outside History: Selected Poems 1980-1990*, ©1990 Eavan Boland. 'An Elegy For My Mother In Which She Scarcely Appears' is from *Domestic Violence*, ©2007 Eavan Boland. Both poems reprinted with permission from Carcanet Press and from W.W. Norton & Co., Inc.

Stephanie Bolster was born in October 1969 in Vancouver, BC and raised in the suburb of Burnaby. Her first book, *White Stone: The Alice Poems*, appeared in 1998, and received the Canadian Governor General's Award and the Gerald Lampert Award. Also the author of *Two Bowls of Milk* and *Pavilion*, Bolster has published in literary journals and anthologies internationally and her poems have been translated into French Spanish and German. She teaches Creative Writing at Concordia University in Montréal, Québec. 'Train Windows' is from *Pavilion*, ©2002 Stephanie Bolster. Published by McClelland & Stewart. Used with permission of the publisher.

Roo Borson was born in Berkeley, California in 1952, and currently lives in Toronto, Canada. Her recent collection, *Short Journey Upriver Toward Oishida*, won the Griffin Poetry Prize and the Canadian Governor General's Award. She also works in collaborative poetry with the group Pain Not Bread (with Kim Maltman and Andy Patton), and in a duo called Baziju. 'Water Memory' is the title poem from that collection, ©1996 Roo Borson. Published by McClelland & Stewart. Used with permission of the publisher.

Catherine Bowman, originally from Texas, is the author of the poetry collections *The Plath Cabinet, Notarikon, Rock Farm*, and *1-800-HOT-RIBS* which was reissued by Carnegie-Mellon University Press as part of its contemporary classics series. She is the editor of *Word of Mouth: Poems featured on National Public Radio's 'All Things Considered'*. Her poems have appeared in six editions of *The Best American Poetry* selected by Richard Howard, A.R. Ammons, James Tate, Donald Hall, Yusef Komunyakaa, and Paul Muldoon. Her poems have appeared in a wide variety of journals, and in several anthologies including *An Exhalation of Forms, The Extraordinary Tide: New Poetry By American Women, Inking Through the Soul: Writers On Writing*, and **Poetry 180** edited by Billy Collins. She is the Ruth Lilly Professor of Poetry and Director of the Creative Writing Program at Indiana University. '1-800-HOT-RIBS' is the title poem of the book of that name, ©1993 Catherine Bowman, and is reprinted with permission from the author.

Peg Boyers (née Margarita O'Higgins Lluriá) was born in San Tomé, Venezuela in 1952, of an Irish father and a Cuban mother. She teaches Creative Writing at Skidmore College in Saratoga Springs, New York, and is Executive Editor of Salmagundi magazine. She is author of two books of poems, *Hard Bread* (2002) and *Honey with Tobacco*. Her poems appear in *The New Republic, Paris Review, Raritan* and many other magazines. 'Tobacco,' is from *Honey with Tobacco*, ©2007 Peg Boyers and reprinted with permission of The University of Chicago Press. All rights reserved.

Lucie Brock-Broido was born in Pittsburgh, Pennsylvania in 1956 and is the author of three collections of poetry, each published by Alfred A. Knopf, *A Hunger* (1988), *The Master Letters* (1995), and *Trouble in Mind* (2004). She has been the recipient of awards from the Guggenheim Foundation, the National Endowment for the Arts, and the American Academy of Arts and Letters. She is Director of Poetry in the School of the Arts at Columbia University and lives in New York City and in Cambridge, Massachusetts. 'Domestic Mysticism' originally appeared in Ploughshares and is reprinted with permission from the author, ©1987 Lucie Brock-Broido.

Gwendolyn Brooks (1917-2000) was born in Topeka, Kansas and raised in Chicago. Brooks is the author of more than twenty books of poetry, including *Annie Allen* (1949) for which she won the Pulitzer Prize. She also wrote a novel, an autobiography and edited *Jump Bad: New Chicago Anthology* (1971). In 1968 she was named Poet Laureate for the State of Illinois and from 1985-86 she was consultant in Poetry to the Library of Congress. Winner of numerous awards, she lived in Chicago until her death. 'The Mother' is from her *Selected Poems* (Harper Collins 2006), 'The Pool Players Seven at the Golden Shovel' is from *The Bean Eaters* (Harper Collins). Both ©Estate of Gwendolyn Brooks and reprinted by consent of Brooks Permissions.

Eleanor Brown was born in 1969, and grew up in Scotland. She read English Literature at York University, and later travelled in France, where she lived for a while in a convent. After working as a barmaid in a North London pub for several years, she served time as a legal secretary before taking up teaching at various universities. In 1997 her first collection *Maiden Speech* was shortlisted for the *Mail on Sunday*/John Llewellyn Rhys Prize, and her new version of Sophocles' play *Philoctetes* was staged by Inigo at the Cockpit Theatre in London. 'Terrible Sonnet' is from *Maiden Speech*, ©1996 Eleanor Brown, reprinted with permission from Bloodaxe.

Elizabeth Barrett-Browning (1806-1861) Lived in Ledbury, near Great Malvern, England and later in London. The last of twelve children, she was educated at home and suffered ill-health, possibly tuberculosis, and was considered an invalid by her family. She began writing poetry as a child and published her first long poem at the age of fourteen. Her first poetry collection appeared in 1826. Her fame grew as she published scholarly works, such as a translation of Aeschylus's **Prometheus Unbound**. Marriage to the poet Robert Browning and a move to Italy proved fruitful, her health improved and she produced such works as her verse-novel *Aurora Leigh*, the story of a woman writer. 'Sonnet 43' is from her best-known work, *Sonnets from the Portuguese*.

Colette Bryce was born in Derry in 1970, and has lived in England, Spain and Scotland. Her first collection, *The Heel of Bernadette* (2000) won the Aldeburgh Prize for best first collection and the inaugural Eithene Strong award in Ireland. She was also awarded first prize in the 2003 National Poetry Competition. 'The Full Indian Rope Trick' is from the book of that title (Picador) ©2004 Colette Bryce and reprinted with permission from Pan Macmillan. Her third collection *Self Portrait in the Dark* appeared in 2008.

Heather Buck (1926-2004) began to write in 1966. Her collections include: *At the Window* (1982), *The Sign of the Water Bearer* (1987), *Psyche Unbound* (1995), and *Waiting for the Ferry* (1998) all published by Anvil. She is also the author of a critical study, *T.S. Eliot's Four Quartets* (Agenda, 1996). 'The Poppy' is taken from *At the Window*, ©The Estate of Heather Buck and reprinted with permission of Anvil Press Poetry.

Mary Baine Campbell was born in Hudson, Ohio in 1954. American poet, scholar and professor, she teaches Medieval and Renaissance Literature as well as Creative Writing at Brandeis University. Her first collection, *The World, the Flesh and Angels* (1989) won the Barnard New Women Poets Prize. Her book *Wonder and Science* won the 2000 James Russell Lowell Prize for the best book of the year in Literary Studies from the Modern Language Society. 'Novocaine' and 'The Wake' are from **Trouble**, © 2003 Mary Baine Campbell and published by Carnegie Mellon University Press.

Siobhán Campbell was born in Dublin in 1962. She spent a number of years in New York and San Francisco and worked as Director of the Wolfhound Press before joining Faculty at Kingston University in London as MA/MFA Course Director, Creative Writing. She is widely published in the UK and USA including journals: *Poetry (Chicago)*, *The Southern Review, Magma, Agenda, Wasafiri*. She has won awards in the Troubadour, Wigtown and National Poetry competitions and has published collections including *The Permanent Wave* (Blackstaff Press), and *That Water Speaks in Tongues* (Templar Poetry); another, entitled *Cross-Talk*, is about to appear. 'Recall' is from *The Cold That Burns* (Blackstaff), ©2000 Siobhán Campbell and reprinted with permission from the author.

Vuyelwa Carlin was born in South Africa in 1949. Raised in East Africa, Carlin has spent the last few decades in Shropshire where she has worked in boarding schools and care homes. She feels rooted both in the English countryside and in Africa, recently revisiting that continent for the first time in thirty years. Her fourth collection of poetry was published in 2008 and she is currently engaged in translating contemporary Polish poetry. 'Lydia' is from the series 'Plaques and Tangles' from *The Solitary*, ©2008 Vuyelwa Carlin and reprinted with permission from Seren.

Melanie Challenger was born in 1977 in Oxford, England. Her first collection of poems, *Galatea* (2006), won the Society of Authors' Eric Gregory Award and received nomination for the Forward Poetry Prize. She is a Fellow at the Centre for the Evolution of Cultural Diversity at University College London, where she is researching a non-fiction book on the theme of extinction. As Artist-in-Residence for the British Antarctic Survey, she spent International Polar Year summer season (October 2007-March 2008) in Antarctica. 'Mother' is from *Galatea*, ©2006 Melanie Challenger, reprinted with permission of Salt Publishing.

Eiléan Ní Chuilleanáin was born in Ireland in 1942, and is married to Macdara Woods; they have a son, Niall. With

Leland Bardwell and Pearse Hutchinson, they are founding editors of the literary review *Cyphers*. She has published six collections of poetry; her awards include the Patrick Kavanagh Prize. Educated in Cork and Oxford, she is a Fellow of Trinity College, Dublin, and a member of Aosdána. 'Translation' is from *The Girl Who Married the Reindeer*, ©2002 Eiléan Ní Chuilleanáin and reprinted with permission from Gallery Press, Ireland, and Wake Forest University Press, USA.

A.V. Christie was born in Redwood City, California in 1963. Christie, co-winner of the 2004 Robert McGovern Publication Prize, is also the winner of the 1996 National Poetry Series for her book *Nine Skies*. She has won Individual Artist Fellowships from the National Endowment for the Arts and from the Maryland and Pennsylvania State Arts Councils as well as from the Ludwig Vogelstein Foundation. 'Evermay-on-the-Delaware' is from *Nine Skies*, ©1997 by A.V. Christie and is reprinted with permission of the poet and the University of Illinois Press.

Amy Clampitt (1920-1994) was born in New Providence, Iowa. Clampitt's first acclaimed collection, *The Kingfisher*, appeared when she was sixty-three, after a life spent in New York City working as a secretary, reference librarian and freelance editor. In the following eleven years until her death, she produced five more critically praised volumes, and received a Guggenheim Fellowship, an Academy Fellowship and was made a MacArthur Foundation Fellow in 1992. 'Meadowlark Country' is from *The Collected Poems of Amy Clampitt* (Knopf) and is reprinted with permission from Random House/Knopf, USA.

Kate Clanchy was born in Scotland in 1965 and now lives in England with her husband and children. Her three collections, *Slattern, Samarkand*, and *Newborn* (all Picador) have brought her a wide audience and Forward and Somerset Maugham Prizes. She edited the anthology, *All The Poems You Need To Say Hello* in 2004, and a first prose book, *What Is She Doing Here?* was published by Picador in 2008. 'War Poetry' is from *Samarkand*, ©1999 Kate Clanchy and reprinted with permission from Pan Macmillan.

Polly Clark was born in Toronto in 1968 and brought up in Lancashire, Cumbria and the Borders of Scotland. She has worked as a zookeeper, a teacher of English in Hungary, and in publishing at Oxford University Press. In 1997 she won an Eric Gregory Award for her poetry and her first collection, *Kiss*, was a Poetry Book Society Recommendation. 'Elvis the Performing Octopus' is from her second collection *Take Me With You*, shortlisted for the 2005 T.S. Eliot Prize. Clark lives on the West Coast of Scotland and is a Royal Literary Fund Writing Fellow at Edinburgh University, ©2005 Polly Clark and reprinted with permission of Bloodaxe Books.

Gillian Clarke was born in Cardiff, Wales in 1937. Clarke is a poet, playwright, editor, broadcaster, lecturer and translator (from Welsh). She edited the *Anglo-Welsh Review* from 1975 to 1984, and has taught creative writing in schools and universities. She is a former president of Ty Newydd, the writers' centre in North Wales which she co-founded in 1990. She has given poetry readings and lectures in Europe and the United States, and her work has been translated into ten languages. She has three children and lives with her husband on a smallholding in west Wales, where they raise a flock of sheep, and care for the land according to organic and conservation practice. Author of a number of collections, most recently: *Making Beds for the Dead* (2004). 'Overheard in County Sligo' is from her *Selected Poems*, ©1996 Gillian Clarke and reprinted with permission of Carcanet Press.

Lucille Clifton was born in 1936 in Depew, New York. Educated at Howard University and the State University of New York, Clifton worked in local government positions, including literature assistant in the Office of Education in Washington D.C. until 1971 when she began to take writer-in-residence positions in academia. She has written over twenty children's books and over half a dozen books of poetry, and won numerous prizes, including an Emmy (for her television work). She has also raised six children. 'The Lost Women' is from *Next*, ©1987 Lucille Clifton. Reprinted with the permission of BOA Editions, Ltd.

Anne Cluysenaar was born in Brussels in 1936, her family moving to England just before the war. She studied at Trinity College, Dublin and worked for some years in academia before leaving to dedicate her time to writing and painting. She now lives in Wales and her new book of poems is *Batu-Angas*, dedicated to the Welsh naturalist and pioneer of evolution, Alfred Russel Wallace. 'Yellow Meadow-Ants in Hallowed Ground' is from *Timeslips: Selected Poems*, ©1997 Anne Cluysenaar and reprinted with permission of Carcanet Press Limited.

Merle Collins was born in 1950 in Aruba and grew up in Grenada. She was educated at St. Joseph's Convent High School, and the University of the West Indies in Jamaica where she gained a BA in English and Spanish. She began teaching, and later gained her Masters from Georgetown University. Her first collection appeared in 1985 and she also joined The African Dawn, a musical group that incorporated poetry and African music. During this time she began to work in England, writing and lecturing and earning a Ph.D in Government from the University of London. She has published three collections of poetry, two novels and a collection of short stories. Collins continues to teach at the University of Maryland in the USA where she is professor of Caribbean Literature. 'No Dialects Please' is from *Watchers and Seekers* (Women's Press) and is reprinted with permission from the author.

Wendy Cope was born in 1945 in Erith, a place that few people have heard of and fewer still can pronounce (first syllable rhymes with beer). It is in North Kent. After university she worked as a London primary school teacher for nearly twenty years and began writing in her spare time. She has published three collections of poems and is now a freelance writer, living in Winchester. 'Men and Their Boring Arguments' is in *Serious Concerns* (Faber, 1992) and 'Strugnell's Haiku' is the second of three haiku from *Making Cocoa for Kingsley Amis* (Faber, 1996). ©Wendy Cope and reprinted in the UK with permission of Faber and Faber Ltd. and in the USA with permission from Peters, Fraser and Dunlop.

Julia Copus was born in 1969 in London. She has worked as a copywriter, a candlemaker, and a clerk in a prosthetics factory. Her publications include *The Shuttered Eye*, which was shortlisted for the Forward Prize for Best First Collection, and *In Defence of Adultery* — both Poetry Book Society Recommendations. In 2002, she won the National Poetry Competition with 'Breaking the Rule'. Her radio work includes an afternoon play, *Eenie Meenie Macka Racka*, which won the BBC's prestigious Alfred Bradley Award. A new play, *The Enormous Radio*, was broadcast on BBC Radio 4 in 2008. She has recently received funding from the Society of Authors for work on her third collection of poetry, and is an Honorary Fellow of Exeter University and an Advisory Fellow for the Royal Literary Fund. 'The Back Seat of My Mother's Car' is reprinted from *The Shuttered Eye* with permission from Bloodaxe Books.

Sarah Corbett was born in Chester in 1970 and grew up in rural north Wales. She has studied at the Universities of Leeds and East Anglia, and is currently at the University of Manchester. Her first collection of poems, *The Red Wardrobe*, was nominated for both the T.S. Eliot and Forward Prizes for Best First Collection. A subsequent collection, *The Witch Bag*, has appeared. The featured poem, 'Kisses' is from her new book, *Other Beasts*, ©2008 Sarah Corbett and reprinted with the permission of Seren.

Frances Cornford (1886-1960) was born and lived for most of her life in Cambridge. She was the granddaughter of Charles Darwin, and on her mother's side was related to William Wordsworth. In 1909 she married the classicist F. Cornford, who became Professor of Ancient Philosophy at Cambridge, and they had five children. Cornford published eight books of poetry and two of translations. Her *Collected Poems* (1954) was a Poetry Book Society Choice, and in 1959 she was awarded the Queen's Gold Medal for Poetry. 'Childhood' is from *Selected Poems*, ©1996 The Estate of Frances Cornford and reprinted with permission from Enitharmon Press.

Roz Cowman was born in Cork, Ireland, in 1942. Her collection, *The Goose Herd* (Salmon) was published in 1989. She received the Arlen House/Maxwell House Award in 1982, and the Patrick Kavanagh Award for Poetry in 1985. She lives in Cork. 'Logic' is from *The Goose Herd*, ©1989 Roz Cowman and reprinted with permission of Salmon Poetry.

Adelaide Crapsey (1878-1914) was born in Brooklyn, New York. She graduated from Vassar in 1901, and taught literature and history from 1902-08, taking one year out to study in Rome. Due to declining health, she spent some years abroad and in the summer of 1911 her condition was diagnosed as tuberculosis. She did not tell her family and continued to teach poetics at Smith College but grew slowly worse and died in 1914. Her poetry was published after her death, as well as a prose work, *A Study in English Metrics*. 'Susanna and the Elders' is from the *Complete Poems and Collected Letters of Adelaide Crapsey* (State University of New York Press, 1977).

Lorna Crozier was born in 1948 in Swift Current, Saskatchewan. She has published seven collections of poetry, had poems published in many journals and anthologies and won a number of prizes. She has been writer-in-residence at several institutions, including the University of Toronto, and currently teaches in the Department of Creative Writing at the University of Victoria. 'What Comes After' originally appeared in *Whetstone* ©2005 Lorna Crozier, and most recently in The Blue Hour of the Day, ©2007 Lorna Crozier, published by McClelland & Stewart. Used with permission of the publisher.

Amanda Dalton was born in 1957 in Coventry. She has worked as a Deputy Headteacher in comprehensive schools, and as Centre Director for Lumb Bank, the Arvon Foundation's Centre in Yorkshire. She is currently Associate Director (Education) at the Royal Exchange Theatre in Manchester. As well as writing poetry, she is a radio and theatre dramatist and has an MA in Writing from the University of Glamorgan. 'How To Disappear' is the title poem from the book of that name, ©1999 Amanda Dalton, and is reprinted here with permission from Bloodaxe Books.

Margaret Esse Danner (1915-1986) Born in Kentucky, Danner's parents moved to Chicago when she was quite young. Educated at Loyola and Northwestern Universities she began to associate with other writers and rose to be Assistant Editor of *Poetry: The Magazine of Verse*. She moved to Detroit in the 1960s to become poet-in-residence at Wayne State University where she also established an Arts Centre for children. She travelled to Africa and found inspiration for much of her later verse, producing two further volumes. 'The Painted Lady' is from her final *Selected Poems* (Country Beautiful).

Julia Darling (1956-2005) was born in Winchester, in the house in which Jane Austen died. She was a prizewinning playwright and the author of two novels as well as a poet. She also co-edited the anthology, *The Poetry Cure*. She was given a Northern Rock Foundation Writer's Award to pursue her writing and was also active in health care issues and was the Fellow in Literature and Health at Newcastle University. She died, tragically young, of breast cancer. 'My Complicated Daughter' is from *Sudden Collapses in Public Places*, ©2000 The Estate of Julia Darling and reprinted with permission from Arc Publications.

Elizabeth Daryush (1887-1977) was born in Chiswell, overlooking Oxford. She was the daughter of Poet Laureate Robert Bridges and grandaughter of a famous nineteenth century architect, Alfred Waterhouse. Although she lived to be ninety, her poetry was somewhat neglected until rediscovered by the New Formalists of recent times, although some critics feel she may best be remembered for her experiments in syllabics. She married and moved to Persia for four years but returned to Chiswell with her husband and lived there until her death. 'Children of Wealth' is from *Selected Poems*, ©1972 Elizabeth Daryush and reprinted with permission from Carcanet Press Ltd.

Toi Derricotte was born in Hamtramck, Michigan, in 1941. She earned her BA in special education from Wayne State University and her MA in English literature from New York University. Her books of poetry include *Tender* (1997), *Captivity* (1989), *Natural Birth* (1983), and *The Empress of the Death House* (1978). She is also the author of a literary memoir, *The Black Notebooks* (W.W. Norton, 1997). Together with Cornelius Eady, she co-founded Cave Canem, a workshop retreat for black poets, in 1996. Her honours include the Lucille Medwick Memorial Award from the Poetry Society of America, two Pushcart Prizes, the Distinguished Pioneering of the Arts Award from the United Black Artists, and fellowships from the National Endowment for the Arts, the New Jersey State Council on the Arts, the Guggenheim and Rockefeller Foundations and the Maryland State Arts Council. She teaches at the University of Pittsburgh. 'Family Secrets' is from *Tender*, ©1997 Toi Derricotte and reprinted with permission from The University of Pittsburgh Press.

Nuala Ní Dhomhnaill was born in 1952 in Lancashire. In 1957, her family returned to Ireland, where the poet grew up. She graduated from University College, Cork, and then lived in Holland and Turkey before returning to Dublin where she currently lives with her husband and four children. Over the years, Ní Dhomhnaill has gained prestige and recognition for her works which focus on Irish folklore, myth and culture. She has won numerous international awards for her writing which has been translated into a plethora of languages. Her books include *Astrakhan Cloak, Selected Poems*, and *Spionain is Roiseanna*. 'The Language Issue' is from *Pharaoh's Daughter*, ©1993 Nuala Ní Dhomhnaill (this poem translated into English by Paul Muldoon) and reprinted with permission from Gallery Press, Ireland and Wake Forest University Press, USA.

Emily Dickinson (1830-1886), was born in Amherst, Massachusetts and attended Mount Holyoke Female Seminary for one year. Upon her death, her family discovered forty handbound volumes of more than eight hundred of her poems. Although relatively secluded, and unpublished in her lifetime, the poet kept up a wide correspondence, read intensively and was very close to her brother (who lived next door) and a sister, who also lived at home. Now considered, along with Walt Whitman, to be one of the founding voices of American poetry, and she remains hugely influential. The depredations of successive editors meant that a volume featuring the poet's original punctuation, characterised by her use of the dash, did not appear until 1981. The selections in this book are from *The Complete Poems by Emily Dickinson* (Little, Brown, 1988).

Josephine Dickinson was born in London in 1957, and has published two previous collections of poetry in the UK: *Scarberry Hill* (The Rialto 2001) and *The Voice* (Flambard 2004). *Scarberry Hill* was the winner in the 2005 Staple Magazine Alternative Generation contest. In 2007 her US debut, *Silence Fell*, was published by Houghton Mifflin. Josephine Dickinson lives on a small hill farm in the high Pennines, close to Alston. 'V. Mass' is from the sequence 'This Night' in the book *Night Journey* (Flambard, 2008) and is reprinted with permission from the author and Flambard Press.

Maura Dooley was born in Truro, grew up in Bristol, and after working for some years in Yorkshire now lives in London. She is a freelance writer and lectures at Goldsmiths College. She edited *Making for Planet Alice: New Women Poets* (1997) and *The Honey Gatherers: A Book of Love Poems* (2002) and *How Novelists Work* (2000). *Life Under Water* (2008) is her recent poetry collection. Her books have been Poetry Book Society Recommendations, and she has been nominated for the T.S. Eliot Prize. 'History' is from *Sound Barrier: Poems 1982-2002*, ©2002 Maura Dooley, and is reprinted here with permission from Bloodaxe Books.

Rita Dove was born in Akron, Ohio in 1952. Dove was educated at Miami University in Ohio, studied as a Fulbright scholar in Tubingen, Germany and earned an MFA at the Iowa Writers' Workshop in 1977. She has published a number of poetry collections, including *Thomas and Beulah*, based on the life of her grandparents, which won the

Pulitzer Prize in 1987. She has also written a book of short stories, a verse drama, and a collection of essays inspired by her time as Poet Laureate of the United States and Consultant in Poetry at the Library of Congress in 1993-5. 'After Reading Mickey in the Night Kitchen for the Third Time Before Bed' is from *Grace Notes*, ©1989 by Rita Dove. Used by permission of the author and W.W. Norton & Company, Inc.

Freda Downie (1929-1993) was born in London, and educated in Britain and Australia. She worked for music publishers and art agents for many years, and only began publishing her poems in the 1970s, in limited editions. Two full collections, *A Stranger Here* (1977) and *Plainsong* (1981) followed from Secker. She completed a further collection, Forty Poems, which was not published. She was living in Berkhamsted in Hertfordshire when she died. 'Great-Grandfather' is from her *Collected Poems* edited by George Szirtes (1995), and is reprinted here with permission from Bloodaxe Books.

Jane Draycott (born 1954) is a British poet, who has worked in sound as well as text. Her poetry collections include *The Night Tree* (2004), *Tideway* - with artist Peter Hay (2002), *Prince Rupert's Drop* (1999), *Christina the Astonishing* (1998) with Lesley Saunders, and *No Theatre* (1997). She has been poet-in-residence at the River and Rowing Museum, Henley-on-Thames and lectures in Creative Writing at the universities of Reading, Oxford, and Lancaster. In 2004, she was named as one of the Next Generation Poets. Draycott is a mentor on the Crossing Borders creative writing system, which was set up by the British Council and Lancaster University. 'The Levitation of St. Christina' is from *Christina the Astonishing* (1998) and is reprinted with permission from Carcanet Press with additional thanks to Two Rivers Press.

Carol Ann Duffy was born in Glasgow in 1955. She grew up in Stafford then attended the University of Liverpool, where she studied Philosophy. She has written for both children and adults, and her poetry has received many awards, including the Signal Prize for children's verse, the Whitbread and Forward Prizes, the Lannan Award and the E.M. Forster Prize in America. In 2005, she won the T.S. Eliot Prize for Rapture. Considered one of the most influential British poets of her generation. 'Mrs Darwin' is from *The World's Wife* ©2000 (new edition) Carol Ann Duffy, and reprinted here with permission from Pan/Macmillan. 'Small Female Skull' is from *Mean Time* ©1993 Carol Ann Duffy. 'Selling Manhattan' is from *Selling Manhattan* ©1987 Carol Ann Duffy. Last two poems reprinted with permission from Anvil Press Poetry.

Denise Duhamel was born in Woonsocket, Rhode Island, in 1961. She received a BFA from Emerson College and an MFA from Sarah Lawrence College. Her recent titles are *Two and Two* (University of Pittsburgh, 2005) and *Mille et un sentiments* (Firewheel Editions, 2005). Her other books currently in print are *The Star-Spangled Banner*, (1999), *Kinky* (1997), *Girl Soldier* (1996), and *How the Sky Fell* (1996). She co-edited with Nick Carbó the anthology *Sweet Jesus: Poems About the Ultimate Icon*. Duhamel teaches Creative Writing and Literature at Florida International University and lives in Hollywood, Florida, with her husband. 'Lawless Pantoum' is from *Two and Two*, ©2005 Denise Duhamel. 'Sex With a Famous Poet' is from *Queen for a Day: Selected and New Poems*, ©2001 Denise Duhamel. Both poems are reprinted with permission of the University of Pittsburgh Press.

Helen Dunmore was born in 1952 in Yorkshire and is a poet, novelist and children's writer. Her poetry books have been Poetry Book Society Choice and Recommendations, and she is the winner of The Cardiff International Poetry Prize, The Alice Hunt Bartlett Award and The Signal Poetry Award, and *Bestiary* was shortlisted for the T.S. Eliot Prize. Her latest poetry title is *Glad of These Times* (2007). She has published nine novels and three books of short stories with Viking Penguin, including *A Spell of Winter* (1995), *Talking to the Dead* (1996), *The Siege* (2001), and *House of Orphans* (2006). She lives in Bristol. 'Safe Period' is from *Out of the Blue: Poems 1975-2001*, ©2001 Helen Dunmore and reprinted with permission from Bloodaxe Books.

Jane Duran was born in Cuba in 1944, brought up in the USA and Chile and now lives in England. Her book *Breathe Now, Breathe* was awarded the Forward Prize for Best First Collection. She also published *Silences from the Spanish Civil War* in 2002, and *Coastal*, a Poetry Book Society Recommendation, in 2005. She received a Cholmondeley Award in 2005. 'Stillborn' is from *Breathe Now, Breathe*, ©1995 Jane Duran and reprinted with permission from Enitharmon Press.

Jean Earle (1909-2002) was born in Bristol but was brought up in the Rhondda Valley, and after her marriage, lived in other parts of Wales. She had written poetry for many years but the best of her work follows the death of her mother, during and after a period of working as an Assistant to the Bishop of St David's. Her latter years were spent in Shrewsbury. Her first collection, *A Trial of Strength*, won the Welsh Arts Council Poetry Prize in 1980, while subsequent books, *Visiting Light* (1987) and *Selected Poems* (1990) were a Poetry Book Society Choice and Recommendation respectively. 'The Way It Goes' is from *The Bed of Memory* (Seren), her final volume, ©2001 Jean Earle and reprinted with permission from her family.

Lauris Edmond (1924-2000) Born in Dannevirke, New Zealand, she published her first volume of poems in 1975 when she was 51. She trained as a teacher but marriage and family (five daughters and one son) intervened. Coming to poetry in later life resulted in considerable success, her *Selected Poems* winning the Commonwealth Poetry Prize in 1985. She wrote sixteen volumes of poetry, three volumes of autobiography, a novel, radio and stage drama, essays and edited a number of other books. 'Trapeze' is from *A Matter of Timing*, ©Lauris Edmond Literary Estate, was originally published by Auckland University Press, 1996.

Menna Elfyn was born in 1951 near Swansea, and is a poet and playwright who writes with passion of the Welsh language and identity. She has published ten collections and also co-edited *The Bloodaxe Book of Modern Welsh Poetry* (2003) with John Rowlands. When not travelling the world for readings and residencies, she lives in Llandysul, Wales where she is Director of the Masters programme in Creative Writing at Trinity College, Carmarthen and also Fellow at Swansea University. Her poetry is now available in two bilingual selections, *Eucalyptus: Detholiad o Gerddi / Selected Poems:1978-1994* from Gomer and *Perfect Blemish: New & Selected Poems / Perffaith Nam: Dau Ddetholiad & Cherddi Newydd:1995-2007*, which features 'Couplings' as translated by Joseph Clancy, ©2007 Menna Elfyn and reprinted here with permission from Bloodaxe Books.

Lynn Emanuel was born in Mt. Kisco, New York, in 1949. She is the author of three books of poetry including: *Then, Suddenly* – (University of Pittsburgh Press, 1999), which was awarded the Eric Matthieu King Award from the Academy of American Poets. She has taught at the Bread Loaf Writers' Conference, The Warren Wilson Program in Creative Writing, and the Vermont College Creative Writing Program. She is currently a Professor of English at the University of Pittsburgh. 'Frying Trout While Drunk' is from *The Dig* (1992) and 'Blonde Bombshell' is from Hotel Fiesta, ©1984 Lynn Emanuel and used with permission of the poet and the University of Illinois Press.

Louise Erdrich was born in 1954, and raised in North Dakota, where her parents worked for the Wahpeton Indian School. Educated at Dartmouth and earning an MFA at Johns Hopkins University, Erdrich is a noted novelist as well as a poet, author of three popular novels that chronicle three generations of Native-American and European-immigrant families in a fictionalised region of North Dakota, and three books of poetry. 'Fooling God' is from *Original Fire: Selected and New Poems*, ©2003 by Louise Erdrich. Reprinted by permission of HarperCollins Publishers, USA.

Carrie Etter was born in 1969, raised in Normal, Illinois, and has since lived thirteen years in southern California and seven in England. In 2003 she was awarded a Ph.D in English from the University of California, Irvine for her thesis, *Class, Gender and the Making of the Criminological Subject in Mid-Victorian Fiction*, and joined the Creative Writing faculty of Bath Spa University in 2004. She now lives in Bradford-on-Avon and wishes ginger were a food group. 'The Daughters of Prospero' first appeared in the *Times Literary Supplement* and will feature in her forthcoming book, *The Tethers* (Seren, 2009); it is reprinted here with the author's permission.

Christine Evans was born in Yorkshire, moved to the Llyn Peninsula in North Wales to teach in the 1960s and has since made her home there. She spends summers on Bardsey "the Island of 20,000 saints," often cut off by tides and weather, a place which features in much of her work. She has published seven collections of verse and read her work on radio and television. 'Case History' is from her prize-winning *Selected Poems*, ©2004 Christine Evans and is reprinted here with the permission of Seren.

Martina Evans was born in Cork in 1961, the youngest of ten children. She studied sciences at University College Cork and worked for fourteen years as a radiographer. She began writing in 1990 and has published three books of poetry and three novels. Her first novel, *Midnight Feast*, won a Betty Trask Award in 1995 and her third novel, *No Drinking No Dancing No Doctors* (Bloomsbury, 2000), won an Arts Council of England Award in 1999. Currently, she teaches Creative Writing at the City Literary Institute, Centreprise Literature Development Project. 'Some Bores Are Just Born' is from *Can Dentists Be Trusted*, ©2004 Martina Evans and reprinted with permission from Anvil Press Poetry.

Bernardine Evaristo was born in London in 1959. Her books fuse poetry with fiction and are *Lara* (1997) and with new material (Bloodaxe, 2009), *The Emperor's Babe* (Penguin, 2001) and *Soul Tourists* (Penguin, 2005). Her first fully-prose novel is *Blonde Roots* (Penguin, 2008). She edited the British Council/Granta anthology *NW15 (New Writing 15)* in 2007 with the novelist Maggie Gee. She has received several awards and was made a Fellow of the Royal Society of Literature in 2004 and the Royal Society of Arts in 2006. 'Amo, Amas, Amat' is taken from *The Emperor's Babe*, ©2001 Bernardine Evaristo, and reprinted with permission of the author.

Ruth Fainlight was born in New York City in 1931, and has lived in England since the age of fifteen. She attended art college, then lived for some years in France and Spain before returning to London. She has published thirteen collections of poems as well as two volumes of short stories and translations from the French, Portuguese and Spanish. Her new translation of Sophocles' *Theban Plays*, done with Robert Littman, will be published by John Hopkins

University Press in 2009. She received the Cholmondeley Award in 1994 and her 1997 collection, *Sugar-Paper Blue* was shortlisted for the Whitbread Prize. 'Moving' is in *Moon Wheels*, ©2006 and reprinted here with permission of Bloodaxe Books. 'Thunder' is from *This Time of Year* (Sinclair-Stevenson, 1994) and is reprinted with permission from the author.

U.A. Fanthorpe was born in Kent in 1929. After boarding school in Surrey, she read English at St. Anne's College, Oxford, before training as a teacher. She taught at Cheltenham Ladies' College for sixteen years and was Head of English for eight before deciding to do something radically different. It was while working as a receptionist at a neurological hospital in 1974 that she began writing poetry. After various residencies (Lancaster 1983-85, Northern Arts Fellow, 1987) she left the hospital in 1989 to pursue her writing full-time. Among her many honours, in 2001 she was awarded the CBE for services to literature and received the Queen's Gold Medal for Poetry in 2003, only the fifth woman in seventy years. She lives in Wotton–Under-Edge, in an Elizabethan cottage, with her partner, Rosie Bailey. 'The Poet's Companion' from *Neck Verse* (1992) is reprinted courtesy of Peterloo Press.

Helen Farish was born in 1962 in Wigton, Cumbria. Her book, *Intimates*, won the Forward Prize for Best First Collection and was short-listed for the T.S. Eliot Prize. She wrote her doctoral thesis on contemporary American women poets and now teaches at Lancaster University. 'Newly Born Twins' is from *Intimates*, ©2005 Helen Farish and reprinted with permission from Cape/Random House publishers in the UK.

Vicki Feaver was born in Nottingham in 1943 and educated at Durham and London Universities. She has published three volumes of poetry, won a Heineman Award, a Cholmondeley, and a Forward Prize for the Best Poem. Her latest collection *The Book of Blood* (Cape, 2006) was shortlisted for the Forward and Costa Prizes. Now living on the edge of the Pentlands, halfway between Ian Hamilton Finlay's Little Sparta and Hugh MacDiarmid's but-and-ben at Brownsbank, she spends her time writing and painting. 'Oi Yoi Yoi' is from *The Handless Maiden*, ©1994 Vicki Feaver and reprinted with permission of Cape/Random House publishers, UK.

Elaine Feinstein was born in Liverpool in 1930, brought up in Leicester, and educated at Newham College, Cambridge. She has worked as a university lecturer, a sub-editor, and a freelance journalist. She has written fourteen novels, all still in print, radio plays, television dramas, and five biographies (subjects include Ted Hughes and Anna Akhmatova). She has travelled worldwide for readings and residencies and her work has been regularly translated. Her versions of the poems of Marina Tsvetaeva were published in 1971, and remain the authoritative versions. Her *Collected Poems and Translations* (2002) was a Poetry Book Society Special Commendation and 'Infidelities' is from that book, ©2002 Elaine Feinstein and reprinted with permission from Carcanet Press Ltd.

Beth Ann Fennelly was born in 1971 in New Jersey but grew up in Illinois. She graduated magna cum laude in 1993 from the University of Notre Dame then taught English on the Czech/Polish border before returning to complete her MFA from the University of Arkansas. Her books of poems are *Open House* (Zoo Press, 2002), *Tender Hooks* (W.W. Norton, 2004), and *Unmentionables* (W.W. Norton, 2008). She's won grants from the United States Artists' Foundation and the National Endowment for the Arts. She currently resides in Oxford, Mississippi where she is Associate Professor English at the University of Mississippi. 'Poem Not To be Read At Your Wedding' is from *Open House*,(Zoo Press, 2001) and is reprinted here with permission from the author.

Catherine Fisher was born in 1957 in Newport, Gwent, Wales and still lives there, with two cats. She has published four collections of poetry, and many novels for children, with the Bodley Head, Red Fox and Hodder Headline. She worked in teaching and archaeology before becoming a full-time writer; she is also an experienced broadcaster and adjudicator and recently taught Writing for Children at the University of Glamorgan. Myth, legend and spiritual concerns play an important part in her writing. Both her poems and novels have won awards, including the Cardiff International Poetry Competition, 1989 and the Tir na n'Og Prize, 1995, and she was shortlisted for the Smarties Book Prize in 1990 and the Whitbread Book Awards in 2006. 'Undertakers' is from *Altered States*, ©1999 Catherine Fisher and reprinted with permission from Seren.

Leontia Flynn was born in County Down in 1974, and recently completed a Ph.D. at Queen's University, Belfast. In 2001 she won an Eric Gregory Award. Her first collection, *These Days*, won the Forward Poetry Prize for best collection in 2004, and was shortlisted for the Whitbread Poetry Prize. In the same year, she was named as one of the Next Generation Poets. Flynn lives in Ireland where she is currently working on a second collection of poems. 'For Stuart, Who Accidentally Obtained a Job in the Civil Service' is from *These Days*, ©2004 Leontia Flynn and reprinted with permission from Cape/Random House publishers in the UK.

Carolyn Forché was born in Detroit, Michigan in 1950. Her early volumes, such as *Gathering the Tribes* (1976) and *The Country Between Us* (1982) won numerous awards and established Forché as a writer with strong political interests. She has published four collections of poems and edited, *Against Forgetting: Twentieth Century Poetry of Witness*. She is Lannan Professor of Poetry and Poetics at Georgetown University in Washington, D.C. and lives in Maryland with her husband, photographer Harry Mattison. 'The Colonel' is from *The Country Between Us*, reprint ©2003 Carolyn Forché and reprinted in the UK with permission from Bloodaxe Books and in the USA,©1981 with permission of HarperCollins Publishers, New York. It originally appeared in *Women's International Resource Exchange*.

Janet Frame (1924–2004) An acclaimed New Zealand writer, Frame was best-known for her prizewinning fiction and the bestselling autobiographical trilogy later adapted by Jane Campion for her film *An Angel at My Table*. Frame's first love was poetry, and her poems appeared in print from childhood onwards, though she published only one book of poetry in her lifetime, *The Pocket Mirror* (1967). 'The Happy Prince' is from the posthumously published volume *The Goose Bath* (2006), first published in the UK in *Storms Will Tell: Selected Poems* (2008) and is reprinted with permission from Bloodaxe Books and the Janet Frame Literary Trust.

Linda France was born in Newcastle and educated at Leeds University. She is the author of a number of collections of poetry, including *Red, The Gentleness of the Very Tall, Storyville, The Simultaneous Dress* and a biography in verse of Lady Mary Wortley Montague. France is also involved in music/art collaborations and edited the influential *Sixty Women Poets* anthology for Bloodaxe. She now lives in the Northumberland countryside with her family. 'Elementary' is from *Red*, ©1992 and is reprinted with permission from Bloodaxe Books.

Daisy Fried was born in Ithaca, New York, in 1967. She is the author of two books of poems, *My Brother is Getting Arrested Again* (University of Pittsburgh Press, 2006), which was a finalist for the National Book Critics Circle Award, and *She Didn't Mean to Do It* (U of Pittsburgh) which won the Agnes Lynch Starrett Prize. She has received Guggenheim, Hodder and Pew Fellowships and a Pushcart Prize. She was recently the Grace Hazard Conkling Writer-in-Residence at Smith College. She lives in Philadelphia with her husband and daughter. 'A Story Having To Do With Walt Whitman' is from *She Didn't Mean To Do It*, ©2001 Daisy Fried and reprinted with permission of the University of Pittsburgh Press.

Leah Fritz has lived in London for more than two decades, so don't ask her why she came here from New York. She can't remember. The author of two prose books on the 'counter-culture' and feminism over there, she has had four collections of poetry published here, *Going, Going...*, in hardback, (Bluechrome), being the most recent. She has no academic credentials at all, but did throw her bra in the famous dustbin in Atlantic City in 1968. 'Rembrandt' is reprinted from *Going, Going...* with permission from the author.

Alice Fulton was born in Troy, New York, was educated at Empire State College and received an MFA from Cornell in 1982. Fulton's recent books have won major prizes. *Felt* (2001) was awarded the 2002 Rebekah Johnson Bobbitt National Prize for Poetry from the Library of Congress. It was also chosen by the *Los Angeles Times* as one of the Best Books of 2001 and as a finalist for the Los Angeles Times Book Award. She is currently the Ann S. Bowers Professor of English at Cornell University. 'My Diamond Stud' and 'What I Like' are from *Dance Script with Electric Ballerina: Poems by Alice Fulton*, ©1983 Alice Fulton and used with the permission of the poet and the University of Illinois Press.

Anne-Marie Fyfe, (b. 1953, Cushendall, County Antrim), organises both the Coffee House Poetry reading series at London's Troubadour and the John Hewitt Spring Festival in the Antrim Glens. She was elected Chair of the Poetry Society (2006) and won first prize in The Cardiff International Poetry Competition (2004). A recent attic-conversion, to house her thirty-five years of *The New Yorker* and other vintage poetry publications, has merely hidden an ongoing problem! 'Novgorod Sidings' is from *The Ghost Twin*, ©Anne-Marie Fyfe 2005 and reprinted with permission from Peterloo Press.

Rhian Gallagher was born in 1961 on the South Island of New Zealand and studied at Victoria University in Wellington, at London University and the London College of Printing. She lived in London for eighteen years and returned to New Zealand to live in 2005. She participated in the pilot mentoring scheme set up by London Arts Board and The Poetry School, and her first collection *Salt Water Creek* (2003) was shortlisted for the Forward Prize. 'Amaryllis' is from *Salt Water Creek*, ©2003 Rhian Gallagher and reprinted with permission from Enitharmon Press.

Tess Gallagher, poet, essayist, short story writer and screenwriter, was born in 1943 in Port Angeles, Washington. She received her BA and MA from Washington University where she studied with Theodore Roethke. She also holds an MFA from the University of Iowa. She has won a number of awards and fellowships and Bloodaxe Books published her most recent poetry collection, *Dear Ghosts*, in 2007. She published *Barnacle Soup and Other Stories from the West of Ireland, the Stories of Josie Gray*, with Blackstaff Press in 2007. She has taught at St. Lawrence University, Kirkland College, Whitman College and the Universities of Montana, Arizona, Syracuse and Williamette. 'Instructions to the Double' is from the book of that name, ©1987 by Tess Gallagher and reprinted with permission of Graywolf Press.

337

Isabella Stewart Gardner (1840-1924) was born to a wealthy family in New York City. She was an influential American art collector, philanthropist and patron of the arts whose collection is now housed in the museum named after her in Boston, MA. Her appearance at a 1912 concert of the Boston Symphony wearing a white headband emblazoned with 'Oh, you Red Sox' was reported at the time to "almost have caused a panic" (Wikipedia). 'In The Museum' is from *The Collected Poems*, ©1990 by The Estate of Isabella Gardner. Reprinted with the permission of BOA Editions, Ltd.

Elizabeth Garrett was born in London and grew up in the Channel Islands. Her first book, *The Rule of Three*, was selected for the Next Generation Poets promotion in 1994. Her second book, *A Two-Part Invention*, appeared in 1998. She works as a professional piano teacher in Oxford. 'Russian Dolly' is from *The Rule of Three* (Bloodaxe), ©1991 Elizabeth Garrett and reprinted with permission of the author.

Deborah Garrison was born in Ann Arbor, Michigan in 1965 and educated at Brown and New York University. She worked for fifteen years on the editorial staff of *The New Yorker*, and is now the Poetry Editor at Alfred A. Knopf and a senior editor at Pantheon Books. Her poetry has been published in a variety of periodicals and in two collections, most recently *The Second Child* (Random House, 2007). She and her family live in Montclair, New Jersey. 'Please Fire Me' is from *A Working Girl Can't Win and Other Poems*, ©1998 Deborah Garrison and reprinted here with the permission of Random House, Inc.

Amy Gerstler was born in 1956. She has a BA in psychology and an MFA in nonfiction. Her book, *Bitter Angel* won the National Books Critics Circle Award. Author of reviews, fiction and various journal articles, she also collaborates with visual artists and her writing has been published in numerous exhibition catalogues. She currently lives in Los Angeles and teaches at Bennington in Vermont and the Art Center College of Design in Pasadena, California. 'A Non-Christian On Sunday' is from *Medicine*, ©2000 Amy Gerstler. Used by permission of Penguin, a division of the Penguin Group (USA) Inc.

Sandra M. Gilbert was born in 1936, in New York. She is a Professor of English Emerita at the University of California, Davis, and an influential and widely published literary critic and poet. Gilbert is also well known for her collaborative work with Susan Gubar, *The Madwoman in the Attic*, widely recognized as a central feminist text. She is the author of numerous other volumes, including seven collections of poetry, most recently *Belongings* (2005). Her most recent prose works are *Wrongful Death: A Memoir* (1995) and *Death's Door: Modern Dying and the Ways We Grieve* (2006). 'Going to Connecticut' is from *Kissing the Bread: New and Selected Poems 1969-1999*, ©2000 by Sandra M. Gilbert. By permission of W.W. Norton & Company, Inc.

Pamela Gillilan (1918-2001) was born in North London and was educated in Finchley (leaving school at 16, to join the Board of Trade in Whitehall as a civil servant; during the war she joined WRAF to serve as an airfield meteorologist.) She won the Cheltenham Festival poetry competition in 1979. Her selected poems, *All-Steel Traveller* (1994) includes work from her first book, *That Winter*, which was shortlisted for the Commonwealth Poetry Prize as the UK's best first collection. Her 'selected' does not include The Turnspit Dog. Her last collection, *The Rashomon Syndrome*, was published by Bloodaxe in 1998. 'Menopause' is from *All-Steel Traveller* (Bloodaxe) ©1994 Pamela Gillilan and is reprinted here by permission of the author's estate. www .pamelagillilan.co.uk.

Nikki Giovanni, a well-known black American poet, essayist and lecturer, was born in Knoxville Tennessee in 1943. She studied at Fisk, Pennsylvania and Columbia Universities. She founded the publishing company Niktom Ltd in 1970. She is currently working as a professor of English at Virginia Polytechnical Institute. 'Nikki-Rosa' is from *Black Feeling, Black Talk, Black Judgment*, ©1968, 1970 by Nikki Giovanni. Reprinted by permission of HarperCollins Publishers, USA.

Diane Glancy was born in 1941 in Kansas City, Missouri, of a Cherokee father and an English/German mother. The mother of two children herself, she obtained her MFA from the University of Iowa Writers' Workshop in 1988. For seventeen years she was a professor at Macalester College in St. Paul, Minnesota. She currently holds the visiting Richard Thomas Chair at Kenyon College. Her recent publications include: *In-Between Places*, essays, *The Dance Partner, Stories of the Ghost Dance*, and a new poetry collection, *Asylum in the Grasslands*. 'Christopher' and 'Kemo Sabe' are from *Rooms: New and Selected Poems*, ©2005 Diane Glancy, reprinted with permission of Salt Publishing.

Louise Glück was born in 1943 in New York City, and is the author of nine books of poetry and won the Pen/Martha Albrand Award for nonfiction for her collection of essays, *Proofs and Theories: Essays on Poetry* (1994). She has won numerous awards and fellowships for her poetry including the Pulitzer Prize and the National Books Critics Circle Award. A resident of Cambridge, MA, she taught at Williams College from 1983-2004. She currently teaches at Yale University. 'Mock Orange' and 'Anniversary' are reprinted in *The First Four Books of Poems* by Louise Glück,

Patricia Goedicke (1931-2006) was born in Boston, MA, and grew up in Hanover, NH. An accomplished downhill skier in High School, she graduated from Middlebury College in 1953. She earned her MFA from Ohio in 1965. She studied under W.H. Auden and Robert Frost, and wrote twelve books of poetry, was a popular teacher, conducting one workshop a year even after her retirement in 2003. 'The Reading Club' is from *The Wind of Our Going*,©1985 Patricia Goedicke. Reprinted with permission of Copper Canyon Press.

Jorie Graham was born in New York City in 1950 and spent her youth in Italy. She was educated at New York University and received an MFA from the University of Iowa. Among her numerous collections, *The Dream of the Unified Field: Selected Poems 1974-94* won the 1996 Pulitzer Prize for Poetry. She has also won a number of other awards and fellowships, edited two anthologies and is currently the Boylston Professor of Rhetoric and Oratory at Harvard University. 'Wanting a Child' is from *The Dream of the Unified Field: Selected Poems 1974-1994*, ©1996 Jorie Graham and reprinted with the permission of Carcanet Press in the UK and by HarperCollins in the USA.

Kathryn Gray was born in 1973 and raised in South Wales. She studied German and Medievalism at the Universities of Bristol and York. *The Never-Never*, her first collection, was nominated for the T.S. Eliot and Forward Prizes and her poems and articles have appeared widely. She is currently working on her first play in association with Sherman Cymru and is the new editor, as of 2008, of *The New Welsh Review*. 'Friend...' is from *The Never-Never*, ©2004 Kathryn Gray and reprinted with permission from Seren.

Linda Gregerson was born in 1950, and educated at Oberlin College, Northwestern University, the University of Iowa (MFA, 1977) and Stanford University (Ph.D, 1987). As well as four books of poetry she has written literary criticism, including *Negative Capability: Contemporary American Poetry* (2000). Waterbourne won the Kingsley Tufts Prize and Magnetic North (2007) was a finalist for the National Book Award. She teaches American Poetry and Renaissance Literature at the University of Michigan. 'Noah's Wife' is from *Waterbourne: Poems* ©2002 Linda Gregerson and reprinted with permission from Houghton Mifflin.

Linda Gregg was born in Suffern, New York and grew up in Marin County, California. She has published a number of collections since her first in 1981 and her honours include: a Guggenheim Fellowship, a Lannan Literary Foundation Fellowship, an NEA Grant, a Whiting Writer's Award, and multiple Pushcart prizes. She has taught at Iowa and Columbia Universities and currently lives in New York and teaches at Princeton. 'Marriage and Midsummer's Night' is from *In the Middle Distance*, ©2006 Linda Gregg and reprinted with permission from Graywolf Press.

Angelina Weld Grimke (1880-1958) was a journalist and poet, born in Boston, MA. From a prominent family, her father was a lawyer who became the second black person to graduate from Harvard Law School and her great-aunts were famous abolitionists. Active during the Harlem Renaissance, she eventually moved to Washington D.C. with her father and taught at Dunbar High School. She wrote essays, short stories and poems which were published in various newspapers and journals. 'Fragment' was found online.

Vona Groarke was born in Edgeworthstown, Co Longford, Ireland in 1964. She is the author of four acclaimed collections of poetry, *Shale, Other People's Houses, Flight* and *Juniper Street*. In 2008, she translated and introduced the eighteenth-century Irish epic poem, 'Lament for Art O'Leary'. She divides her teaching time between the Centre for New Writing at the University of Manchester and Wake Forest University in North Carolina. 'Call Waiting' is from *Juniper Street*, ©2006 Vona Groarke and is reprinted with permission from Gallery Press and Wake Forest University Press, USA.

Barbara Guest (1920-2006) was born in Wilmington, North Carolina and was educated at UCLA and UC Berkeley, where she graduated in 1943. Early in her career she was known as a writer of the New York School, a group of poets that included Ashbery, Koch, O'Hara, Schuyler. She wrote for Art News in the 1950s and her book *Dürer in the Window* (Roof Books, New York) includes many of her art reviews. She was on the board of the literary magazine *Partisan Review* in the 60s. She published numerous collections of poetry, several plays and one novel, *Seeking Air* (1978). 'Parachutes, My Love, Could Carry Us Higher' is from *Collected Poems*, ©2008 Barbara Guest and reprinted by permission of Wesleyan University Press.

Marilyn Hacker was born in New York City in 1942. Author of eleven collections, most recently *Essays on Departure, New and Selected Poems* (Carcanet, 2006), and eight collections of poetry translated from the French, including Venus Khoury-Ghata's *Nettles* (Graywolf Press, 2008). Her honours include the National Book Award, an Award in Literature from the American Academy of Arts and Letters, the Prix Max Jacob Etranger (France) and the 2007 Robert Fagles

Translation Prize. She currently lives in New York City and Paris. 'Mythology' is from *Love, Death and the Changing of Seasons* (W.W. Norton), ©1986 Marilyn Hacker. 'Square du Temple II' is from *Desperanto* (W.W. Norton), ©2003 Marilyn Hacker. 'Ghazal: min al-hobbi ma khatal' first appeared in *Modern Poetry in Translation*. Poems reprinted with permission from the author.

Rachel Hadas was born in New York City in 1948. Author of numerous books of poetry, essays and translations, the book in which this poem appears was a finalist for the Lenore Marshall Poetry Prize. Hadas studied classics at Harvard, poetry at Johns Hopkins and comparative literature at Princeton. Four years spent in Greece had a profound impact on her work. Since 1981 she has taught in the English Department of the New Jersey campus of Rutgers University as well as occasional courses at Columbia and Princeton. Recent titles include: *Laws* (2004), *The River of Forgetfulness* (2006) and *Classics* (2007). She is currently co-editing an anthology of Greek poetry in translation from Homer to the present. She lives in New York City. 'The Red Hat' is from *Halfway Down The Hall: New and Selected Poems*, ©1998 Rachel Hadas and reprinted by permission of Wesleyan University Press.

Kimiko Hahn was born in Mt. Kisco, New York, in 1955, the child of two artists, a Japanese American mother from Hawaii and a German American father from Wisconsin. She is the author of seven collections of poetry and has won numerous awards and fellowships including from the NEA, and the New York Foundation for the Arts, a Lila Wallace Reader's Digest Prize, the Theodore Roethke Memorial Poetry Prize, and an American Book Award. She is Distinguished Professor in the English Department at Queens College/CUNY and lives in New York. 'In Childhood' is from *The Artist's Daughter*, ©2002 by Kimiko Hahn. Used by permission of W. W. Norton & Company, Inc.

Saskia Hamilton was born in 1967 in Washington, D.C. She is the author of *Canal: New and Selected Poems* as well as two American collections, *As for Dream* (Graywolf, 2001) and *Divide These* (Graywolf, 2005). She is the editor of *The Letters of Robert Lowell* (Faber & Faber, 2005). The recipient of fellowships from the Radcliffe Institute and the National Endowment for the Arts, she teaches at Barnard College, Columbia University. 'Elegy' comes from *Divide These* (Graywolf, 2005), reprinted in *Canal: New and Selected Poems* (Arc, 2005).

Mary Stewart Hammond was born in 1947 and raised in Roanoke, VA and Baltimore, MD. Her poems have appeared in many magazines including *The Atlantic Monthly, American Poetry Review, Boulevard, The Gettysburg Review, Field, The New Criterion, The New England Review, The New Yorker, The Paris Review, The Yale Review*, and numerous anthologies. Among her awards are MacDowell and Yaddo fellowships, a Poet-in-Residence fellowship from the Writers Community in New York City and the New Writers Award for the best first collection for *Out of Canaan* from the GLCA. She conducts master classes in poetry under the auspices of The New York Writers Workshop. 'Making Breakfast' originally appeared in *The New Yorker* and is included in her collection *Out of Canaan*, ©1991 Mary Stewart Hammond. It is reprinted with permission from W.W. Norton & Company, Inc.

Sarah Hannah (1966-2007) was born in Massachusetts. Her mother was the painter Renee Rothbein; Nathan Goldstein, her father and also an artist, is the author of art books such as *Design and Composition* (Prentice Hall) and *Drawing to See*, co-authored with Harriet Fishman, Sarah's step-mother. Hannah received a BA from Wesleyan and an MFA and Ph.D from Columbia University. Widely published, she was also an editor at Barrow Street Press and Poet Laureate of the Friends of Hemlock Gorge, an organization of nature conservators in Newton, MA. She was awarded a Governor's Fellowship for residencies at the Virginia Center for the Creative Arts for the summers of 2001, 02, and 06. The original ms. for her first collection was a semi-finalist for the Yale Younger Poets Prize in 2002. She died young, while this book was being compiled, but not before "having been kissed by three out of the four members of The Monkees band, a fact of which she was inordinately proud.". Her book *Inflorescence* appeared posthumously in 2007. 'Cassetta Frame' and 'The Linen Closest' are from *Longing Distance* ©2004 Sarah Hannah and reprinted with permission from the estate and Tupelo Press.

Sophie Hannah, poet and novelist, has won awards for her short stories and her poetry. She was selected for the Next Generation poetry promotion and Penguin have recently published her *Selected Poems*. She has published three psychological thrillers - *Little Face, Hurting Distance* and *The Point of Rescue* - and a collection of short stories, *The Fantastic Book of Everybody's Secrets*. Her recent collection, *Pessimism for Beginners*, was a Poetry Book Society Choice and was shortlisted for the 2007 T.S. Eliot Prize. From 1997-99 she was Fellow Commoner in Creative Arts at Trinity College, Cambridge, and from 1999-2001, a fellow at Wolfson College, Oxford. She currently lives in West Yorkshire with her family. 'The End of Love' is from *The Hero and the Girl Next Door*, ©1995 Sophie Hannah and is reprinted by permission of Carcanet Press Ltd.

Choman Hardi was born in Iraqi Kurdistan in 1974, just before the collapse of the Kurdish revolution and the flight of her family to Iran. Following an Iraqi government amnesty for the Kurds, she returned to her hometown at the age of five and lived there until she was fourteen. When the Iraqi government gassed Halabja in 1988, in tandem with the genocide campaign known as Anfal, her family fled to Iran again. She came to England in 1993 where she was educated at Queen's College, Oxford (BA, Philosophy and Psychology), University College London (MA, Philosophy) and the University of Kent in Canterbury (Ph.D, Mental Health). Currently, she is researching the lives and survival strategies of the Anfal widows. 'My Children' is from *Life for Us*, ©2004 Choman Hardi and reprinted here with permission from Bloodaxe Books.

Joy Harjo is an internationally known poet, performer, writer and musician. She was born in Tulsa, Oklahoma in 1951. She received her B.A. from the University of New Mexico and her MFA from the University of Iowa Writers Workshop. She has published seven books of award-winning poetry, most recently *How We Became Human:New and Selected Poems* from W.W. Norton. In Harjo's music CDs, she is featured as poet and saxophone player and has performed internationally. Her photographs were displayed in the May 2007 art show *Looking Indian* at the Untitled ArtSpace Gallery in Oklahoma City. She writes a monthly column for her tribal newspaper, the *Muscogee Nation News*. She was recently the Joseph M. Russo endowed professor at UNM in Creative Writing. When not teaching and performing she lives in Honolulu, Hawaii where she belongs to the Hui Nalu Canoe Club. 'She Had Some Horses' is from the book (and CD) of that name and is reprinted here with permission from the author.

Gwen Harwood, Australian poet and librettist, was born in Taringa, Queensland and brought up in Brisbane where she was an organist at All Saints Church. She moved to Tasmania upon marriage and her first book of poems was published in 1963. Her early work is notable for the use of numerous pseudonyms, some of which have only been uncovered by literary detective work. She is also known for her series of poems with recurring characters, two of the most notorious being Professor Eisenbart and Kröte. 'In The Park' is from *Selected Poems*, ©2001 John Harwood, published and reprinted with permission by Penguin Group (Australia).

Lyn Hejinian was born in the San Francisco Bay area in 1941. Poet, essayist and translator (from Russian), she is the author of a number of books of poetry and also *The Language of Inquiry* (University of California Press, 2000), a collection of essays. From 1976-84 she was an editor at Tuumba Press and since 1981 she has been the co-editor of Poetics. She is also the co-director of Atelos, a literary project commissioning cross-genre work by poets. She has won fellowships from the NEA and from the Academy of American Poets. She lives in Berkeley, California. 'Come October, It's the Lake Not the Border' is from *The Fatalist*, (Omnidawn), ©2003 Lyn Hejinian and reprinted with the permission of the author and the publisher, Omnidawn.

Ruth Herschberger was born in 1917 in Philipse Manor, New York and grew up in Chicago. She was educated at the University of Chicago and Black Mountain College. She also studied theatre and poetry at the University of Michigan and Playwriting at the Dramatic Workshop of the New School for Social Research in New York City. She is the author of two collections of poetry, *Nature & Love Poems* (1969) and *A Way of Happening* (1948), and a book of feminist essays, *Adam's Rib* (1948). She won a number of awards for her poetry, including: a Hopwood Award, The Midland Authors Award, The Harriet Monroe Memorial Prize, a Rockefeller grant and a Bolligen grant for her translations of Vladimir Mayakovsky. She lives in Westbeth's artists' residence, Greenwich Village, New York City. 'The Huron' is from *Nature & Love Poems* (Eakins Press), 1969.

H.D. (1886-1961) Hilda Doolittle was born in Bethlehem, Pennsylvania. Her mother was a Moravian and her father, an astronomer. As a young woman she began life-long friendships with Ezra Pound and Marianne Moore. She dropped out of Bryn Mawr University and made her way to England in 1913 where she became well-known as essentially an 'imagist' poet but her style evolved away from this over quite a lengthy and volatile personal and professional life. Although she suffered a breakdown after World War II, she experienced some of her most prolific writing years then, in her sixties. She died from the complications of a stroke. 'Helen' is from *Trilogy*, ©1997 estate of Hilda Doolittle and reprinted in the UK with the permission of Carcanet Press Limited, and in the USA by New Directions.

Rita Ann Higgins was born in 1955 in Galway, Ireland, where she still lives. One of thirteen children, she left school at fourteen, and was in her late twenties when she started writing poetry. She has since published seven collections including: *Sunny Side Plucked: New & Selected Poems*, a Poetry Book Society Recommendation She has performed her work throughout the world. Peter Porter called her 'A quite untameable poet'. 'The Did-You-Come-Yets of the Western World' is from *Throw in the Vowels: New and Selected Poems* ©2005 Rita Ann Higgins and reprinted here with permission from Bloodaxe Books.

Selima Hill was born in 1945 and grew up in rural England and Wales. She read Moral Sciences at New Hall, Cambridge and regularly collaborates on multi-media projects with the Royal Ballet, Welsh National Opera and BBC Bristol. She is a tutor at the Poetry School in London and has taught creative writing in hospitals and prisons. In 1988 she won first prize in the Arvon Foundation/Observer International Poetry Competition for her long poem: 'The Accumulation of Small Acts of Kindness' and her collection, *Violet*, was shortlisted for the Forward, the T.S. Eliot and the Whitbread Poetry prizes. *Bunny* (2001) won the Whitbread Poetry Award. Her recent book is *Red Roses* (2006). 'Please Can I Have A Man' is from *Violet*, ©1997 Selima Hill and reprinted with permission from Bloodaxe Books.

Brenda Hillman was born in Tucson, Arizona, in 1951. She was educated at Pomona College and received her MFA from the University of Iowa. She is the author of seven collections of poetry and is also the co-editor of *The Grand Permission: New Writings on Poetics and Motherhood* (Wesleyan University Press 2003) and has edited a collection of Emily Dickinson's poems. She has received fellowships from the Guggenheim Foundation, and the NEA, as well as the William Carlos Williams Prize from the Poetry Society of America. She is the Olivia Flippi Professor of Poetry at St Mary's College in Moraga, California and does anti-war activism with CodePink. 'Trois Merceaux En Forme De Poire' is from *White Dress*, ©1985 Brenda Hillman and reprinted by permission of Wesleyan University Press, and 'november moon' appeared in the *Electronic Poetry Review* and is forthcoming in *Practical Water*, (2009) also from Wesleyan University Press.

Jane Hirshfield was born in New York City in 1953. After receiving her BA from Princeton (in their first graduating class to include women) she went on to study at the San Francisco Zen Center. Hirshfield's sixth poetry collection, *After*, was a finalist for the T.S. Eliot Prize, a Poetry Book Society Choice, and named a best book of 2006 by the *Washington Post, Financial Times* (UK), and *San Francisco Chronicle*. Other honours include major fellowships from the Guggenheim and Rockefeller Foundations, National Endowment for the Arts, and Academy of American Poets. Hirshfield's other books include three now-classic anthologies of work by women poets from the past and a book of essays on poetry, *Nine Gates*. She lives in Northern California. 'In Praise of Coldness', 'Burlap Sack', and 'The Bell Zygmunt' are all from *Each Happiness Ringed by Lions: Selected Poems,* ©2005 Jane Hirshfield and reprinted with permission from Bloodaxe Books.

Linda Hogan was born in Denver in 1947, spent most of her childhood in Oklahoma and Colorado and although she did not grow up within a Native American community (her tribal affiliation is Chickasaw), the main focus of her work is the traditional indigenous view of and relationship to the land, animals and plants. She has received numerous awards for her poetry and fiction, as well as Guggenheim and NEA grants. *Mean Spirit* was one of three finalists for the Pulitzer Prize in 1990. She is currently a Lecturer in International Peace Studies at the Irish School of Ecumenics at Trinity College, Dublin. 'Skin' is from *The Book of Medicines*, ©1993 by Linda Hogan. Reprinted with permission of Coffee House Press.

Jane Holland is a poet, novelist and editor, born Essex, 1966. She won an Eric Gregory Award for her poetry in 1996. Her first collection, *The Brief History of a Disreputable Woman,* was published by Bloodaxe in 1997. A first novel, *Kissing the Pink,* followed from Sceptre in 1999. Her second poetry collection *Boudicca & Co.* was published by Salt in 2006. She is currently living in Warwickshire with her husband and five children, where she edits the online literary magazine *Horizon Review* and is the Warwick Poet Laureate for 2008. In a previous incarnation, she was a professional snooker player on the women's circuit, ranked 24th in the world, until she was banned for life in 1995 for 'bringing the game into disrepute'. 'The Knife' is from *Camper Van Blues* (Salt 2008), ©Jane Holland and reprinted with permission from the author and Salt Publishing.

Fanny Howe was born in Buffalo, New York, in 1940. She is the author of more than twenty books of poetry and prose including a *Selected Poems* which won the Lenore Marshall Poetry Prize in 2001, and a collection of literary essays: *The Wedding Dress: Meditations on Word and Life* (University of California Press, 2003). She was shortlisted for the Griffin Poetry Prize in 2001 and 2005 and she has lectured in Creative Writing at Tufts, Emerson College, Columbia, Yale and the Massachusetts Institute of Technology. '9-11-01' is from *Selected Poems: New California Poetry,* ©2000 Fanny Howe (U of California Press), reprinted with permission from the author.

Marie Howe was born in 1950. She is the author of two volumes of poetry and co-editor of a book of essays, *In the Company of my Solitude: American Writing from the AIDS Pandemic* (1994). She has won NEA and Guggenheim fellowships, and was selected for a Lavan Younger Poets Prize from the American Academy of Poets. She has taught Creative Writing at Sarah Lawrence College, Columbia and New York University. Her first collection, *The Good Thief* was a National Poetry Series selection. Her second book was inspired by the loss of two close relatives, a mother and a brother, within a short space of time. 'Death, The Last Visit' is from *The Good Thief,* ©1988 by Marie Howe. Reprinted by permission of Persea Books, Inc. (New York).

Sue Hubbard, at various times an antique dealer and a smallholder, Hubbard has published two collections of poetry, *Everything Begins with the Skin* (Enitharmon) and *Ghost Station* (Salt). A Hawthornden Fellow, she has been awarded two bursaries to Yaddo and twice won the London Writers' Competition as well as third prize in the National, the Cardiff, the Peterloo and the *Times Literary Supplement* competitions. The Poetry Society's first Public Art Poet she was responsible for London's largest public art poem at Waterloo. Her first novel *Depth of Field* is published by Dewi Lewis and her collection of short stories, *Rothko's Red* will appear in 2008 from Salt. She also writes on art for *The Independent* and *The New Statesman*. 'A Necklace of Tongues' is from *Ghost Station,* ©2004 Sue Hubbard reprinted with permission from Salt Publishing.

Colette Inez was born in Belgium, the "unexpected outcome of a love affair between a French archivist and a French-American priest" and grew up with Catholic sisters, and managed to land in Long Island before the outbreak of World War II. She has published nine books of poetry and has won Guggenheim, Rockefeller, and two NEA fellowships and Pushcart Prizes. She teaches in Columbia University's Undergraduate Writing Program and has recently released a memoir: *The Secret of M Dulong*, (University of Wisconsin Press.) 'The Chairs', ©2006 Colette Inez, originally appeared in *Louisville Review*.

Josephine Jacobsen (1908-2003) was born in Cobourg, Ontario. Poet, short story writer and critic, she served as poetry consultant to the Library of Congress from 1971-73, and as honorary consultant in American letters from 1973-9, amongst other appointments. Her awards include: an Academy of American Poets Fellowship and the Shelley Memorial Award for lifetime service to literature. 'Of Pairs' is from *In the Crevice of Time: New and Collected Poems*, ©1995 Josephine Jacobsen. Reprinted with permission of Johns Hopkins University Press.

Kathleen Jamie was born in Renfrewshire, Scotland in 1962. She studied philosophy at Edinburgh University, and has published several collections of poetry and a travel book about Northern Pakistan, *The Golden Peak*, which was recently updated and reissued as *Among Muslims* (2002). She has also written for the radio, travel-scripts and specially commissioned long poems. She lives in Fife and in 1999 was appointed Lecturer in Creative Writing at St. Andrews University. She has won various prizes including a Somerset Maugham Award, the Forward Prize for Best Individual Poem and for Best Collection, and two Geoffrey Faber Memorial awards. 'Ultrasound' is from *Jizzen*, (Picador) ©1999 Kathleen Jamie and reprinted with permission from Pan Macmillan, UK.

Carolyn Jess-Cooke was born in 1978 in Belfast, Northern Ireland. She holds a Ph.D in Shakespearean Cinema and is Senior Lecturer in Film Studies at the University of Sunderland. Her work has appeared in *Poetry London, Magma, Ambit, Poetry Ireland Review, The Wolf, Poetry New Zealand, Stand, The Stinging Fly*, amongst others. Her work has won various awards, including a Gregory Award, a major Arts Council award, the Tyrone Guthrie Prize, and recently a Northern Promise Award. A vehement chocoholic, her medical record includes the eternally damning statement, "avoids even trivial exercise". 'Inroads' first appeared in *The Shop* and is the title poem from her forthcoming collection from Seren. Reprinted with permission from the author and Seren.

June Jordan (1936-2002) was born in Harlem, New York to Jamaican immigrants. She was an African-American bisexual political activist, writer, poet and teacher. Author of 28 books, her *Directed By Desire: The Collected Poems of June Jordan* (2005) appeared posthumously. She began a distinguished teaching career in 1967 at the City College of New York and went on to become professor in the Departments of English, Women's Studies and African American Studies at UC Berkeley. She also taught at Yale. She won many awards and fellowships including the Achievement Award for International Reporting from the National Association of Black Journalists in 1984. 'The Reception' is from *Naming Our Destiny: New and Selected Poems*, ©2006 June Jordan Literary trust; reprinted by permission; www.junejordan.com.

Jenny Joseph was born in Birmingham in 1932 and read English at St. Hilda's College, Oxford. Her much-anthologised dramatic monologue 'Warning' was written in 1961 and was recently found by a BBC poll to be the most popular twentieth century poem. Before and since then she has written prose and poetry using various forms, for adults and children. Her 'story in prose and verse', *Persephone*, won the James Tait Black Award for fiction in 1986. She has worked with painters, photographers, musicians, actors and dancers. Her latest book of poems, *Extreme of Things*, came out in 2006 from Bloodaxe Books. 'Warning', ©Jenny Joseph and is reprinted with permission of the author.

Sylvia Kantaris was born in 1936 in the Derbyshire Peak District. She studied French at Bristol University, taught in Bristol and London and then spent ten years in Australia where she taught French at Queensland University, had a family and completed her MA and Ph.D theses on French Surrealism. In 1974 she moved to Helston, Cornwall, from where she taught for the Open University, Exeter University, The Arvon Foundation and various schools and colleges. She has published six collections of poetry since 1975, including *Dirty Washing: New and Selected Poems* (Bloodaxe 1989). Her recent full collection is *Lad's Love* (Bloodaxe 1993). 'Annunciation' was first published in the *Times Literary Supplement* and then in *The Tenth Muse* (Peterloo) reprint *Menhir*, ©1986 Sylvia Kantaris.

Martha Kapos won the Jerwood/Aldeburgh Prize for Best First Collection for her book, *My Nights in Cupid's Palace* which also received a Poetry Book Society Special Commendation. Born in 1941, in America, she came to London for a gap year following her Classics degree from Harvard, and never returned. She is Assistant Poetry Editor of *Poetry London*. Her second collection, *Supreme Being,* is due from Enitharmon in 2008. 'Accomplice' is from *My Nights in Cupid's Palace*, ©2003 Martha Kapos and reprinted with permission from Enitharmon Press.

Joy Katz was born in Newark, New Jersey in 1963 and raised in various places on the east coast of the USA. She is the author of two poetry collections, *Fabulae* (Southern Illinois University Press, 2002) and *The Garden Room* (Tupelo Press, 2006). She is editor-at-large for *Pleiades* and presently teaches at The New School and New York University. She lives in Brooklyn, New York, with her husband and young son. 'The Family, One Week Old' first appeared in *Blackbird* and is reprinted with the author's permission.

Shirley Kaufman. Born in Seattle in 1928 and resident of San Francisco for some years, Kaufman is the author of eight books of poetry and several translations from the Hebrew. Her awards include the Shelley Memorial Award from the Poetry Society of America and the Alice Fay di Castagnoia Award. She has also won two NEA Fellowships. A native of Seattle, she has made her home in Jerusalem since 1973. 'Jealousy' is from *Rivers of Salt*, ©1993 Shirley Kaufman. Reprinted with the permission of Copper Canyon Press.

Jackie Kay was born in Edinburgh in 1961 to a Scottish mother and Nigerian father. She was adopted and brought up in Glasgow, studying at the Royal Scottish Academy of Music and Drama and Stirling University where she read English. As well as prize-winning collections of poetry, her first novel, *Trumpet* (1998) inspired by the story of a Scottish jazz trumpeter Joss Moody whose death revealed that he was, in fact, a woman, was awarded the Guardian Fiction Prize. She lives in Manchester. 'The Shoes of Dead Comrades' is from *Darling: New & Selected Poems*, ©2008 Jackie Kay and is reprinted with permission of Bloodaxe Books. 'I Am The Child' is reprinted with permission from the author.

Judith Kazantzis, born in 1940, is a Londoner of Irish-English parentage. She has published ten collections of poetry including her midway *Selected Poems 1977-1992*, and a novel, *Of Love And Terror* (2002). Her latest collection is *Just After Midnight* (Enitharmon, 2004). She received a Cholmondeley Award in 2007. After much time in Key West and London, she lives in Lewes, Sussex. 'The Dose' was first published in *Poetry Review*, ©2006 Judith Kazantzis. See www.judithkazantzis.com.

Brigit Pegeen Kelly was born in Palo Alto, California in 1951. Among her publications, *Song* was the 1994 Lamont Poetry Selection of the Academy of American Poets. *To The Place of Trumpets* (1987) was selected by James Merill for the Yale Series of Younger Poets. Among her many other honours are the Cecil Hemley Award from the Poetry Society of America, a Pushcart Prize and the Theodore Roethke Prize. She is currently a professor of English at the University of Illinois, Urbana-Champaign. 'Imagining Their Own Hymns', ©1988 Brigit Pegeen Kelly reprinted from *To The Place of Trumpets* with permission of Yale University Press.

Jane Kenyon (1947-1995) was born in Ann Arbor, Michigan and grew up in the midwest. Kenyon earned a BA from the University of Michigan and an MA in 1972. She published four collections of poems in her lifetime and spent some years translating the poems of Anna Akhmatova. She was New Hampshire's poet laureate when she died from leukemia. She had been working on *Otherwise: New and Selected Poems*, which was published posthumously in 1996. 'Things' and 'Otherwise' are both from *Collected Poems*, ©2007 The Estate of Jane Kenyon and reprinted here with permission from Graywolf Press.

Mimi Khalvati was born in 1944 in Tehran and grew up on the Isle of Wight. She trained at The Drama Centre, London and then worked as a theatre director in Tehran, translating from English into Farsi and devising new plays as well as co-founding the Theatre in Exile group. She is the founder of The Poetry School in London, where she teaches. Her collections include *Selected Poems* (2000) and *The Chine* (2002). She received a Cholmondeley Award in 2006, and 'Ghazal:The Servant' is from her recent book, *The Meanest Flower*, which is a Poetry Book Society Recommendation, and was shortlisted for the T.S. Eliot Prize, ©2007 Mimi Khalvati and reprinted with permission from Carcanet Press Limited.

Carolyn Kizer was born in Spokane, Washington in 1925. She is the author of eight books of poetry including *Yin* which won the Pulitzer Prize in 1984. In 1959 she founded *Poetry Northwest* and served as its editor until 1965. From 1966-70 she served as the first Director of the Literature Program for the National Endowment of the Arts. A former Chancellor of the Academy of American Poets, she lives in Sonoma, California and Paris. 'Parent's Pantoum' and 'Bitch' are from *Cool, Calm & Collected: Poems 1960-2000*, ©2001 Carolyn Kizer. Reprinted with the permission of Copper Canyon Press.

Maxine Kumin was born in 1925, attended Radcliffe College where she obtained a BA and an MA, and has lectured at many universities, including Princeton, Tufts and Brandeis. She has written a number of poetry collections including *Up Country* (1972) which won a Pulitzer Prize. She has also published several novels, collections of essays and short stories and more than twenty children's books, several of them in collaboration with the poet Anne Sexton. 'In The Root Cellar' is from *Selected Poems: 1960-1990*, ©1975 by Maxine Kumin. Used by permission of W.W. Norton & Company, Inc.

Deborah Landau was born in Colorado and grew up in Ann Arbor, Michigan. She was educated at Stanford, Columbia and Brown where she was a Javits Fellow and earned a Ph.D in English and American Literature. Her poems, essays, and reviews have appeared widely and her book *Orchidelirium* won the Anhinga Prize for Poetry. She is a two-time winner of the Los Angeles Poetry in the Windows Contest and a National Poetry Series finalist, and has been nominated three times for a Pushcart Prize. She is Director of the Creative Writing Program at NYU. 'August in West Hollywood' is reprinted from a sequence called 'Lola and the Grape' from *Orchidelirium*, courtesy of Anhinga Press, ©2004 Deborah Landau.

Ann Lauterbach is the author of seven poetry collections including *If In Time: Selected Poems 1975-2000* (2001) and *Hum* (2005), and a book of essays: *The Night Sky: Writings on the Poetics of Experience* (2005). She is the co-chair of Writing in the Milton Avery Graduate School of the Arts and Schwab Professor of Languages and Literature at Bard College. She has received fellowships from the Ingram Merrill, Guggenheim, and John D. and Catherine T. MacArthur foundations. 'Hum' is the title poem from that collection, ©2005 Ann Lauterbach reprinted by permission of Penguin Group, USA, Inc.

Dorianne Laux was born in 1952 in Augusta, Maine and is of Irish, French and Algonquin Indian heritage. She worked in a number of jobs, including sanatorium cook and gas station manager, before receiving her BA in English from Mills College in 1988. A finalist for the National Book Critics Circle Award, Laux's fourth book of poems, *Facts about the Moon* (W.W. Norton), was the recipient of the Oregon Book Award and short-listed for the Lenore Marshall Poetry Prize. Her other collections are: *Awake* (1990), *What We Carry* (1994), *Smoke* (2000) and *Superman: the Chapbook* (2008). She lives in Raleigh, North Carolina where she is Poet-in-Residence at North Carolina State University. 'The Shipfitter's Wife' is from *Smoke*, ©2000 by Dorianne Laux. Reprinted with the permission of BOA Editions.

Emma Lazarus (1849-1887) was born in and grew up around New York City's Union Square. Fluent in German and French, she was encouraged by her family to write verse and her father published her first book, *Poems and Translations Written Between the Ages of Fourteen and Seventeen*. She wrote 'The New Colossus' in 1883 for an art auction, in aid of the Bartholdi Pedestal Fund, dedicated to raising funds for the pedestal for the Statue of Liberty. In 1903, sixteen years after her death, her sonnet was engraved on a plaque and placed in the pedestal.

Phillis Levin was born in Paterson, New Jersey in 1954. Levin met Allen Ginsberg at a party when she was twelve, an encounter that sparked her poem, 'Dancing with Allen Ginsberg,' in her third collection. She is the author of four books of poetry, *Temples and Fields* (1988), *The Afterimage* (1995), *Mercury* (2001), and *May Day* (2008), and is the editor of *The Penguin Book of the Sonnet* (2001). Her honours include a Fulbright Fellowship to Slovenia, the Amy Lowell Poetry Travelling Scholarship, a Guggenheim Fellowship, and a 2007 National Endowment for the Arts Fellowship. She lives in New York, is a professor of English and Poet-in-Residence at Hofstra University, and also teaches in the graduate creative writing program at New York University. 'Acorn' ©2007 Phillis Levin, first appeared in *Poetry Northwest* and has recently been published, along with 'Keep Reading' and 'Box in Eden' in *May Day*, ©Phillis Levin and reprinted with permission from Penguin, New York, and the author.

Denise Levertov (1923-1997) was born in Ilford, Essex. Her mother was Welsh, her father had immigrated from Germany and became an Anglican parson. Levertov was educated at home and developed an early desire to be a writer. After serving as a nurse in London during the Blitz, she moved to America upon marriage. In the 1960s and 70s she was politically active, influenced by the Black Mountain School of poets. She was also Poetry Editor for *The Nation* magazine and wrote many anti-Vietnam war poems. She taught at Brandeis, MIT and Tufts Universities and was full professor at Stanford from 1982-93. 'Despair', 'To The Reader' and 'Hypocrite Women' are from *New Selected Poems*, ©2003 The Estate of Denise Levertov and are reprinted here with permission from Bloodaxe Books in the UK and New Directions/Pollinger Ltd. for the USA.

Gwyneth Lewis was born in 1959 in Cardiff, Wales, educated at Girton College, Cambridge and received a D.Phil in English from Oxford for her thesis on eighteenth century literary forgery. She has published six books of poetry in Welsh and English and has written several prose titles including *Sunbathing in the Rain: A Cheerful Book on Depression* and *Two in a Boat* recounting a voyage she made on a small boat from Cardiff to North Africa. Among her many awards and grants, she was appointed Wales' First National Poet from 2005-06. 'Advice on Adultery', (from 'Welsh Espionage') and 'Pentecost' are all reprinted in *Chaotic Angels: Collected Poems*, ©2005 Gwyneth Lewis and reprinted with permission from Bloodaxe Books.

Kate Lilley was born in Perth, in Western Australia, in 1960. After studying at the University of Sydney she completed a Ph.D on Masculine Elegy at the University of London and was then Julia Mann Junior Research Fellow at St Hilda's College, Oxford. She is the editor of the Penguin Classics edition of Margaret Cavendish's *Blazing World* and has published widely on early modern women's writing, Australian literature and feminist theory. She is a senior lecturer in the English Department at the University of Sydney. Her first volume of poems, *Versary* appeared from Salt Publishing in 2002 and won the Grace Leven Prize. 'Cento/Around Vienna' was first published in *Jacket* magazine, ©2005 Kate Lilley.

Hilary Llewellyn-Williams was born in 1951 in Kent but made her home in Carmarthenshire, Wales for a number of years before moving to Pontypool. Widely published, she is the author of five collections of poems, has read her work at a variety of venues worldwide and has taught in universities, schools, workshops and seminars. She is also a qualified counsellor, and is into Gestalt, allotments, cats and Sufism. 'Making Man' is from *Greenland*, ©2003 Hilary Llewellyn-Williams and reprinted with the permission of Seren.

Amy Lowell (1874-1925) was born into a prominent Boston family. Denied college due to her sex, she compensated for this with avid reading and near-fanatical book-collecting. She travelled to Europe, lived as a socialite, smoked cigars and was influenced by Ezra Pound and Elenora Duse. She died of a cerebral haemorrhage at the age of 51. The following year, she was awarded the Pulitzer Prize for her book, *What's O'Clock*. There has been a resurgence of interest in her work in part because of its focus on lesbian themes and her imagistic style. 'Penumbra' is from *Amy Lowell: Selected Poems* (Library of America, 2004).

Catherine Phil MacCarthy was born in 1954 in Crecora, Co. Limerick. She is the author of four books of poems, a first joint-book and three collections: *How High the Moon* (Poetry Ireland/Co-Operation North 1991); *This Hour of the Tide* (Salmon 1994); *the blue globe* (Blackstaff Press 1998); and *Suntrap* (Blackstaff Press 2007). She has won prizes and awards and is a former editor of *Poetry Ireland Review*. She was Writer-in-Residence for the City of Dublin in 1994, and University College, Dublin in 2002. Her first novel, *One Room an Everywhere* was published by Blackstaff Press in 2003. She works regularly at the Irish Writers Centre as a tutor of creative writing and lives in Dublin. 'Rag Doll' is from *This Hour of the Tide*, ©1994 Catherine Phil MacCarthy and reprinted with permission of the author.

Gwendolyn MacEwen (1941-1987) was born in Toronto, Canada. Author of many poetry collections, among them the Governor General's Award winning collections *The Shadow Maker* (Macmillan 1969), and *Afterworlds*. Her poetry explores magic, history and the writing of verse. She also wrote novels, short stories, two children's books and a travel narrative: *Mermaids and Ikons: A Greek Summer* (House of Anansi 1978). 'Let Me Make This Perfectly Clear' is from *Afterworlds* (McClelland & Stewart) ©1987 and permission for use is granted by the author's family.

Elizabeth Macklin was born in Poughkeepsie, New York in 1952, and is the author of *A Woman Kneeling in the Big City* and *You've Just Been Told*. She worked on the editorial staff of *The New Yorker* from 1974 until 1999, when an Amy Lowell Poetry Travelling Scholarship allowed her to begin studying the language of the Basque Country; her translation of the Basque poet Kirmen Uribe was published in 2007. She has also received an Ingram Merrill Foundation Prize and a Guggenheim Fellowship. She works as a freelance editor in New York City. 'Despite the Temptation' appeared in *Epiphany* and 'How To Wait' initially appeared in *The New Yorker*, both reprinted with permission from the author.

Sarah Maguire was born in west London in 1957. She has published four poetry collections, including *The Invisible Mender* (1997), *The Florist's at Midnight* (2001) and *The Pomegranates of Kandahar* (2007). She is the editor of *Flora Poetica: The Chatto Book of Botanical Verse*. The first writer to be sent to Palestine and Yemen by the British Council, she is the only living English language poet with a book in print in Arabic; her selected poems, *Haleeb Muraq*, translated by Saadi Yousef, was published in Damascus in 2003. Founder and Director of the Poetry Translation Centre, she is currently translating the Sudanese poet Al-Saddiq Al-Raddi. 'Spilt Milk' is the title poem of her first collection, which was republished in 2007 as part of the Poetry Book Society's 'Back in Print' series ©1991, 2007 Sarah Maguire and reprinted with permission from the author.

Kathryn Maris was born in 1971, in Long Island, New York, and is the author of *The Book of Jobs* (Four Way Books, 2006). She has received several fellowships and awards, most recently a Pushcart Prize. Maris credits her university professor, Kenneth Koch, who shouted "Help! Somebody call the Biology Department" on discovering a live bird's nest in his New York City classroom, with influencing her decision to become a poet despite her ignorance of the natural world. 'Goddess' and 'The Boatman' are from *The Book of Jobs*, ©2006 Kathryn Maris. Reprinted with permission of Four Ways Books, Inc. All rights reserved.

Cleopatra Mathis was born in 1947 and raised in Ruston, Louisiana. She has published six collections of poetry including *What to Tip the Boatman* which won the Jane Kenyon Award for Outstanding Book of Poems in 2001. Her recent title is *White Sea* (Sarabande, 2005). Her numerous awards include two NEA grants, The Peter Lavin Award for Younger Poets from the Academy of American Poets, two Pushcart Prizes, The Robert Frost Award, The May Sarton Award, and a number of fellowships. Since 1982 she has been Professor of English and Creative Writing at Dartmouth College. 'Getting Out' is from *Aerial View of Louisiana* (Sheep Meadow Press), ©1979 by Cleopatra Mathis.

Gail Mazur was born in 1937 in Cambridge, Massachusetts, has a BA from Smith College and an MA from Lesley College (now University) is the author of five books of poetry including *They Can't Take That Away from Me* (University of Chicago Press) which was a finalist for the National Book Award in 2001 and her *New & Selected Poems* which won the Massachusetts Book Award and was a finalist for *The Los Angeles Times* Book Prize and the Paterson Poetry Prize. She lives in Cambridge and Provincetown, MA. She is Distinguished Writer-in -Residence in the Graduate Writing Program of Emerson College and Founding Director of the Blacksmith House Poetry Series in Cambridge, a weekly poetry reading series she ran for twenty-nine years. She has been appointed a Fellow at the Radcliffe Institute for Advanced Study for 2008-09. 'Bluebonnets' is from *Zeppo's First Wife: New & Selected Poems* ©2005 Gail Mazur, (University of Chicago Press).

Medbh McGuckian was born in 1950 in Belfast, and educated at a Dominican convent and at Queens University, Belfast. She came to public notice when her poem 'The Flitting', submitted under a pseudonym, won the National Poetry Prize, ahead of a well-known poet. When the organisers 'rearranged the prize money' the *Times Literary Supplement* demanded to know whether she received less because she was "Irish, or Catholic, or a woman, or unknown". Now the author of a dozen or so collections of poetry published to widespread critical acclaim, including the recent *The Book of the Angel* (2004), she has worked as an editor and a teacher and was visiting poet at the University of California, Berkeley. 'Hand Reliquary, Ave Maria Lane' is from *The Book of the Angel*, ©2004 Medbh McGuckian and reprinted with permission from Gallery Press, Ireland and Wake Forest University Press in the USA.

Heather McHugh was born to Canadian parents in San Diego, California, in 1948. She was raised in Virginia and educated at Harvard University. Her books of poetry include *Eyeshot* (Wesleyan University Press, 2004), which was shortlisted for the Pulitzer Prize; *The Father of Predicaments* (2001); *Hinge & Sign: Poems 1968-1993* (1994), a finalist for the National Book Award and named a 'Notable Book of the Year' by the *New York Times Book Review; Shades* (1988); *To the Quick* (1987); *A World of Difference* (1981); and *Dangers* (1977). Her honours include two grants from the NEA, a Lila Wallace/Reader's Digest Award, a Guggenheim Foundation fellowship, and one of the first United States Artists' awards. For over twenty years, she has served as a visiting faculty member in the MFA Program for Writers at Warren Wilson College, and since 1984 as Milliman Writer-in-Residence at the University of Washington in Seattle. 'Ghazal of the Better-Unbegun' is from *The Father of Predicaments*, ©2001 Heather McHugh and reprinted by permission from Wesleyan University Press.

Sandra McPherson. Born in 1943 and raised in California, she received her BA from San Jose University and she studied at graduate level with Elizabeth Bishop and David Wagoner at the University of Washington. Author of ten collections, including *The Year of our Birth*, which was nominated for the National Book Award, she has also published ten chapbooks. Her awards and honours include NEA grants, a Guggenheim Fellowship and an award in literature from the American Academy and Institute of Arts and Letters. She has taught at the University of Iowa's Writer's programme. She currently teaches English at the University of California, Davis. 'Eschatology' is from *The Spaces Between Birds*, ©1996 Sandra McPherson and reprinted by permission of Wesleyan University Press.

Valeria Melchioretto was born in Winterthur, Switzerland, in 1967. Melchioretto has lived in the UK since the early 1990s and holds a BA in Modern Drama and a MA in Fine Art. In 2005 she won the New Writing Ventures Award. She received a bursary from the Arts Council of England to complete her first full collection which has recently appeared from Salt. 'The Girl With The Shoe Fetish' is in *The End of Limbo*, ©2007 Valeria Melchioretto and is reprinted with permission from Salt Publishing.

Hilary Menos was born in Luton, Bedfordshire in 1964, studied Philosophy, Politics and Economics at Wadham College, Oxford and worked as a food journalist and restaurant critic in London before moving to rural South Devon to co-run Beenleigh Manor Organics, a 75-acre organic farm producing pedigree Red Ruby Devon cows and no-shear Wiltshire Horn sheep, with her husband and four children, various cats, one pet Vietnamese pot-belly pig called Titus, a handful of die-hard chickens and three psychotic guinea fowl. She was one of five first stage winners of The Poetry Business Book and Pamphlet Competition 2004 and her pamphlet, *Extra Maths*, was published by Smith/Doorstop Books in 2005. Her first collection will be published by Seren. 'Berg' won runner up in BBC *Wildlife Magazine* Poet of the Year Competition, 2006 (titled, 'The Last Dance').

Charlotte Mew (1869-1928) had a difficult youth: two of her siblings suffered from mental illness and three others died in early childhood. Her first collection was published in 1916, and in the US under a different title in 1921. Her poems are varied: some are passionate discussions of faith and the possibility of belief, others are proto-modernist in form and atmosphere. Despite gaining the patronage of notable literary figures, among them Thomas Hardy, Virginia Woolf and Siegfried Sasoon and a small Civil List pension to help ease her financial difficulties, she never achieved the level of fame she might have deserved. After the death of her sister she was admitted to a nursing home where she committed suicide by drinking Lysol. 'The Farmer's Bride' is from *Collected Poems and Selected Prose of Charlotte Mew* (Fyfield Books, Carcanet, 2003).

Josephine Miles (1911-1985) was born in Chicago and eventually moved to Southern California. Due to a disabling arthritis, she was educated at home by tutors but was able to graduate from Los Angeles High School and earned a BA from UCLA and a Ph.D from Berkeley where she eventually became the first woman to be tenured in the English Department. She wrote over a dozen books of poetry and several works of criticism, and was a noted champion of the Beat poets, helping Allen Ginsberg publish 'Howl'. 'Ride' is from *Collected Poems, 1930-83*, ©1983 Josephine Miles. Reprinted with permission from the University of Illinois Press.

Edna St. Vincent Millay (1892-1950) was born in Rockford, Maine in 1892. She suffered a peripatetic childhood after her parents divorced. With her mother's encouragement, she began writing poems in Camden High School, Maine, and rose to public notice with her poem 'Renascence' (1912) which gained her a scholarship to Vassar College. She moved to New York City after college and won the Pulitzer Prize in 1923 for *The Harp Weaver and Other Poems*. Curiously, her reputation suffered after she wrote poetry in support of the Allied War effort during World War Two. After a colourful private life that included relationships with both sexes, she married and moved to a farmhouse in Austerliz, New York that the state purchased in 2006 and plans to turn into a museum. 'Sonnet' is from *The Harp Weaver and Other Poems* (HarperCollins) and is reprinted here with permission of the Millay Society.

Vassar Miller (1924-1998) was born in Houston, Texas where she lived all her life. She was the daughter of a prominent architect and began writing as a child, composing on a typewriter due to the cerebral palsy which affected her speech and movement. She attended the University of Houston, receiving a BA and MA in English. She published ten volumes of poetry and also edited a collection of poems and short stories about people with disabilities titled *Despite this Flesh*. Nominated for the Pulitzer Prize in 1961 and in 1982, in 1988 she was named Poet Laureate of Texas. 'On Approaching My Birthday' is from *Onions and Roses*, ©1968 Vassar Miller and reprinted by permission of Wesleyan University Press.

Elma Mitchell was born at Airdrie, Scotland in 1919. She has worked as a professional librarian and in broadcasting, publishing and journalism in London and as a freelance writer and translator in Somerset. 'Thoughts After Ruskin' is from *People Etcetera: Poems New & Selected*, ©Elma Mitchell 1987 and reprinted with permission from Peterloo Press.

Lyn Moir was born in 1934 in Glasgow, although her maternal ancestors' families were in New England before 1635. Her collections, *Me and Galileo* (2001) and *Breaker's Yard* (2003) are published by Arrowhead Press. Her new collection, *Velázquez's Riddle*, a sequence on the painting 'Las Meninas' and Picasso's versions of it, is to be published by Bluechrome in September, 2008. She is bilingual in Spanish, has translated prose and plays in that language as well as translations of seven Simenon novels from French. 'Velázquez on Picasso's Pigeons' has appeared in *Stand* and is reprinted with permission from the author.

Honor Moore was born in 1945 in New York City and is author of three collections of poetry, editor of *Amy Lowell: Selected Poems* and co-editor of *At the Stray Dog Cabaret*, a book of Russian poems translated by Paul Schmidt. Her biography, *The White Blackbird, A Life of the Painter Margarett Sargent by her Granddaughter*, was a *New York Times* Notable Book in 1996 and she received a Guggenheim Fellowship in 2004 for *The Bishop's Daughter*, a memoir. Her play, *Mourning Pictures* was produced on Broadway and published in *The New Women's Theatre: Ten Plays by Contemporary American Women*, which she edited. She is also a theatre critic for *The New York Times*. 'First Time: 1950' is from *Memoir* (Chicory Blue Press), ©1988 Honor Moore and reprinted with the author's permission.

Marianne Moore (1887-1972) was born in Kirkwood, Missouri, educated at Bryn Mawr College, and taught until 1915 when she began to publish her poetry. Travelling extensively in Europe before the first world war, she came to the notice of a prominent generation of poets including Wallace Stevens, William Carlos Williams, H.D., T.S. Eliot and Ezra Pound. She served as influential editor and tastemaker at the literary and cultural journal *The Dial*, known to encourage young poets, including Elizabeth Bishop, Allen Ginsberg, John Ashbery and James Merrill. Her *Collected Poems* of 1951 won the Pulitzer Prize, the National Book Award and the Bollingen Prize. Moore became a minor celebrity in New York society, attending boxing matches, baseball games and other public events. 'Poetry' is reprinted here with the permission of Faber and Faber, London, and Scribners in the USA, an imprint of Simon & Schuster Adult Publishing Group and is from *The Complete Poems of Marianne Moore*, ©1935 by Marianne Moore; copyright renewed ©1963 by Marianne Moore & T.S. Eliot. All rights reserved.

Thylias Moss was born in 1954 in Cleveland, Ohio, to a poor family. Moss suffered discrimination at her school (due to her race, African American) and withdrew, age nine. Around this time she began to write poetry. She graduated from Oberlin College in 1981 and later received an MFA in writing from the University of New Hampshire. She has published eight books of poetry, including a *New and Selected Poems*, a memoir, two plays and two books for young people. Among her awards are a MacArthur Fellowship, A Guggenheim Fellowship and the Witter Bynner Award for poetry. 'The Warmth of Hot Chocolate' was originally published in *Rainbow Remnants in Rock Bottom Ghetto Sky*, ©1993 by Thylias Moss. Reprinted with permission of Persea Books, Inc.

Sinead Morrissey was born in Portadown in 1972 and studied English and German at Trinity College, Dublin, from which she took her Ph.D in 2003. Author of three collections of poetry, she won a Patrick Kavanagh Award in 1990 and an Eric Gregory Award for the manuscript of her first collection, *There Was a Fire in Vancouver*. Her second book, *Between Here and There* (2002) was shortlisted for the T.S. Eliot Prize. She has lived and worked in Japan and New Zealand and now lives in Northern Ireland. Her recent book, *The State of the Prisons* was a Poetry Book Society Recommendation. She won the Michael Hartnett Award for Poetry in June 2005. '& Forgive Us Our Trespasses' is from *Between Here and There*, ©2002 Sinead Morrissey and reprinted with permission from Carcanet Press Limited.

Joan Murray (1917-1942) was born to Canadian parents in London during a dirigible air raid in World War One. Despite the lasting effects of rheumatic fever, she studied acting and dancing, and began to write after taking a class with W. H. Auden at the New School in New York City in 1940. She wrote all her poems the following year, before dying of a heart valve infection just short of her twenty-fifth birthday. During his first year as judge of the Yale Younger Poets series, Auden chose Murray's posthumous *Poems* as the winning title. 'You Talk of Art' is from *Poems: 1917-1945*, (Yale University Press).

Marilyn Nelson was born in Cleveland, Ohio in 1946 to a military family. She earned her BA from the University of California, Davis and has an MA from the University of Pennsylvania and a Ph.D from the University of Minnesota. Her *The Fields of Praise: New and Selected Poems* (1997) was a finalist for the 1998 Lenore Marshall Poetry Prize, the 1997 National Book Award and the PEN Winship Award. As well as her collections of poetry for adults she has published two for children. Her honours include two Pushcart Prizes, two fellowships from the NEA, and a Guggenheim Fellowship. She taught for many years at the University of Connecticut, Storrs, where she is now an emerita professor of English. 'Chopin' is reprinted by permission of Louisiana State University Press from *The Homeplace: Poems*,©1990 by Marilyn Nelson Waniek.

Grace Nichols was born in 1950 in Georgetown, Guyana. She worked there as a journalist and reporter before coming to Britain in 1977. She has written three collections of poetry for adults, the first of which, *I is a Long Memoried Woman*, won the 1983 Commonwealth Poetry Prize. Her other two poetry books are: *The Fat Black Woman's Poems* and *Lazy Thoughts of a Lazy Woman*, (both Virago). She has also written a novel set in Guyana, *Whole of a Morning Sky*, and her books for children include two collections of short stories and a book of poems. She has also edited a poetry anthology called *Poetry Jump Up*. She lives with her family in Brighton. 'Because She Has Come' is from *Everybody Got a Gift: New and Selected Poems* (A & C Black), ©2006 Grace Nichols and reprinted with permission from Curtis Brown, London.

Lorine Niedecker (1903-1970) was born on Black Hawk Island near Fort Atkinson, Wisconsin. She lived most of her life here in rural isolation. The only woman associated with the Objectivist poets, she is widely credited with demonstrating how an Objectivist poetic could handle the personal as subject matter. She attended Beloit College to study literature but dropped out after two years to care for her ailing mother. A brief marriage lasted only two years. The 1960s saw a revival of interest in her work, she was befriended by a number of poets, and starting writing and publishing again. A comprehensive *Collected Works* was published in 2002 and a centennial celebration of her work was held in Wisconsin in 2003. 'What Horror to Awake at Night' is from *The Granite Pail: The Selected Poems of Lorine Niedecker* as published by Gnomon, 1996. Reprinted with permission by Bob Arnold, Executor for the Literary Estate of Lorine Niedecker.

Alice Notley was born in Arizona in 1945, and raised in California. She has a BA from Barnard College and an MFA from the University of Iowa. She is a visual artist as well as a poet, and hopes that her work will instill social awareness in the reader. Her collection of poems, *Mysteries of Small Houses* was a finalist for the Pulitzer Prize. Another collection received the San Francisco Poetry Center Book Award and in 2001 she was presented with an award from the American Academy of Arts and Letters as well as the Poetry Society of America's Shelley Memorial Award. After some years in New York City, she now lives in Paris. 'II-The Person That You Were Will Be Replaced' is from *Mysteries of Small Houses*, ©1998 Alice Notley. Used by permission of Viking Penguin, division of Penguin Group, (USA) Inc.

Naomi Shihab Nye, poet and songwriter, was born in 1952 to a Palestinian father and an American mother. She grew up in St. Louis, Missouri, Jerusalem, and San Antonio, Texas. As well as several collections of poetry, she has published a book of essays entitled *Never in a Hurry*; a young adult novel called *Habibi* and a picture book *Lullaby Raft*, which is also the title of one of her two albums of music. She has also edited a number of anthologies the most recent being *Is This Forever, Or What?: Poems and Paintings from Texas*. Among her awards are four Pushcart Prizes, The Jane Addams Children's Book Award, and the Paterson Poetry Prize. She lives in San Antonio with her family. 'Small Vases From Hebron' and 'Making a Fist' are from *Words Under Words: Selected Poems* by Naomi Shihab Nye, ©1995, reprinted with permission of Far Corner Books.

Julie O'Callaghan was born in Chicago in 1954 and has lived in Ireland since 1974. Her collections of poems include *Edible Anecdotes*, a Poetry Book Society Recommendation, *What's What*, a PBS Choice, *No Can Do*, another Poetry Book Society Recommendation for which she was also awarded the Michael Hartnett Poetry Prize. She has also written a number of collections for children. She was awarded Irish Arts Council Bursaries in 1985, 1990, and 1998 and is now a resident in Co. Kildare. 'Schmooze-Fest' is from *Tell Me This Is Normal: New & Selected Poems*, ©2008 Julie O'Callaghan and reprinted with permission from Bloodaxe Books.

Sharon Olds was born in San Francisco in 1942, and studied at Stanford and Columbia Universities. Her first collection, *Satan Says*, received the inaugural San Francisco Poetry Center Award. Her second book, *The Dead & The Living* (1983) received the Lamont Poetry Selection and the National Books Critics Circle Award. She has also published other collections including, *Strike Sparks: Selected Poems* (2004). Her numerous honours include an NEA grant and a Guggenheim Fellowship. She currently teaches poetry workshops in NYU's Graduate Creative Writing Programme and in 2007 she was elected a Chancellor of the Academy of American Poets. Her ninth collection, *One Secret Thing*, will appear from Knopf in 2008. She lives in New York City. 'I Go Back To May 1937' is from *The Gold Cell* ©1987 Sharon Olds and is reprinted with permission of Cape, UK and Alfred A. Knopf, a division of Random House, Inc.

Alicia Ostriker was born in New York City in 1937. Her mom (an English major in college) poured Shakespeare, Browning and Tennyson into her baby ears, so she had no choice but to become a poet. Ostriker has published eleven volumes of poetry, including *The Little Space* (a New and Selected), and *The Volcano Sequence*. She is also the author of *Stealing the Language: The Emergence of Women's Poetry in America*. 'Liking It' is from *No Heaven* by Alicia Ostriker, ©2005. Reprinted by permission of the University of Pittsburgh Press.

Alice Oswald was born in 1966 lives in Dartington, Devon and works as a gardener on the Dartington Estate. She trained as a classicist at Oxford and was the recipient of an Eric Gregory Award in 1994. Her first collection, *The Thing in the Gap-Stone Stile* (1996) won a Forward Poetry Prize for Best First Collection. Her second book, *Dart*, won the T.S. Eliot Prize in 2002. Her third collection, *Woods*, was published in 2005 and shortlisted for both prizes. In 2004 she was chosen to participate in the Poetry Society's 'Next Generation' promotion. 'Wedding' and 'The Thing In The Gap Stone Stile' are from, in the UK, *The Thing In The Gap Stone Stile*, copyright ©1996 Alice Oswald and reprinted with permission from Faber and Faber, London. In the USA, they appear in *Spacecraft Voyager 1* and are reprinted with the permission of Graywolf Press.

Ruth Padel was born in 1947 in London. Padel is a freelance writer who has lived extensively in Greece. Previous jobs include singing in an Istanbul nightclub, teaching opera in Princeton's Modern Greek Department and teaching ancient lyric poetry at Oxford. She has won the National Poetry Competition and published six poetry collections (four shortlisted for T.S. Eliot and Forward Prizes). Her non-fiction includes books on rock music and Greek myth, tiger-jungles in Asia, and reading contemporary poetry – most recently, *The Poem and the Journey*. "Brilliant, unpretentious, wonderfully apt and lively, it answers questions an anxious reader wants to ask and makes a powerful case for poetry as a living art form," wrote Peter Forbes in *The Independent*. 'Blown Ruby' is reprinted with permission from the author.

P.K. (Patricia Kathleen) Page was born in England in 1916 and brought up on the Canadian prairies. She is the author of more than a dozen books of poetry, fiction, non-fiction, and several books for children. She won The Governor General's Award for Poetry in 1957, and she was appointed a companion of the Order of Canada in 1999. In 2002, her selected poems, *Planet Earth*, was shortlisted for the Griffin Poetry Prize. As P.K. Irwin, she is also a painter and has had one woman shows in Mexico and Canada and is represented in permanent collections in the National Gallery of Canada and in the Art Gallery of Ontario. She lives in Victoria, British Columbia. 'Brazilian Fazenda' is from *The Hidden Room: Collected Poems* ©1997 P.K. Page and reprinted with permission from Porcupine Quill.

Dorothy Parker (1893-1967) was born Dorothy Rothschild in Long Branch, New Jersey and was raised in New York City. Her career took off while writing theatre criticism for *Vanity Fair*. She became part of the famous Algonquin Round Table group along with other New York writers and editors like Harold Ross, Robert Benchley and Alexander Woollcott. During her life she published seven volumes of short stories and poetry, and was also a noted screenwriter, nominated for an Academy Award for *A Star is Born* (1937). An advocate for left-wing causes, she helped to found the Anti-Nazi League in Hollywood. Investigated by the FBI for supposed Communist links in the McCarthy era, she was blacklisted by movie studio bosses. In the late 50s and early 60s she wrote book reviews and returned to Manhattan. Famous for her caustic wit, her epitaph reads: "excuse my dust". 'Oscar Wilde' and 'Unfortunate Coincidence', ©1926 and renewed ©1954 by Dorothy Parker are from *The Portable Dorothy Parker*, edited by Marion Meade, ©1928 and renewed in ©1956 by Dorothy Parker. Used by permission of Viking Penguin, (USA) Inc. and G. Duckworth Publishers in the UK.

Molly Peacock is an ex-New Yorker who has adopted Canada and lives in Toronto. She helped create the Poetry in Motion program on New York's buses and subways and now she is Poetry Editor of the *Literary Review of Canada*. She is the author of six volumes of poetry, and her poems have appeared in the *Times Literary Supplement, The New Yorker, The Paris Review,* as well as *The Oxford Book of American Poetry.* She crosses genres as well as borders, and has written about her choice not to have children in a memoir, *Piece by Piece,* as well as writing and performing an Off Broadway one-woman show in poems, *The Shimmering Verge.* 'Why I Am Not A Buddhist' and 'Cutting Tall Grass' are from *Cornucopia: New and Selected Poems,* ©2002 by Molly Peacock. Used by permission of W.W. Norton & Company, Inc.

Pascale Petit was born in Paris and grew up in France and Wales. She trained as a sculptor at the Royal College of Art. Her last two collections, *The Huntress* (2005) and *The Zoo Father* (2001), were both shortlisted for the T.S. Eliot Prize and were Books of the Year in the *Times Literary Supplement.* A pamphlet *The Wounded Deer – Fourteen poems after Frida Kahlo* was also published in 2005. Two new collections are forthcoming from Seren: *The Treekeeper's Tale* (2008) and *The Thorn Necklace – Forty poems after Frida Kahlo* (with the paintings). In 2004 she was selected as a Next Generation Poet. Website: www.pascalepetit.co.uk. 'My Mother's Perfume' is from *The Huntress,* ©2005 Pascale Petit. 'The Second Husband' initially appeared in *Poetry Review* and is from *The Treekeeper's Tale,* ©2008 Pascale Petit, both reprinted with permission from Seren.

Katherine Pierpoint studied languages at Exeter University then worked in publishing and television. Her collection *Truffle Beds* (Faber, 1995) won a Somerset Maugham Award and was shortlisted for the T.S. Eliot Prize. She was Royal Literary Fund Writing Fellow at the University of Kent at Canterbury and in 2006 was poet-in-residence at the King's School, Canterbury. With sponsorship from the British Council, she has attended literary festivals in Macedonia, Sweden, Spain and Mexico. 'This Dead Relationship' is from *Truffle Beds,* ©1995 Katherine Pierpoint and reprinted with permission from Faber and Faber, London.

Ruth Pitter (1897-1992) was born in Ilford and began writing poetry in early life inspired by her schoolteacher parents. In 1920 she published her first book, with the help of Hilaire Belloc. She went on to publish numerous volumes of poetry and enjoyed considerable fame as both author and broadcaster. She won the Hawthornden Prize in 1937 and in 1954 she won the William E. Heinemann Award. She was the first woman to receive the Queen's Gold Medal for Poetry (in 1955), and was appointed a CBE in 1979. A traditionalist in the matter of rhyme and metre (although also sometimes unexpectedly experimental), her work was admired by Philip Larkin, C.S. Lewis, W.B. Yeats and Thom Gunn. 'Morning Glory' is from *Collected Poems,* ©Ruth Pitter 1996, reprinted with permission of Enitharmon Press.

Sylvia Plath (1932-1963) was born in Jamaica Plain, Massachusetts. Plath published her first poem in the *Boston Herald's* children's section when she was eight. Her father died the same year and the family moved to Wellesley, MA. She graduated from Smith College with honours in 1955 despite a breakdown and suicide attempt recorded in her book, *The Bell-Jar.* She received a Fulbright scholarship to Cambridge University, taught for several years at Smith College in the States, and also moved for a time to Boston where she attended seminars given by Robert Lowell along with the poet Anne Sexton, early champions of what became known as the Confessional style of verse. She returned to England with her husband, the poet Ted Hughes, where she started a family and lived in London and Devon. While there, she published her first collection, *The Colossus.* She was working on the book which would make her name, *Ariel,* when she committed suicide, in 1963. Her *Collected Letters and Journals* have also been published. 'Lady Lazarus' and 'Sheep in Fog' are from *Ariel,* ©1961,62,63,64,65,66 by Ted Hughes. Foreward by Robert Lowell. Reprinted by permission of HarperCollins Publishers in the USA and by Faber and Faber, London.

Clare Pollard was born in Bolton in 1978. Her first book, *The Heavy Petting Zoo* (1998) was written when she was still at school, and she has since published two other collections, the latest of which is *Look, Clare! Look!* (2005). Her first play, *The Weather* (Faber, 2004) was performed at the Royal Court. Pollard currently teaches at the City Lit, and lives in East London. She enjoys the testicles at her local kebab house. 'The Chain' is from *Look, Clare! Look!,* ©2005 Clare Pollard and reprinted with permission from Bloodaxe Books.

Katha Pollitt was born in New York City in 1949. Educated at Harvard and Columbia, Pollitt is well-known for her 'Subject to Debate' column in *The Nation – The Washington Post* called it "The best place to go for original thinking on the left". Her poems have appeared widely and her book, *Antarctic Traveller* won the National Book Critics Circle Award in 1982. Amongst her many publications are: *Virginity or Death!* (Random House, 2006) and *Learning to Drive,* a collection of personal essays. 'Trying To Write a Poem Against the War' was originally published in *The Nation* and will be in her forthcoming collection *The Mind-Body Problem,* ©Katha Pollitt and reprinted with permission from Knopf (Random House) New York.

Marie Ponsot, a native New Yorker, was born in 1921. Her numerous books include *True Minds* (1957), *Admit Impediment* (1981), and *The Bird Catcher* (1998) which won a National Books Critics Circle Award and was a finalist for the Lenore Marshall Poetry Prize. Ponsot, who also translates books from French, has taught in the graduate programs at Queens College, Bejing United University, the Poetry Center of YMHA, NYU and Columbia. She has had an NEA grant, a Delmore Schwartz Memorial Prize and the Shaughnessy Medal of the Modern Language Association. 'Living Room' is from *Springing: New and Selected Poems,* ©2003 Marie Ponsot and reprinted with permission from Knopf (Random House) New York.

Katrina Porteous was born in Aberdeen in 1960, grew up in County Durham, read history at Cambridge and studied in the US on a Harkness Fellowship. She has lived as a freelance writer on the Northumberland coast since 1987, and is particularly concerned with the inshore fishing communities and the cultural and natural history of that area. Her publications include *The Lost Music, The Wund an' the Wetter, Dunstanburgh, Longshore Drift* and *The Blue Lonnen.* One of her main interests is in radio poetry: 'Seven Silences' is an excerpt from 'An Ill Wind', commissioned by BBC Radio 3 as part of the Poetry Proms in 2001. It is published in *Seven Silences,* (Selkirk Lapwing Press, 2008), originally ©2001 Katrina Porteous, and reprinted with the author's permission.

Deborah Randall was born in 1957 in Hampshire, and is now living in Scotland. Her first collection, *The Sin Eater* was a Poetry Book Society Recommendation and won a Scottish Arts Council Book Award. In 1987 she won first prize in the Bloodaxe and Bridport poetry competitions. Also the author of an unconventional portrait of John Ruskin, the renowned, nineteenth century art critic titled: *White Eyes, Dark Ages.* 'Ballygrand Widow' is from *The Sin Eater* (Bloodaxe) ©1997 Deborah Randall and reprinted with permission from the author.

Kathleen Raine (1908-2003) was born in London. She won a scholarship to study at Girton College, Cambridge where she read natural sciences and psychology rather than English literature which she already knew well. Despite a tempestuous personal and professional life, she produced more than a dozen books of poetry, four volumes of autobiography, and substantial scholarly work on Blake and Yeats. In 1980 she was one of the founding editors of the *Temenos Review* and Academy, dedicated to 'learning of the Imagination' in deliberate contrast to the prevailing Thatcherite ethos of the day. She was awarded the Queen's Gold Medal for Poetry in 1992 and in 2000 was made both a CBE and A Commandeur de L'Ordere des Arts et des Lettres. 'The Moment' is from *The Collected Poems of Kathleen Raine,* ©2001 Kathleen Raine.

Deryn Rees-Jones was born in 1968. After reading English at the University of Wales, Bangor, she did doctoral research at Birkbeck College, University of London, on post war women's poetry and now lectures in literature at the University of Liverpool. Her first collection, *The Memory Tray* (1994) was shortlisted for a Forward Prize, her second book, *Signs Around a Dead Body,* was a Poetry Book Society Special Commendation. She is also the author of *Quiver* (2004) a murder mystery in verse, a book of critical essays, *Consorting with Angels,* and the editor of a companion anthology, *Modern Women Poets* (both Bloodaxe). 'I Know Exactly the Sort of Woman I'd like to Fall in Love With' is from *The Memory Tray,* ©1994 Deryn Rees-Jones and reprinted with permission from Seren.

Adrienne Rich was born in 1929 in Baltimore, Maryland. She began writing poetry as a child. By the time she graduated from Radcliffe College her first book had been selected by W.H. Auden for the Yale Younger Poets Prize. In her early work she tended towards the use of modernist formalism but *Snapshots of a Daughter-in-Law* (1963) marked a significant shift towards political, topical and feminist poems in freer forms, and thereafter her books reflect social upheavals in society. 'Diving into the Wreck', the title poem from her 1974 collection, is widely acknowledged as one of the most significant poems of the twentieth century. A respected teacher and winner of numerous awards, she has also been known to refuse a few, including the National Medal of the Arts in 1997, given at the White House, because "[Art] means nothing if it simply decorates the dinner table of the power which holds it hostage." 'The Insusceptibles' is from *Collected Early Poems: 1950-1970,* ©1993, 1955 Adrienne Rich. 'Diving into the Wreck' is from *The Fact of a Doorframe: Selected Poems 1950-2001,* ©2002 Adrienne Rich. Reprinted with the permission of author and W.W. Norton & Company, Inc.

Denise Riley was born in 1948 in Carlisle, England. A poet, critic, linguist, editor, and researcher, her interests extend to politics, history, philosophy, feminist theory and visual art. She lectures at the University of East Anglia in several of these areas. She has also been Writer in Residence at the Tate Gallery. A recent title is: *Impersonal Passion: Language as Affect* (Duke University Press, 2005). 'Shantung' is from *Selected Poems,* ©2000 Denise Riley and reprinted with permission from Reality Street Editions.

Lynette Roberts (1909-1995) was born in Buenos Aires, of Welsh stock. She published two collections of poems in her lifetime, both with Faber: *Poems* (1944) and *Gods with Stainless Ears* (1951) She was part of the artistic and literary scene of her day, working with T.S. Eliot, Robert Graves, Alun Lewis and (her husband) Keidrych Rhys. Dylan Thomas was best man at her wedding. A recent edition of her work has revived interest in her ambitious modernist poetry. 'Englyn' is from *Collected Poems,* ©2006 Estate of Lynette Roberts and reprinted with permission from Carcanet Press Ltd.

Judith Rodriguez was born in 1936 in Perth, Australia and grew up in Brisbane. She has published numerous volumes of poetry, some illustrated by her own woodcuts, edited an anthology and the *Collected Poems of Jennifer Rankin*. During the 1990s she was poetry editor with Penguin, Australia. The play *Poor Johanna* co-written with Robyn Archer, was produced in 1994 and her libretto for Moya Henderson's opera *Lindy*, about the Azaria Chamberlain disappearance, was performed at the Sydney Opera House in 2003. She is the recipient of the Christopher Brennan Award and currently teaches at Deakin University. Her *Collected Poems* appeared in 1990. 'How Come The Truck Loads' is from *Water Life*, ©1976 Judith Rodriguez and reprinted with permission from University of Queensland Press.

Pattiann Rogers was born in Joplin, Missouri, in 1940. She is a graduate of the Universities of Missouri (BA) and Houston (MA), and has published a dozen award-winning collections of poetry. She has received two NEA grants, a Guggenheim Fellowship, a Lannan Poetry Fellowship in 1991 and a Lannan Literary Award in 2005. She has been a visiting writer at the Universities of Texas, Montana and Arkansas and a member of the faculty of Vermont College. She currently teaches with the MFA program in Writing at the Pacific University in Oregon. Her most recent book, *Wayfare*, appeared in 2008. She has two sons and three grandsons and lives with her husband, a retired geophysicist, in Colorado. 'When You Watch Us Sleeping', ©2005 Pattiann Rogers, is included in *Firekeeper,* an expanded edition of her *Selected Poems* (Milkweed Editions) and is reprinted with permission from the author.

Christina Rossetti (1830-1894) Born in London, educated mostly at home, Rossetti suffered from bouts of depression and illness throughout her life. Although she began writing at age seven, her first publication, the critically acclaimed, *Goblin Market and Other Poems* did not appear until she was thirty-one. A scrupulous evangelical religiosity prevented at least two romantic engagements and led her to do such things as give up chess because she "enjoyed winning too much". Despite spending most of her life at home, she frequented the company of her brother (painter Dante Gabriel Rossetti), the Pre-Raphaelite circle, and others such as Whistler, Swinburne and Charles Dodgson (Lewis Carroll). We feature her Christmas poem, 'In The Bleak Midwinter' which was set to music by Gustav Holst and is now a famous hymn.

Anne Rouse was born in Washington D.C. in 1954 and grew up in Virginia. After reading History at the University of London, she worked as a nurse and health worker. Since becoming a freelance writer, she has had many residencies and now lives in Hastings. She has published three collections of poetry, *Sunset Grill* and *Timing*, both Poetry Book Society Recommendations, and *The School of Night* (2003). 'Sum' and 'Virginia Arcady' are from *Sunset Grill*, ©1993 Anne Rouse and reprinted with permission from Bloodaxe Books.

Jane Routh is a professional photographer and writer from the Forest of Bowland, North Lancashire, where she manages woodlands and a flock of geese. Her first poetry collection, *Circumnavigation* (2002) won the Poetry Business Book & Pamphlet Competition, and was shortlisted for the Forward Prize. 'Tell Me What Else' is from her second collection, *Teach Yourself Mapmaking* (A Poetry Book Society Recommendation) ©2006 Jane Routh and reprinted with permission from Smith/Doorstop Books (The Poetry Business).

Mary Ruefle was born outside Pittsburgh in 1952 but spent her early life travelling around the USA and Europe. She graduated from Bennington College in 1974 with a BA in Literature. She is the author of ten collections of poetry and one book of prose, and has received an NEA Fellowship, a Whiting Writer's Award, a Guggenheim Fellowship, amongst many honours. She teaches in the MFA Writing program at Vermont College and lives in New England. 'The Last Supper' is from *The Adamant* (Carnegie Mellon) ©1989 Mary Ruefle, 'Perfume River' is from *Apparition Hill* (CavanKerry Press) ©2002 Mary Ruefle. Both reprinted with permission from the author.

Muriel Rukeyser (1913-1980) attended a progressive private school in the Bronx, then Vassar College in Poughkeepsie, NY, then Columbia University in Manhattan. A political activist as well as a poet, she wrote for the *New Masses* as well as a variety of other publications, literary and political. One of her best-known poem sets is *The Book of the Dead*, based on her reporting of a deadly silicosis lung disease outbreak amongst miners in Gauley Bridge, West Virginia. She gave lectures and workshops and taught at Sarah Lawrence College, but never became a career academic. In the 1960s and 70s her feminism and Vietnam War opposition drew a new generation to her poetry. In the mid 70s she presided over PEN's American center. 'Myth' is from *The Collected Poems of Muriel Rukeyser*, Pittsburgh University Press, 2005. Reprinted by permission of International Creative Management, Inc., ©1973 by Muriel Rukeyser.

Carol Rumens. Born south London in 1944, she has published fourteen collections of poetry and is currently Professor in Creative Writing at the University of Wales, Bangor. As her ex-husband and current partner could testify, she has never ironed a man's shirt in her life. On the other hand, she has never ironed a woman's shirt, either. She has no iron. A recent title is *Self into Song* (three essay-lectures about poetry), Bloodaxe Books, 2007. 'Two Women' is from *Selected Poems 1968-2004*, ©2004 Carol Rumens and reprinted here with the permission of Bloodaxe Books. 'Women, Veiled' is from her new collection, *Blind Spots,* (Seren, 2008) and is reprinted with permission from the author.

Donna Kate Rushin. 'The Bridge Poem' is from *The Bridge Called My Back: Writing by Radical Women of Colour*: Ed. by Cherrie Moraga & Gloria Zaldua (Kitchen Table Press, 1983).

Kay Ryan was born in California in 1945 and grew up in the small towns of the San Joaquin Valley and the Mojave Desert. She received a BA and MA from UCLA. Her awards include a Ruth Lilly Poetry Prize, a Guggenheim Fellowship, an Ingram Merril Award, an NEA Fellowship and four Pushcart Prizes. She has recently been chosen as the sixteenth Poet Laureate of the USA. She lives in Marin County, California. 'A Bad Time for the Sublime' is from *Strangely Marked Metal*, (Copper Beech Press, ©1985 Kay Ryan); and 'Blandeur' is from *Say Uncle*, (Grove Press, © 2000 Kay Ryan). Reprinted with permission from the author.

Eva Salzman - see (*About the Editors*)
'Alex, Tiffany, Meg' was first printed in *Bargain with the Watchman* (OUP 1997), 'The Refinery' first appeared in *The English Earthquake* (Bloodaxe, 1992) and 'Brooklyn Bridge' was first published in *One Two II* (Wrecking Ball Press). All the poems appear in *Double Crossing: New and Selected Poems*, ©2004 Eva Salzman and are reprinted here with permission from Bloodaxe Books.

Fiona Sampson was born in 1968, and grew up in Wales. Sampson has published fourteen books – poetry, philosophy of language and books on the writing process – of which the most recent are: *Common Prayer* (Carcanet, 2007), shortlisted for the 2007 T.S. Eliot Prize), *On Listening* (essays: 2007) and *Writing: Self and Reflexivity* (Macmillan, 2005). Her awards include the Newdigate Prize and the 2006 Forward Prize (shortlist); and she has been widely translated, with eight books in translation, including *Travel Diary*, awarded the Zlaten Prsten (Macedonia). She contributes regularly to *The Guardian, The Irish Times* and other publications; and is the editor of *Poetry Review*. 'Hay-On-Wye' is from *Common Prayer* and is reprinted with permission from Carcanet Press Limited.

Carole Satyamurti was born in Farnborough, Kent, in 1939. Her career has been as a sociologist interested in the social application of psychoanalytic ideas. She started writing poetry late, following an Arvon course, and won the National Poetry Competition in 1986. She has published five volumes of poetry, initially with Oxford University Press and then, after the demise of their poetry list, with Bloodaxe. She is an experienced tutor for the Arvon Foundation, the Poetry School, and other organisations, and often co-tutors with Gregory Warren Wilson. She lives in London and Paris, and is allergic to country walks. 'My First Cup of Coffee' is from *Stitching the Dark: New and Selected Poems,* ©2005 Carole Satyamurti and reprinted with permission from Bloodaxe Books.

Grace Schulman's newest poetry collection is *The Broken String* (from Houghton Mifflin, 2007). Her other recent books of poems are *Days of Wonder: New and Collected Poems* (2002) and *The Paintings of Our Lives* (2001). She is editor of *The Poems of Marianne Moore* (Viking, 2003), and Distinguished Professor of English, Baruch College, CUNY. Honours for her poetry include a Guggenheim Fellowship, the Aiken Taylor Award, and the Delmore Schwartz Award. 'Eve's Unnaming' is from *Paintings Of Our Lives: Poems by Grace Schulman*, ©2001 by Grace Schulman. Reprinted by permission of Houghton Mifflin Harcourt Publishing Company. All rights reserved.

E.J. (Edith Joy) Scovell (1907-1999) was born in Sheffield, England, studied in Westmorland and at Somerville College, Oxford but did not publish a collection of poems until 1944 when she was thirty-seven. She went on to publish three more collections and translated the work of Giovanni Pascoli, but was always reserved about presenting herself and her work. She regained popularity during the formalist revival in the 1980s and Carcanet published two books, a *Selected* and a *Collected Poems*. 'Deaths of Flowers' is from *Selected Poems*, ©1991 E.J. Scovell and reprinted with permission from Carcanet Press Limited.

Olive Senior was born in Jamaica in 1941. She is the author of ten books of poetry, fiction and non-fiction. Her poetry book *Over the Roofs of the World* was shortlisted for Canada's Governor-General's Award for Literature and *Gardening in the Tropics* is a textbook in Caribbean schools. Her short story collection *Summer Lightning* won the Commonwealth Writers Prize and was followed by *Arrival of the Snake-Woman* and *Discerner of Hearts*. She now divides her time between Toronto, Canada and Montego Bay, Jamaica. 'Join-the-Dots' is from her collection *Shell*, ©2007 Olive Senior and reprinted with permission from Insomniac Press, Canada.

Anne Sexton (1928-1974) was born Anne Gray Harvey in Newton, Massachusetts and spent most of her life in Boston. One of the foremost poets of the 'Confessional' school, she attended Robert Lowell's poetry workshops with Sylvia Plath and took up poetry at suggestion of a doctor who was treating her for what would later become known as bi-polar disorder. She was the author of eight collections of poetry, often focusing on controversial themes specific to women such as menstruation and abortion. She also worked with musicians to set her prose to music, and won numerous awards including the Pulitzer Prize for *Live or Die* (1967). She committed suicide in 1974. 'The Fury of Cocks' is from the *Selected Poems of Anne Sexton*, ©1988 by Linda Gray Sexton, as Literary Executor of the Estate of Anne Sexton. Thanks also to Virago, UK.

Jo Shapcott was born in London in 1953, and educated at Trinity College, Dublin. *Her Book: Poems 1988-1998* consists of a selection of poetry from her three earlier collections: *Electroplating the Baby* (1988) which won the Commonwealth Poetry Prize, *Phrase Book* (1992) and *My Life Asleep* (1998) which won the Forward Poetry Prize. She has won the National Poetry Competition twice and has edited an anthology of contemporary poetry with Matthew Sweeney called *Emergency Kit: Poems for Strange Times*, (1996). She has worked on a number of collaborative projects with musicians, published versions of Rilke's French poems (*Tender Taxes*, Faber, 2002) and currently teaches on the MA course in Creative Writing at Royal Holloway, University of London. 'Muse' is from *Her Book: Poems 1988-1998*, ©2006 Jo Shapcott and reprinted with permission of Faber and Faber, London.

Penelope Shuttle was born in Middlesex in 1947 and had a fabulous 60th birthday party in Falmouth in May 2007, with over 60 guests. Her most recent collections are *Redgrove's Wife* (2006 and 2007), shortlisted for the Forward Prize and for the T.S. Eliot Award, and the reprint of her 1988 collection, *Adventures With My Horse*, (Poetry Book Society, 2007). Her hobbies are friendships, dieting, and wishing she was thirty years younger but knowing what she knows now. (Not much). 'Poem' is from *Redgrove's Wife* (Bloodaxe) ©2006 Penelope Shuttle and reprinted with permission from David Higham Associates.

Peggy Shumaker was born in La Mesa, California in 1952 and grew up in Tucson, Arizona. She earned her BA in English and her MFA in Creative Writing from the University of Arizona. She has published six collections of poetry. A recent title is *Blaze*, a collaboration of her poems and the paintings of Alaskan artist Kesler Woodward. *Just Breathe Normally*, a book of lyrical non-fiction, is available from University of Nebraska Press. Professor emerita from the University of Alaska, Fairbanks, Shumaker was chair of English Department and Director of their MFA programme. She currently teaches in the low-residency Rainier Writing Workshop and lives in Fairbanks, Alaska. 'Oatmeal', ©2005 first appeared in the *Iowa Review* and is reprinted with permission from the author.

Kathryn Simmonds was born in Hertfordshire in 1972. Her short stories and poems have appeared in periodicals and been broadcast on Radio 4. A pamphlet, *snug*, was published in 2004 and her first full collection, *Sunday at the Skin Launderette* (Seren, 2008), is a Poetry Book Society Recommendation and has been nominated for the Forward, Glen Dimplex and the *Guardian* First Book Prizes. 'The Men I Wished I'd Kissed' is from *snug*, ©2003 Kathryn Simmonds and reprinted with permission from Smith/Doorstop Books (The Poetry Business) and is also included in *Sunday at the Skin Launderette*.

Zoë Skoulding's most recent collection is *Remains of a Future City,* published by Seren in 2008, following *The Mirror Trade* in 2004. *Dark Wires,* a collection of collaborative poems co-authored with Ian Davidson, was published by West House Books in 2007. She is a member of the group Parking Non-Stop, whose debut album, *Species Corridor*, was released by Klangbad in 2008. She holds an AHRC Fellowship in the Creative and Performing Arts in the School of English at Bangor University, where she also teaches in the School of Lifelong Learning. Having edited *Skald* since its launch in 1994, she became editor of *Poetry Wales* in 2008. 'The Mirror Trade' is the title poem of that collection, ©2004 Zoë Skoulding and reprinted with permission from Seren.

Stevie Smith (1902-1971) Florence Margaret Smith, born in Kingston upon Hull, was nicknamed 'Stevie' after a jockey. She moved to London, age three, and was raised by an aunt after her father left home and her mother became ill. Smith suffered illness herself and was sent to a sanatorium on and off for several years as a child. Educated at Palmers Green High School and North London Collegiate for Girls, she spent the rest of her life living with her aunt, working as private secretary to Sir Neville Pearson at Newnes Publishing Company in London. Famously eccentric, described as 'naive and selfish in some ways and formidably intelligent in others', she wrote three novels as well nine volumes of poetry. Among her awards is the Queen's Gold Medal for poetry (1969). 'Not Waving But Drowning' is from *Selected Poems* (Penguin) reprinted with permission from James & James in UK. In the USA the poem appears in the *Collected Poems of Stevie Smith*, ©1972 by Stevie Smith. Reprinted by permission of New Directions Publishing Corp.

Rommi Smith, born in London in 1973, is a poet and playwright. Her work has been nominated for a South Bank Show Award. She has held numerous residencies including recently, Parliamentary Writer-in-Residence - the first in history; her specific focus was an exploration of the Parliamentary act to abolish the slave trade. Her other residencies include: British Council Poet-in-Residence at California State University in Los Angeles and BBC Writer-in-Residence for the Commonwealth Games. Her chapbook of poems selected from her forthcoming book, *Mornings and Midnights* (Peepal Tree Press) was a Poetry Book Society Pamphlet Choice. 'Tide' is from *Dance the Guns To Silence,* an international anthology exploring the legacy of Ken Saro Wiwa and published by Flipped Eye in 2005. It was first performed on 'The Verb' on BBC Radio 3 as part of Smith's role as Writer-in-Residence for BBC's Africa Season. Reprinted with permission from the author: www.rommi-smith.co.uk.

Sandy Soloman was born and raised in Baltimore, Maryland, earned a BA in History from the University of

Chicago and went on to do graduate work on early modern England. She worked in Washington D.C. where she was Director of Government Affairs for the National Urban Coalition, which she helped found. She later returned to study poetry and received an MA and MFA in writing. A freelance writer now for many years she works on projects for voluntary sector organisations as well as her poetry in Washington, London and Princeton. Her book of poems, *Pears, Lake, Sun*, won the Agnes Lynch Starrett award. 'My Friend Seems Near Tears' is from *Pears, Lake, Sun* ©Sandy Solomon 1996 and reprinted with permission from Peterloo Press.

Elizabeth Spires was born in 1952 in Lancaster, Ohio, earned a BA from Vassar College and an MA from Johns Hopkins University. Her six volumes of poetry are *Globe, Swan's Island, Annonciade, Worldling, Now the Green Blade Rises* and, forthcoming in 2008, *The Wave-Maker*. She has also written six books for children, including *The Mouse of Amherst*. Her awards include a Guggenheim Fellowship, the Amy Lowell Travelling Poetry Scholarship, a Whiting Award, and the Witter Bynner Prize for Poetry from the American Academy of Arts and Letters. She is currently a professor of English at Goucher College in Baltimore where she holds a Chair for Distinguished Achievement. 'Waving Goodbye' is from *Swan's Island*, (Carnegie Mellon) ©1985 Elizabeth Spires and reprinted with permission from the author.

Jean Sprackland was born in 1962 and brought up in Burton-on-Trent, and now lives in Southport, Merseyside. She studied English and Philosophy at the University of Kent and taught before beginning to write poetry at the age of thirty. She has held residencies in schools and universities, tutored for the Arvon Foundation, and also works in education, training and consultancy for organizations including the Poetry Society and the Poetry Archive. She is the author of three collections of poetry, the second *Hard Water* (2003) was a Poetry Book Society Recommendation and was shortlisted for both the T.S. Eliot Prize and the Whitbread Book Award. Her third collection is *Tilt*, which won the 2007 Costa Prize. 'The Apprentice' is from *Hard Water*, ©2003 Jean Sprackland and reprinted with permission of Cape/Random House publishers in the UK.

Pauline Stainer was born in Burslem, Stoke-on-Trent in 1941. She has a degree in English from St. Anne's College, Oxford and has an M.Phil from the University of Southampton. She has published a number of collections including *The Lady and the Hare: New and Selected Poems* (2003) and was nominated for the Whitbread Poetry Award for her fourth collection, *The Wound-Dresser's Dream*. She is noted for her neo-romantic, neo-symbolist, highly compact poetry. She raised her four children in Essex and also lived on the Orkney island of Rousay. She now lives in Suffolk, England. 'The White Shell' is from *Lady and the Hare: New Selected Poems*, ©2003 Pauline Stainer and reprinted with permission of Bloodaxe Books.

A.E. Stallings was born in 1968, grew up in Decatur, GA and studied at the Universities of Georgia and Oxford. She is the author of two collections of poetry, *Archaic Smile*, which received the 1999 Richard Wilbur Award, and *Hapax*, which received the 2008 Poets' Prize; she was also recently awarded the 2008 Benjamin H. Danks award from the American Academy of Arts and Letters. She composed the Latin lyrics for the opening music of the film *The Sum of All Fears*. Her new verse translation of Lucretius, *The Nature of Things*, is published by Penguin Classics. Stallings resides in Greece, with her husband, the journalist John Psaropoulos, and their small argonaut, Jason. 'Listening to the Monkeys of the Nearby Yerkes Regional Primate Research Center' is from *Archaic Smile* ©1999 A.E. Stallings (University of Evansville Press). Reprinted with permission from the author.

Gertrude Stein (1874-1946) was born in Allegheny, Pennsylvania to a wealthy family who later moved to Vienna and then to France where she would spend most of her life. She attended Radcliffe College where she studied under psychologist William James and went to Johns Hopkins medical school but left without obtaining a degree. Considered one of the primary figures in the development of modernism and an early champion of cubism, her Paris salon attracted the cream of artistic talent of her day including Picasso, Hemingway, Pound, and Matisse. An openly gay feminist, Stein was nevertheless politically conservative. She wrote novels, plays, stories, libretti and poems in her unique and highly idiosyncratic style. 'America' is from *Tender Buttons*. Recent edition from Dover Publications in 1998.

Anne Stevenson was born in 1933 of American parents in Cambridge, England and was raised in the USA, educated at Ann Arbor, University of Michigan where her father was professor of Philosophy. After obtaining her BA and MA (hons) degrees she returned to Great Britain where she has lived most of her life. She is the author of over a dozen volumes of poetry, several books of essays and literary criticism including a biography of Sylvia Plath and two critical studies of Elizabeth Bishop. Among her many honours are The Neglected Masters Award from The Poetry Foundation of America and The Lannan Lifetime Achievement Award, both in 2007. 'The Spirit Is Too Blunt An Instrument' is from *Poems: 1955-2005*, ©2005 Anne Stevenson and reprinted here with permission from Bloodaxe Books.

Ruth Stone was born in 1915 in Roanoke, Virginia, and has been a resident of Vermont since 1957. She has published numerous collections, the most recent being *In the Next Galaxy* (Copper Canyon, 2002). She won the 2002 Wallace Stevens Award, and her many awards include Guggenheim Fellowships, the Bess Hokin Award, the Shelley

Memorial Award, the National Books Critics Circle Award, and the National Book Award. For the last fifteen years she has been professor at Binghamton University. 'Resonance' is from *Ordinary Words* (Paris Press) ©2000 Ruth Stone.

Sara Teasdale (1883-1933) was born in St. Louis, Missouri, and was educated at home as a child, in the Victorian manner, continuing to live at home throughout her twenties, with the occasional trip to Europe. Throughout her life she struggled with ill-health and what would be probably be diagnosed today as bi-polar disorder. A very popular poet during the early twentieth century, in 1918 she won the Columbia University Poetry Prize (forerunner of the Pulitzer) and the annual prize of the Poetry Society of America for her volume, *Love Songs*. She committed suicide in 1933. 'The Look' and 'Let It Be Forgotten' are from her *Collected Poems,* (Buccaneer Books, 1998).

Rosemary Tonks was born in London in 1932, and educated at Wentworth School, London. Expelled in 1948, she published a children's story that same year. Married at nineteen, she moved to Karachi where she began to write poetry. Ill-health forced a return to England where she worked for the BBC, writing stories and reviews for the European Service. She published collections and also wrote poetic novels but stopped publishing in the early 70s, at about the same time as her conversion to fundamentalist Christianity. Nothing is known publicly about her subsequent life. 'Done For!' is from *Poetry Library 50 Years.*

Chase Twichell was born in 1950 in New Haven, Connecticut and is the author of six books of poetry, most recently *Dog Language* (Copper Canyon, Bloodaxe). Her work has been awarded grants from the Guggenheim Foundation, the National Endowment for the Arts, the Poetry Society of America, the Artists' Foundation, the Smart Family Foundation, and the American Academy of Arts and Letters. In 1999 she quit teaching at Princeton University to start Ausable Press, which publishes contemporary poetry. 'Horse' is from *The Snow Watcher*, ©1999 Chase Twichell and reprinted with permission from Bloodaxe Books.

Jean Valentine was born in 1934 in Chicago. She earned her BA from Radcliffe College and has lived most of her life in New York City. She won the Yale Younger Poets Award for her first book, *Dream Barker*, in 1965. The book from which her poem is taken from was winner of the 2004 National Book Award for Poetry. She is the author of nine other books, has received numerous prizes and fellowships including the Maurice English Prize, the Teasdale Poetry Prize and the Poetry Society of America's Shelley Memorial Prize in 2000. She has taught at Sarah Lawrence College, the Graduate Writing Programme of NYU, Columbia University and the 92nd Street Y in Manhattan. 'Annunciation' is from *Door in the Mountain: New and Collected Poems: 1965-2003*, ©2004 Jean Valentine and reprinted by permission of Wesleyan University Press.

Ellen Bryant Voigt was born in 1943 and grew up on a farm in Virginia. She is the author of seven collections of poetry including *Shadow of Heaven* (2002) and *Messenger: New and Selected Poems 1976-2006*, both of which were finalists for the National Book Award. She has also written a collection of essays on craft, *The Flexible Lyric* (2001). Amongst her many awards include: grants from the NEA and the Guggenheim Foundation, Pushcart Prizes, and the O.B. Hardison Award. She designed the low-residency MFA program at Goddard College, which has served as a model for other institutions, and in 1981 moved the program to Warren Wilson, where she continues to teach. Voigt was elected a Chancellor of the Academy of American Poets in 2003. She lives in Cabot, Vermont, and is a former Vermont Poet Laureate. 'The Lotus Flowers' is the title poem of the collection first published by W.W. Norton and reprinted by Carnegie Mellon University Press in 2000, originally ©1987 Ellen Bryant Voigt and reprinted with permission of the author.

Amy Wack (see *About the Editors*)
'The Tooth Fairy' first appeared in *Agenda*, Vol 37, No. 4 and was reprinted in *The Year's Best Fantasy and Horror* anthology, St. Martin's Press, 2001.

Diane Wakoski was born in Whittier, California in 1937, and studied at Berkeley where she participated in Thom Gunn's poetry workshops. Her early work was part of the 'deep image' movement that also included Jerome Rothenberg and Robert Kelly. Although best known for the series of poems collectively known as 'the Motorcycle Betrayal Poems', she has published over forty volumes of verse, a book of essays, *Towards a New Poetry* (1980) and was embroiled in controversy in the 80s for her comments linking New Formalism with Reaganism. She teaches creative writing at Michigan State University. 'Meeting An Astronomer On The Buddah's Birthday' is from *Dancing on the Grave of a Son of a Bitch*, (Black Sparrow Press, 1973). 'The Conjurer' was published in *The Magellanic Clouds* (Black Sparrow Press, 1971). Both ©Diane Wakoski and reprinted with permission of the author.

Anne Waldman was born in 1945 in Millville, New Jersey and grew up in New York City. She gained a BA from Bennington College in 1966. During the 60s, along with Gregory Corso and Allen Ginsberg, she beccame part of East Coast poetry scene, and was associated with the group sometimes known as the Beat Generation. She gave frequent readings at St. Mark's Church Poetry Project which she ran from 1966-78. Waldman published more than forty books, became a practicing Buddhist and founded the Jack Kerouac School of Disembodied Poetics at the Naropa Institute in Boulder Colorado, now Naropa University where she is Distinguished Professor of Poetics. 'The Lie' is from *Helping the Dreamer: New & Selected Poems 1966-1988*, ©1989 by Anne Waldman. Reprinted with permission of Coffee House Press.

Margaret Walker (1915-1998) was born in Birmingham, Alabama. She received a BA from Northwestern University in 1935 and began work with the Federal Writers' Project under Roosevelt's Works Progress Administration. She earned her MA in creative writing from the University of Iowa in 1942 and returned to complete an Ph.D in 1965. She also served for a time as professor at what is today Jackson State University. Her work featured African-American themes, among her most popular poems was 'For My People' which won the Yale Younger Poets Competition (the first woman to do so). She sued Alex Haley in 1988, claiming that his novel *Roots: The Saga of an American Family*, had violated the copyright of her popular novel *(Jubilee)*. The case was dismissed. 'Childhood' is from *This Is My Century: New and Collected Poems,* ©1989 by Margaret Walker Alexander. Reprinted with permission of the University of Georgia Press, Athens, Georgia.

Sarah Wardle born in London in 1969, and studied classics at Oxford University and English at Sussex. In 1999 she won the Geoffrey Dearmer Prize. Her first collection, *Fields Away*, was published in 2003 and was shortlisted for the Forward Prize. She has also written reviews and articles for leading publications and currently is a lecturer at Middlesex University and lives in London where she has been Poet-in-Residence for Tottenham Hotspur, F.C. Her second collection is *SCORE!* (2005) and her third collection, *A Knowable World*, is forthcoming from Bloodaxe Books in 2009. 'Author, Author!' is from *A Knowable World*.

Sylvia Townsend Warner (1893-1978) was born in Harrow near London and educated at home. An accomplished musician, the outbreak of World War One prevented her from going abroad to study under Arnold Schoenberg. She developed a circle of literary friends, including T.F. Powys and David Garnett who gathered around Chaldon Herring, in Dorset. It was there she met her partner, the poet Valentine Ackland. The two moved in together and Warner produced her best work. A highly individual writer of novels, short stories and poems, she also translated Proust's *Contre Saint-Beuve* and wrote a biography of the novelist T.H. White and a guide to Somerset. She was active in the Communist Party of Great Britain but later renounced Stalin. 'Quiet Neighbours' is originally from *The Espalier* and is reprinted in her *Selected Poems,* ©1986 estate of Sylvia Townsend Warner and reprinted with permission from Carcanet Press Limited.

Rachel Wetzsteon was born in Manhattan in 1967. Author of three collections of poems, *The Other Stars* (Penguin, 1994), *Home and Away* (Penguin, 1998), and *Sakura Park* (Persea, 2006) and a critical book, *Influential Ghosts: A Study of Auden's Sources* (Routledge, 2007). She has received an Ingram Merrill grant and the 2001 Witter Bynner Prize for Poetry from the American Academy of Arts and Letters, and currently lives in Manhattan, teaching at William Paterson University and the Unterberg Poetry Center of the 92nd Street Y. 'Young Love' is from *The Other Stars*, National Poetry Series, Penguin Books, ©1994 by Rachel Wetzsteon and reprinted with permission of Penguin, a division of Penguin Group (USA) Inc.

Susan Wheeler was born in 1955, grew up in Minnesota and New England and has lived in New York for over twenty years. Her first collection, *Bag o' Diamonds* (University of Georgia Press) received the Norma Farber First Book Award from the Poetry Society of America and was short-listed for the *Los Angeles Times* Book Award. Her second book, *Smokes*, won the Four Ways Book Award in 1998. She has published two further collections of poetry and a novel. Wheeler has had fellowships from the Guggenheim Foundation and the New York Foundation for the Arts and her poems have appeared in six editions of *Best American Poetry* anthologies. She teaches at Princeton University. 'The Stable Earth, The Deep Salt Sea' is from *Bag o' Diamonds*, ©1993 Susan Wheeler and reprinted with permission from the author.

Anna Wickham (1884-1947) is the pseudonym of Edith Alice Mary Harper, born in London and raised in Australia. Back in London in 1904 she took singing lessons and had a drama scholarship (at the future RADA, just founded). She pursued a singing career in Paris, but returned to London. Encouraged by Harold Monro at his Poetry Bookshop, she published her first collection in 1911. She established herself as a literary figure in London and Paris, particularly in the 1930s. Despite a tempestuous marriage and the birth of four sons (one of whom died of scarlet fever, aged four) she wrote a lot of poetry, quite a bit of which was lost in Word War Two. She committed suicide during the exceptionally brutal winter of 1947. 'The Fired Pot' is from *Selected Poems,* ©1971 Anna Wickham (Chatto & Windus, UK). Reprinted by permission of Random House Group Ltd.

Carolyn Beard Whitlow was born in Detroit, Michigan in 1945. She wrote her first poem while a Ph.D candidate at Cornell University and subsequently completed an MFA at Brown University where she won the Rose Low Rome

Memorial Prize in Poetry. She has had two residencies at Yaddo, a residency at Hedgebrook, and has also been a fellow at Cave Canem. She is currently Charles A. Dana Professor of English at Guilford College in Greensboro, NC where she teaches Creative Writing and African-American literature. In 2006 she won the Naomi Long Madgett Prize in Poetry for the manuscript. of her book, *Vanished*. 'Rockin' a Man, Stone Blind' is from her first collection, *Wild Meat*, (Lost Roads Publishers) ©1986 Carolyn Beard Whitlow and reprinted with permission from the author.

Susan Wicks, poet and novelist, was born in Kent, England in 1947. She read French at the Universities of Hull and Sussex and wrote a D. Phil thesis on Andre Gide. She has lived and worked in France, Ireland and America and has taught at University College, Dublin and the University of Kent. She is the author of five collections of poetry including *Singing Underwater* (1992), which won the Aldeburgh Poetry Festival Prize and *The Clever Daughter*, which was shortlisted for both the T.S. Eliot and Forward Prizes and was a Poetry Book Society Choice. She has also written two novels and a short memoir. Her most recent collection is *De-iced*, (Bloodaxe, 2007). A collection of short stories, *Roll Up for the Arabian Derby*, came out in 2008. 'Pistachios' has appeared in *Poetry London* magazine, ©Susan Wicks and reprinted with permission from the Author.

Frances Williams was born in South Wales in 1968, she received a BA in Fine Art from Liverpool University and an MA in Sculpture from Chelsea College of Art, London. *Flotsam*, her first collection, appeared when she was nineteen. Her reviews and articles about art and literature have appeared in a number of major publications. She has worked at Tate Britain as Curator for Informal Activities and is currently Education and Outreach Manager at the South London Gallery. Her other collections include *Wild Blue* (2000) and the book from which 'The Actress' is taken from, *The Red Rubber Ball of Happiness* ©2003 Frances Williams and reprinted with permission from Seren.

Judith Wright (1915-2000) was born in Armidale, New South Wales, Australia. She lived for many years on a rainforest mountain near Brisbane. She studied philosophy and history at the University of Sydney. Her first collection, *The Moving Image*, appeared in 1946 while she was working at the University of Queensland as a research officer and also on the literary magazine *Meanjin*. Author of a number of collections of poetry and a respected critic and essayist, she was particularly noted for her keen focus on the Australian environment and as an advocate for the rights of indigenous Australians. She received the Queen's Gold Medal for Poetry in 1992. 'Request to a Year' is from *Collected Poems: 1942-85* (Carcanet) ©1994 Judith Wright and reprinted with permission from her estate.

Elinor Wylie (1885-1928) was born in New Jersey, and raised in Washington D.C. in a socially prominent family. Her work was particularly popular before World War Two. Despite a colourful private life that featured three marriages, she wrote eight novels and a number of collections of verse and was particularly known for her preoccupation with the sonnet form. Her last novel, *Orphan Angel*, explores what Shelley's life would have been like if he had escaped his early death and moved to America. Her *Collected Poems* appeared in 1932. 'Wild Peaches IV' is from an edition published by Random House in 1986.

Samantha Wynne-Rhydderch was born in Aberystwyth, Wales in 1966. She read classics at Cambridge before gaining her MA in Creative Writing from Cardiff University. Her first collection, *Rockclimbing in Silk*, appeared in 2001 and a further book, *Not in These Shoes*, was published in 2008. In 2003 she won the London Writers' Award's poetry prize. She has read her poetry at festivals and events worldwide, and currently lives in New Quay, west Wales. 'The X-Ray Room' is from *Rockclimbing in Silk*, ©2001 Smanantha Wynne-Rhydderch and reprinted with permission from Seren.

Jane Yeh was born in the USA in 1971 and educated at Harvard, Iowa and Manchester Metropolitan universities. Her collection, *Marabou*, appeared in 2005 and was shortlisted for the Whitbread Poetry Award, the Forward Prize for Best First Collection, and the Jerwood Aldeburgh First Collection Prize. She frequently contributes articles on books and sport to various publications. 'Correspondence' is from *Marabou*, ©2005 Jane Yeh and reprinted with permission from Carcanet Press Limited.

Tamar Yoseloff was born in the USA in 1965, but has lived in the UK since 1987. Her three collections are *Sweetheart* (Slow Dancer Press, 1998), *Barnard's Star* (Enitharmon 2004) and most recently, *Fetch* (Salt 2007). She is also the author of *Marks* (Pratt Contemporary Editions, 2007), a collaborative book with the artist Linda Karshan, and the editor of *A Room to Live In: A Kettle's Yard Anthology* (Salt, 2007). She is the Poetry Editor of *Art World* magazine. 'The Saints' is from *Barnard's Star*, ©2004 Tamar Yoseloff and reprinted with permission of Enitharmon Press.

Every attempt has been made to locate the copyright holders of these works. Our apologies to anyone we may have failed to contact or acknowledge. Do write to us if you want to provide further information.

About the Editors

Eva Salzman was born in 1960 in New York City, growing up in Brooklyn and Long Island where – from the age of ten until twenty-two – she was a dancer and later a choreographer, exericise director at a diet center in Brooklyn for Orthodox Jews, an out-of-print book searcher, waitress, antique wheeler-and-dealer and cleaner of rich ladies' houses, which eclectic background continues to inform her cross-arts and cross-discipline projects. She was educated at Bennington College and Columbia University, moving to Britain in 1985. A co-deviser of Start Writing Poetry for the Open University, her teaching work – for all ages – has included a residencies in London's East End and at Springhill Prison, a Royal Literary Fund Fellowship and teaching for the MA programmes at Goldsmiths and Warwick University. She has received a Cholmondeley from the Society of Authors, and a Writer's Award from the Arts Council of Great Britain. All her books – *The English Earthquake* (Bloodaxe), *Bargain With The Watchman* (Oxford University Press), *One Two II* (Wrecking Ball Press) and her most recent, *Double Crossing: New and Selected Poems* (Bloodaxe) – won Poetry Book Society Recommendations/ Special Commendations. She is also co-editor of *True to Life: Memoirs from the 'Working Class College* – Ruskin College, Oxford. (Heaventree Press), and has written of lyrics/libretti for singer Christine Tobin, and composers Gary Carpenter and Eric Salzman, her father.

Amy Wack was born in 1960 in Florida, and raised in California. One of five children, her father is a retired Navy pilot and her mother is an attorney. She has a BA in English from San Diego State University and an MFA in writing from Columbia, NYC. She has been Poetry Editor for Seren, based in Wales, since the early 90s and has edited a number of anthologies featuring the poets of Wales including *Burning the Bracken* (1996), *Oxygen* (with Grahame Davies) (2000) and *Seren Selections* (2006). From 1989-2005 she was also Reviews Editor for *Poetry Wales* magazine. Her poems have appeared in a number of periodicals and anthologies in the UK and USA. She lives in Cardiff, Wales with her husband and daughter. Her interests include politics, music, art, history and exploring the beautiful coastline of Pembrokeshire in West Wales.

Index of Authors